The Guided Reader t and Learning History

The Guided Reader to Teaching and Learning History draws on extracts from the published work of some of the most influential history education writers, representing a range of perspectives from leading classroom practitioners to academic researchers, and highlighting key debates surrounding a central range of issues affecting secondary history teachers.

This book brings together key extracts from classic and contemporary writing and contextualises these in both theoretical and practical terms. Each extract is accompanied by an introduction, a summary of the key points and issues raised, questions to promote discussion and suggestions for further reading to extend thinking.

Taking a thematic approach and including a short introduction to each theme, the chapters include:

- the purpose of history education;
- pupil perspectives on history education;
- assessment and progression in history;
- inclusion in history;
- diversity in history;
- teaching difficult issues;
- technology and history education;
- change and continuity;
- historical interpretations;
- professional development for history teachers.

Aimed at trainee and newly qualified teachers including those working towards Master's-level qualifications, as well as existing teachers, this accessible but critically provocative text is an essential resource for those that wish to deepen their understanding of history education.

Richard Harris is Lecturer in History Education at the University of Reading.

Katharine Burn is Senior Lecturer in History Education at the Institute of Education, University of London.

Mary Woolley is Senior Lecturer in History Education at Canterbury Christ Church University.

The Guided Reader to Teaching and Learning History

Edited by

Richard Harris, Katharine Burn
and Mary Woolley

Routledge
Taylor & Francis Group

LONDON AND NEW YORK

First published 2014
by Routledge
2 Park Square, Milton Park, Abingdon, Oxon OX14 4RN

and by Routledge
711 Third Avenue, New York, NY 10017

Routledge is an imprint of the Taylor & Francis Group, an informa business

British Library Cataloguing in Publication Data
A catalogue record for this book is available from the British Library

Library of Congress Cataloging in Publication Data
The guided reader to teaching and learning history/[edited by] Richard Harris, Katharine Burn, Mary Woolley.
pages cm
1. History--Study and teaching (Secondary) I. Harris, Richard, 1966- II. Burn, Katharine. III. Woolley, Mary.
D16.25.G78 2013
907.1'2—dc23
2013014181

ISBN: 978–0-415–50344-0 (hbk)
ISBN: 978–0-415–50345-7 (pbk)
ISBN: 978–0-203–12931-9 (ebk)

Typeset in Helvetica and Bembo
by Swales & Willis Ltd, Exeter, Devon

Contents

Acknowledgements

We are grateful to all those who have granted us permission to reproduce the extracts listed below. While every effort has been made to trace and acknowledge ownership of copyright material used in this volume, the publishers will be glad to make suitable arrangements with any copyright holders whom it has not been possible to contact.

QCA (2007) *History: Programme of Study for Key Stage 3*. Coventry: QCA.

Lee, P. (1992) History in schools: Aims, purposes and approaches. A reply to John White. In P. Lee, J. Slater, P. Walsh, P. and J. White, *The Aims of School History: the National Curriculum and beyond*. London: Tufnell Press, 20–34. With thanks to Peter Lee.

Barton, K. and Levstik, L. (2004) *Teaching History for the Common Good*. Mahwah, NJ: Lawrence Erlbaum Associates Publishers; see pp. 28, 35, 38.

Husbands, C., Kitson, A. and Pendry, A. (2003) *Understanding History Teaching*. Maidenhead: Open University Press; see p. 123.

Rogers, P. (1987) The past as a frame of reference. In C. Portal (ed.) *The History Curriculum for Teachers*. Lewes: The Falmer Press, 3–21.

Hirsch, E.D. (1987) *Cultural Literacy: What every American needs to know*. Boston: Houghton Mifflin; see pp. 19, 113, 127–8, 132–3.

Counsell, C. (2000) Historical knowledge and historical skills: A distracting dichotomy. In J. Arthur and R. Phillips (eds) *Issues in History Teaching*. London: Routledge, 54–71.

Seixas, P. (1993) The community of inquiry as a basis for knowledge and learning: The case of history. *American Educational Research Journal*, 30 (2), 305–24.

Bellinger, L. (2008) Cultivating curiosity about complexity: What happens when Year 12 start to read Orlando Figes' *The Whisperers*? *Teaching History*, 132, 5–13.

Foster, R. (2011) Using academic history in the classroom. In I. Davies (ed.) *Debates in History Teaching*. London: Routledge, 199–211.

Haydn, T. and Harris, R. (2010) Pupil perspectives on the purposes and benefits of studying history in high school: A view from the UK. *Journal of Curriculum Studies*, 42 (2), 241–61.

Traille, E.K.A. (2007) 'You should be proud about your history. They made me feel ashamed': Teaching history hurts. *Teaching History*, 127, 31–7.

Grever, M., Haydn, T. and Ribbens, K. (2008) Identity and school history: The perspectives of young people from the Netherlands and England. *British Journal of Educational Studies*, 56 (1), 76–94.

Barton, K. and McCully, A. (2005) History, identity, and the school curriculum in Northern Ireland: An empirical study of secondary students' ideas and perspectives. *Journal of Curriculum Studies*, 37 (1), 85–116.

Epstein, T. (2009) *Interpreting National History: Race, identity, and pedagogy in classrooms and communities*. New York: Routledge; see pp. 86–8.

Barton, K. (2009) The denial of desire: how to make history education meaningless. In L. Symcox and A. Wilschut (eds) *National History Standards: The problem of the canon and the future of teaching history*. Charlotte, NC: Information Age Publishing, 265–82.

Kinloch, N. (2001) Parallel catastrophes? Uniqueness, redemption and the Shoah. *Teaching History*, 104, 8–14.

Short, G. (2003) Lessons of the Holocaust: A response to the critics. *Educational Review*, 55 (3), 277–87.

Salmons, P. (2010) Universal meaning or historical understanding? The Holocaust in history and history in the curriculum. *Teaching History*, 141, 57–63.

Rüsen, J. (2006) Historical consciousness: Narrative structure, moral function and ontogenetic development. In P. Seixas (ed.) *Theorizing Historical Consciousness*. Toronto: University of Toronto Press, 70–8. Reprinted with permission of the publisher.

Lee, P. (2004) Walking backwards into tomorrow: Historical consciousness and understanding history. *International Journal of Historical Learning, Teaching and Research*, 4 (1), 69–114. With thanks to Peter Lee.

Foster, S., Ashby, R., Lee, P. and Howson, J. (2008) *Usable Historical Pasts: A study of students' frameworks of the past: Non-technical summary* (Research Summary). ESRC End of Award Report, RES-000-22-1676. Swindon: ESRC.

Fines, J. (1994) Evidence: The basis of the discipline. In H. Bourdillon (ed.) *Teaching History*. London: Routledge, 122–5.

Ashby, R. (2011) Understanding historical evidence: Teaching and learning challenges. In I. Davis (ed.) *Debates in History Teaching*. London: Routledge, 137–47.

Pickles, E. (2010) How can students' use of historical evidence be enhanced? A research study of the role of knowledge in Year 8 to Year 13 students' interpretations of historical sources. *Teaching History*, 139, 41–51.

Cercadillo, L. (2001) Significance in history: Students' ideas in England and Spain. In A. Dickinson, P. Gordon and P. Lee (eds) *Raising Standards in History Education: International review of history education, Volume 3*. London: Woburn Press, 116–45.

Counsell, C. (2004) Looking through a Josephine-Butler-shaped window: Focusing pupils' thinking on historical significance. *Teaching History*, 114, 30–6.

Brown, G. and Woodcock, J. (2009) Relevant, rigorous and revisited: Using local history to make meaning of historical significance. *Teaching History*, 134, 4–11.

Chapman, A. (2011) Historical interpretations. In I. Davies (ed.) *Debates in History Teaching*. London: Routledge, 96–105.

Card, J. (2004) Seeing double: How one period visualises another. *Teaching History*, 117, 6–11.

Moore, R. (2000) Using the Internet to teach about interpretations in Years 9 and 12. *Teaching History*, 101, 35–9.

Stow, W. and Haydn, T. (2000) Issues in the teaching of chronology. In J. Arthur and R. Phillips (eds) *Issues in History Teaching*. London: Routledge, 83–97.

Lee, P. (1991) Historical knowledge and the National Curriculum. In R. Aldrich (ed.) *History in the National Curriculum*. London: Kogan Page, 39–65.

Howson, J. and Shemilt, D. (2011) Frameworks of knowledge: Dilemmas and debates. In I. Davies (ed.) *Debates in History Teaching*. London: Routledge, 73–83.

Foster, R. (2009) Speed cameras, dead ends, drivers and diversions: Year 9 use a 'road map' to problematise change and continuity. *Teaching History*, 131, 4–8.

Corfield, P. (2009) Teaching history's big pictures: Including continuity as well as change. *Teaching History*, 136, 53–9.

Counsell, C. (2011) What do we want students to *do* with historical change and continuity? In I. Davies (ed.) *Debates in History Teaching*. London: Routledge, 109–23.

Lee, P. (2005) Putting principles into practice: Understanding history. In S. Donovan and J. Bransford (eds) *How Students Learn: History in the classroom*. Washington: The National Academies Press, 49–54.

Chapman, A. (2003) Camels, diamonds and counter-factuals: A model for teaching causal reasoning. *Teaching History*, 112, 6–13.

Howells, G. (1998) Being ambitious with the causes of the First World War: Interrogating inevitability. *Teaching History*, 92, 16–19.

Portal, C. (1987) Empathy as an objective for history teaching. In C. Portal (ed.) *The History Curriculum for Teachers*. London: The Falmer Press, 89–99.

Lee, P. and Shemilt, D. (2011) The concept that dares not speak its name: Should empathy come out of the closet? *Teaching History*, 143, 39–49.

Cunningham, D. (2004) Empathy without illusions. *Teaching History*, 114, 24–9.

Bradshaw, M. (2009) Drilling down: How one history department is working towards progression in pupils' thinking about diversity across Years 7, 8 and 9. *Teaching History*, 135, 4–12.

Banks, J.A. (1989) Integrating the curriculum with ethnic content: Approaches and guidelines. In J. Banks and C. McGee Banks (eds) *Multicultural Education: Issues and perspectives*. Boston: Allyn and Bacon, 189–207. Reprinted by permission of Pearson Education, Inc., Upper Saddle River, NJ.

Bracey, P., Gove-Humphries, A. and Jackson, D. (2011) Teaching diversity in the history classroom. In I. Davies (ed.) *Debates in History Teaching*. London: Routledge, 172–85.

Riley, M. (2000) Into the Key Stage 3 history garden: Choosing and planting your enquiry questions. *Teaching History*, 99, 8–13.

Dawson, I. (2009) *Developing Enquiry Skills*. Available at: www.thinkinghistory.co.uk/EnquirySkill/Index.html.

Barton, K. and Levstik, L. (2004) *Teaching History for the Common Good*. Mahwah, NJ: Lawrence Erlbuam Associates; see pp. 188–91.

Husbands, C. (1996) *What Is History Teaching? Language, ideas and meaning in learning about the past*. Buckingham: Open University Press; see pp. 30–42.

Counsell, C. (2004) *History and Literacy in Year 7: Building the lesson around the text*. London: HodderMurray, see pp. 1 and 107–13. Reproduced by permission of Hodder Education.

Fullard, G. and Dacey, K. (2008) Holistic assessment through speaking and listening: An experiment with causal reasoning and evidential thinking in Year 8. *Teaching History*, 131, 25–9.

Lee, P. and Shemilt, D. (2003) A scaffold, not a cage: Progression and progression models in history. *Teaching History*, 113, 13–23.

Vermeulen, E. (2000) What is progress in history? *Teaching History*, 98, 35–41.

Counsell, C. (2000) Historical knowledge and historical skills: A distracting dichotomy. In J. Arthur and R. Phillips (eds) *Issues in History Teaching*. London: Routledge, 54–71.

Kitson, A. and Husbands, C. with Steward, S. (2011) *Teaching and Learning History 11–18: Understanding the past*. Maidenhead: Open University Press; see pp. 97–8.

Burnham, S. and Brown, G. (2004) Assessment without level descriptions. *Teaching History*, 115, 5–15.

Facey, J. (2011) 'A is for assessment'… Strategies for A-level marking to motivate and enable students of all abilities to progress. *Teaching History*, 144, 36–43.

Harris, R., Downey, C. and Burn, K. (2012) History education in comprehensive schools: Using school level data to interpret national patterns. *Oxford Review of Education*, 38 (4), 413–36.

Hart, S., Dixon, A., Drummond, M.J. and McIntyre, D. (2004) *Learning without Limits*. Maidenhead: Open University Press; see pp. 138–46.

Harris, R. (2005) Does differentiation have to mean different? *Teaching History*, 118, 5–12.

Counsell, C. (2003) History for all. In M. Riley and R. Harris (eds) *Past Forward*. London: Historical Association, 25–32.

Kitson, A. (2001) Challenging stereotypes and avoiding the superficial: A suggested approach to teaching the Holocaust. *Teaching History*, 104, 41–8.

Rollett, S. (2010) 'Hi George. Let me ask my leading historians …': Deconstructing lazy analogies in Year 9. *Teaching History*, 139, 24–9.

Counsell, C. (2003) The forgotten games kit: Putting historical thinking first in long-, medium- and short-term planning. In T. Haydn and C. Counsell (eds) *History, ICT and Learning in the Secondary School*. London: RoutledgeFalmer, 52–108.

Martin, D. (2003) Relating the general to the particular: Data handling and historical learning. In T. Haydn and C. Counsell (eds) *History, ICT and Learning in the Secondary School*. London: RoutledgeFalmer, 134–51.

Thompson, D. and Cole, N. (2003) Keeping the kids on message ... One school's attempt at helping sixth form students to engage in historical debating using ICT. *Teaching History*, 113, 38–43.

Porat, D. (2001) A contemporary past: History textbooks as sites of national memory. In A. Dickinson, P. Gordon and P. Lee (eds) *Raising Standards in History Education: International review of history education, Volume 3*. London: Woburn Press, 36–45.

Nicholls, J. (2006) Beyond the national and the transnational: Perspectives of WWII in U.S.A, Italian, Swedish, Japanese, and English School History Textbooks. In S. Foster and K. Crawford (eds) *What Shall We Tell the Children? International perspectives on school history textbooks*. Charlotte, NC: Information Age Publishing, 89–112.

Edwards, C. (2008) The how of history: Using old and new textbooks in the classroom to develop disciplinary knowledge. *Teaching History*, 130, 39–45.

Husbands, C. (2011) What do history teachers (need to) know? In I. Davies (ed.) *Debates in History Teaching*. London: Routledge, 84–95.

Counsell, C. (2011) Disciplinary knowledge for all, the secondary history curriculum and history teachers' achievement. *Curriculum Journal*, 22 (2), 201–25.

Burn, K. (2012) 'If I wasn't learning anything new about teaching I would have left it by now!' How history teachers can support their own and others' continued professional learning. *Teaching History*, 146, 40–9.

Nature and purposes of history education

The purposes of history teaching

One of the fundamental questions that needs to be asked of any subject and its place in the curriculum is 'what is its purpose?' There must be a reason why a subject or topics within a subject have been chosen for study. For a subject such as history, which is seen as hugely important by a range of educationalists and politicians, this is especially pertinent, as history could be taught to present partisan points of view or could be used to promote a particular sense of identity – the potential for distortion and manipulation is a serious concern. Hence the need to be clear about the purpose of teaching history, yet it is difficult to find a consensus. This chapter explores some of the reasons put forward for the study of the past.

Extract 1

Source

QCA (2007) *History: Programme of Study for Key Stage 3*. Coventry: QCA.

Introduction

This extract comes from the 2007 revision of the National Curriculum for England. As part of the documentation, an importance statement was included, which was to underpin the thinking behind the content to be taught and the concepts and processes that were to be developed within the subject. The document was a product of a consultation between people within the history education community and government advisers and civil servants. It tries to capture a sense of the value of the subject in a way that could appeal to a range of audiences.

Key words & phrases

National Curriculum; importance statement; purpose; aims

Extract

History fires pupils' curiosity and imagination, moving and inspiring them with the dilemmas, choices and beliefs of people in the past. It helps pupils develop their own identities through an understanding of history at personal, local, national and international levels. It helps them to ask and answer questions of the present by engaging with the past.

Pupils find out about the history of their community, Britain, Europe and the world. They develop a chronological overview that enables them to make connections within and across different periods and societies. They investigate Britain's relationships with the wider world, and relate past events to the present day.

As they develop their understanding of the nature of historical study, pupils ask and answer important questions, evaluate evidence, identify and analyse different interpretations of the past, and learn to substantiate any arguments and judgements they make. They appreciate why they are learning what they are learning and can debate its significance.

History prepares pupils for the future, equipping them with knowledge and skills that are prized in adult life, enhancing employability and developing an ability to take part in a democratic society. It encourages mutual understanding of the historic origins of our ethnic and cultural diversity, and helps pupils become confident and questioning individuals.

Summary

This statement identifies the ways in which history should engage young people and the value of studying the past in terms of developing a sense of identity (with a recognition that there will be multiple identities), the understanding of the world in which they live and the knowledge and skills that will be useful in adult life. The statement also outlines the types of values and dispositions that a study of the past can promote. It is a very broad justification for the importance of studying the past, and attempts to relate this to the types of knowledge and understanding young people need to develop. Like any such official document, it was written within a particular context and needed to be acceptable to a range of individuals and groups, hence the broad range of ideas and ideals covered.

Questions to consider

1. Given the range of ideas contained within this statement, which (if any) do you feel are the more important reasons for the study of history?

2. In what ways do you feel the study of history contributes to the development of personal identity and to dispositions such as tolerance? Do you feel these aims are intrinsic to the study of history? If not, are they appropriate extrinsic aims for teaching history?

Extract 2

Source

Lee, P. (1992) History in schools: Aims, purposes and approaches. A reply to John White. In P. Lee, J. Slater, P. Walsh and J. White, *The Aims of School History: The National Curriculum and Beyond*. London: Tufnell Press, 20–34.

Introduction

This extract comes from a book that presents a discussion about the aims of school history at the time of the introduction of the National Curriculum for England in the late 1980s. However, the issues raised are highly pertinent for any discussion about the purposes of history. The particular extract from Peter Lee is a response to ideas presented by John White; White argues that there is a need for much greater clarity about the aims of a national curriculum, and feels that there is a need for history to serve broader educational aims to help students become successful citizens within a liberal–democratic society. These views are challenged by Lee. Lee argues that broader educational aims, such as using history to promote patriotism or democratic values are 'contingent' aims, because learning history has no necessary connection with such aims; it is perfectly possible to become patriotic or to develop a commitment to democracy without studying history. Instead, Lee argues that the point of studying history is to get better at history, and that the power of learning history lies in its transformative powers, i.e. it has the power to alter the way people perceive the world in which they live.

Key words & phrases

Purpose; disciplinary knowledge; second-order concepts

Extract

The reason for teaching history in schools is not so that pupils can use it for making something else, or to change or preserve a particular form of society, or even to expand the economy, but that it changes *pupils*; it changes what they see in the world, and how they see it ....

History is a way of acquiring rational knowledge and understanding of the past – any or all of the past. And since the present, however specious, is, from the point of view of knowledge and understanding, rather short, history bears on much of what is construed as present. To say someone has learnt history is to say something very wide-ranging about the way in which he or she is likely to make sense of the world. History offers a way of seeing almost any substantive issue in human affairs, subject to certain procedures and standards, whatever feelings one may have. Patriotism, on the other hand, is a set of feelings and dispositions, underpinned by a cognitive (or sometimes quasi-cognitive) foundation consisting of substantive beliefs and values to which people subscribe, localised to a particular place and time. Being patriotic cannot be generalised. It makes no sense to educate people to be patriotic in general – towards America, Angola and Antigua, Belgium, Bolivia, Britain and Brazil ... and so on.

The change of view one acquires from history is not just a matter of picking up a new set of beliefs, or even new substantive knowledge. It is also taking on a set of second-order understandings, together with the 'rational passions' (e.g. for truth and respect for evidence) which give historical understanding a universality that patriotism does not have. Learning history is like learning a science: it is transformative in a radically different way from becoming patriotic or even socialised. (Socialisation arguably has a universal component, since all humans belong to societies. But any universal meanings which could be given to socialisation would be either very abstract or very basic: socialisation has to be socialisation into some particular society.) ...

It is not just that learning history and producing patriotism or nurturing democratic citizens are aims which belong to different categories; it is also that the relation of learning history to becoming patriotic or being likely to see the world from a democratic perspective is a contingent one: learning history has no necessary connection with becoming patriotic or seeing the world from a democratic perspective. It is perfectly possible for students to learn history and be less patriotic than they were before they began. (Indeed it is precisely the claim that this was what was happening in schools that led the far right to get so excited about history teaching.)

What aims can or should history have? ... There is little point in going for aims which have no discernible connection with history: how can they be aims of *history* teaching? And among the many contingent aims which might be plausibly asserted to have some sort of connection with history, those which are not linked to history by decent empirical evidence have little claim to be taken seriously: they lie somewhere along the continuum running from pious hopes through self-deception to deliberate misrepresentation.

Summary

Lee puts forward a case for the aims of teaching history to be focused primarily on those that are directly related to history teaching and are not necessarily broader goals such as engendering a sense of democratic values. The focus is thus on the disciplinary nature of the subject; pupils need to understand how the past is constructed, therefore there needs to be a focus on second-order concepts such as change and continuity and causation and the way in we can make claims about the past, based on evaluation of evidence, the construction of reasoned judgements and so forth.

Questions to consider

1. To what extent do you feel learning history 'for its own sake', is a valid justification for the study of the past?
2. How might an emphasis on the disciplinary nature of history shape the content of the curriculum and the teaching and learning approaches adopted?
3. What do you see as the goals of a general education, and to what extent should history meet these general goals?

Extract 3

Source

Barton, K. and Levstik, L. (2004) *Teaching History for the Common Good*. Mahwah, NJ: Lawrence Erlbaum Associates Publishers; see pp. 28, 35, 38.

Introduction

Keith Barton and Linda Levstik argue that teaching history has a strong focus on developing students as citizens. They critically discuss at length the nature of democratic citizenship and its relationship to public education, and highlight the shortcomings of some notions of democratic citizenship. For them democracy is pluralistic and an adequate preparation must include an element of humanistic education. Again they discuss different models of humanistic education before arguing that it must entail a social dimension.

Key words & phrases

Purpose; democratic citizenship; citizenship education; humanistic education

---

Extract

We assume that the overarching goal of public education in the United States is to prepare students for participation in democratic life. We cannot justify an assertion like this by reference to a single, authoritative source, because we do not have a national system of education, and therefore, the purpose of schooling is not established by federal legislation, judicial mandate, or executive order. However, public schools in the United States share an origin in the common school movement of the 19th century, and the ideology of that movement revolved around the need to prepare citizens for a democratic, republican form of government: schools were meant to be, as Carl Kaestle [1983] puts it, 'pillars of the republic.' State and local curriculum guides still pay homage to citizenship education as a fundamental purpose of schooling, and the United States has a long tradition of philosophical reflection on the relationship between education and democracy. Democracy has never been the only goal of education in the United States; economic productivity and individual development have provided rival conceptions of the purpose of schooling. Yet throughout our history, the need to prepare students for citizenship in a democracy has furnished one of the most frequent and persuasive arguments in support of public education …

We believe that students will be best prepared for democratic citizenship if they receive a broadly humanistic education …

The final characteristic of the humanistic study of history – and the most controversial – is that it involves deliberation over the common good. This has not been a significant part of either the classical or romantic humanist traditions, both of which emphasize individual judgement rather than joint deliberation, and individual standards of moral and ethical behaviour rather than collective visions of the common good. However, our view of humanity is a more social one, and we believe both the format and objective of humanistic study should be social in nature. Dewey [1966] argues that '"humanism" means at bottom being imbued with an intelligent sense of human interests,' and he equates such interests with the good of society. For Dewey, a study of humanity that simply involves the accumulation of knowledge 'is on a level with the busy work of children.' For any study to be truly humane, he argues it must produce 'greater sensitiveness to social well-being and greater ability to promote that well-being.'… Discussions about how to promote social well-being and how to care for the public realm are at the heart of participatory democracy, and we believe history has an important role to play in preparing students to take part in such deliberation.

Summary

For Barton and Levstik, the teaching of history is explicitly related to the promotion of democratic citizenship. How this is achieved can vary and they present a range of 'stances' or positions relating to purpose, which they name as identification, analytical, moral response and exhibition, and explore how these relate to democratic citizenship.

They acknowledge that there are different understandings about humanistic education, but argue that it should have a social emphasis. Within this, history provides an important sense of context, engages students with critical thinking and judgement forming, which should provide a valuable grounding in the promotion of a pluralist democracy.

Questions to consider

1. To what extent should preparation for life in a democratic society be the goal of education?
2. How far is it possible to use history as a form of education for democratic participation?
3. How might an emphasis on education for democratic participation shape the content of the curriculum and teaching and learning approaches adopted?

Extract 4

Source

Husbands, C., Kitson, A. and Pendry, A. (2003) *Understanding History Teaching.* Maidenhead: Open University Press; see p. 123.

Introduction

This extract is from a book that is based upon in-depth interviews and lesson observations of eight history teachers in English schools. The book itself covers a range of issues including a general discussion about the state of history education, an examination of the practice of these eight teachers and a section on the nature and purpose of history education. The book therefore presents the views of teachers across a range of issues, including the point of teaching history.

Key words & phrases

Purpose; teacher perspective; moral education; citizenship education

---

Extract

The extent to which history teachers should view moral education as a legitimate aim has been subject to debate and not inconsiderable disagreement. At the heart of this debate lies a crucial distinction between those who believe that history brings with it its own intrinsic goals (for example, Lee 1991) and those who challenge the notion that 'knowledge for its own sake' is possible – or desirable – given that knowledge has to be selected and therefore certain criteria must be applied (for example, White 1994). Lee accepts that history is transformative, but he argues that it is the pupils who change, not society as a whole. Therefore, the argument goes, history should not be made hostage to goals extrinsic to the discipline itself. 'Good citizens' and 'socialization' are 'contested slogans, not appeals to historical criteria' (Lee 1991).

There is no doubt where most of our teachers [in this study] stand in relation to this debate. The majority of our teachers used the language of moral education to articulate their views on the purposes of the history curriculum. The kinds of values informing their curriculum choices and their teaching in general were transparent, drawing on notions of plurality, diversity, respect for humanity and fundamental tolerance combined with an understanding of how individual action can impact on others either negatively or positively in profound ways. To borrow from a discourse that has informed so much of citizenship education, the perspectives we encountered in the interviews therefore combined ideas of rights and responsibilities, in other words, the rights to freedom and the responsibility of others to help defend and protect that freedom. To this extent, then, our teachers assumed a set of shared values. Perhaps none of this is very surprising. After all, what is history teaching about if not to make judgements and how is this ever possible without a degree of moral reasoning? (Arthur et al. 2001). As Slater writes, 'Judgements and moral attitudes lie at the heart of historical language' (Slater 1989). How, for example, can we teach the slave trade or the Holocaust in a moral vacuum (Husbands 1996)? Should we be presenting the case *for* Auschwitz (Slater 1989)? Choices have to be made about what to teach and how to teach it and, for most of our teachers, the kinds of moral reasoning and social values it can thereby promote were an important factor in these choices. What was less clear was the extent to which the teaching of values such as toleration, respect for diversity, understanding of different attitudes and beliefs should be approached entirely historically or linked more explicitly with issues specifically relevant to today.

Summary

Although a range of purposes are discussed by teachers, the idea of history education as part of a broader development of citizenship was seen as important. In this case, history teaching as an explicit form of moral education was regarded as a central goal by the majority of teachers. The teachers present a case for teaching about 'difference' to develop empathy, promote tolerance and respect for diversity, as well as learn from the morally dubious actions of people in the past. This is seen as having a direct impact on content selection and how to teach such content (e.g. do teachers adopt a neutral stance?).

Questions to consider

1. To what extent should the teaching of history education have an explicit moral agenda?
2. What challenges are there for teachers who adopt an explicit focus on a moral agenda in teaching?
3. How might an emphasis on education for moral development shape the content of the curriculum and teaching and learning approaches adopted?

Investigations

Teacher understanding of purpose: Working with a group of history teachers, write your own importance statement to outline your rationale for the study of history.

Teacher understanding of purpose II: Working with history teachers, examine the extent to which they see the purpose of history teaching as study of the past 'for its own sake', as education for democratic participation or as a form of moral education.

Analysis of selected content: Using the findings from the examination of purpose, analyse the selected topics in the curriculum and the extent to which these actually reflect the identified purposes of history teaching.

Pupil understanding of purpose: To what extent do pupils have a clear sense of the purpose of history teaching and how far does this match the views expressed by their history teachers? Conduct a survey with pupils and/or look at ways you might build this into lessons so you are able to identify pupils' preconceptions about the purpose of history.

Think deeper

This issue is extremely important as it underpins debates about what should be taught and how the subject should be taught. It is therefore worth reading this chapter in conjunction with other chapters as many of the issues overlap. For example Chapter 4 examines pupils' perspectives on the purposes of studying history, and Chapter 6 on teaching controversial, emotional and moral issues is fundamentally based upon debates around the purpose of teaching history in order to establish how and what should be taught. In many ways the issue of the purpose of history is deeply philosophical but has a major impact on practice. There are a range of positions that can be adopted within this debate and the suggestions below are not exhaustive, but serve to illustrate different perspectives.

An interesting argument that touches upon both the nature and purpose of history education has been developed by Jörn Rüsen (2004), who distinguishes between common-sense assumptions about the past and more developed ways of thinking about it. This distinction is important because of the ways in which people's historical consciousness serves to orient them in time, and acts as a frame of reference that informs their understanding of the present and shapes their thinking about possible future actions. In this sense, history education is about orientation in time and allows people to look forward (an idea discussed more fully in Chapter 7).

John Tosh (2008) argues very specifically for the central role of history education in developing informed, well-rounded citizens. According to Tosh, history provides an in-depth and invaluable insight into the present world and is therefore crucial in making any informed decisions about present and future actions.

For E.D. Hirsch (1987), knowledge (and, by implication, knowledge of the past) per se is important as a form of 'cultural literacy'. Hirsch (whose argument is examined in detail in Chapter 2) claims that without a shared common knowledge it is difficult for young people to understand things that others, such as writers, refer to and take for granted. While doing research into university students' written composition, he noticed how some students struggled to make sense of texts simply because they lacked basic knowledge of the issue being written about, for example Robert E. Lee's surrender to Ulysses S. Grant in the American Civil War. Hirsch (1999) argues that knowledge can become a form of 'mental Velcro' to which other knowledge can stick. From this students can make greater sense of what is said about the world around them and are thus better able to participate effectively in democratic life. Such a view emphasises factual knowledge rather than an understanding of history as a discipline or how claims about the past are validated and therefore open to challenge.

Think wider

This issue fits into wider debates about the curriculum. Richard Harris and Katharine Burn (2011) place the discussion about the history curriculum within the wider debates about curriculum, in particular highlighting the consequences of curriculum policies that are ill-conceived. Drawing on the social realist theory of knowledge and arguments propounded by Michael Young (2008), they argue that the rapid spread of alternative curricular arrangements, implemented in the absence of an understanding of curriculum theory, undermines the value of disciplined thinking to the detriment of many young people, particularly those in areas of social and economic deprivation.

Clearly the purpose of any curriculum has a fundamental impact upon the nature of the curriculum. It is valuable therefore to explore some of the materials relating to these debates. Howard Gardner's (2007) book *Five Minds for the Future* offers an interesting perspective. There has been much debate about the value of a traditional subject-based curriculum, but Gardner argues that the debate needs to focus on the types of thinking or 'minds' that society wishes to cultivate in young people. Thus he argues for a disciplinary basis to a curriculum, e.g. arguing that scientific thinking and historical thinking are very different yet valuable 'minds' that should be at the heart of a curriculum.

Others have gone further and argued the case that a curriculum based around subjects no longer serves the needs of young people in the twenty-first century and that there needs to be an emphasis on developing key competencies. Advocates of such thinking include John White and Guy Claxton. Such ideas have manifested themselves in a range of alternative curriculum models such as 'Opening Minds' (RSA n.d.).

The impact of different curricula models and their appropriateness is contested, reflecting often very entrenched views on all sides, but it is worth exploring the range of models and reflecting carefully upon their purpose and proposed value as a means of developing your own understanding of the place of history within the educational curriculum.

References

Arthur, J., Davies, I., Wrenn, A., Haydn, T. and Kerr, D. (2001) *Citizenship through Secondary History*. London: RoutledgeFalmer.

Dewey, J. (1966) *Democracy and Education: An introduction to the philosophy of education*. New York: Free Press.

Gardner, H. (2007) *Five Minds for the Future*. Boston: Harvard Business School Press.

Harris, R. and Burn, K. (2011) Curriculum theory, curriculum policy and the problem of ill-disciplined thinking. *Journal of Education Policy*, 26 (2), 245–61.

Hirsch, E.D. (1987) *Cultural Literacy: What every American needs to know*. New York: Vintage Books.

Hirsch, E.D. (1999) *The Schools We Need and Why We Don't Have Them*. New York: Bantam Doubleday Dell Publishing Group.

Husbands, C. (1996) *What Is History Teaching? Language, ideas and meaning in learning about the past*. Buckingham: Open University Press.

Kaestle, C. (1983) *Pillars of the Republic*. New York: Hill and Wang.

Lee, P. (1991) Historical knowledge and the national curriculum. In R. Aldrich (ed.) *History in the National Curriculum*. London: Kogan Page, 35–65.

RSA (Royal Society for the Encouragement of Arts, Manufactures and Commerce) (n.d.) *Opening Minds Framework (first piloted in 2000)*. Available at: www.rsaopeningminds.org.uk/ (accessed 13 May 2013).

Rüsen, J. (2004) Historical consciousness: Narrative structure, moral function, and ontological development. In P. Seixas (ed.) *Theorizing Historical Consciousness*. Toronto: University of Toronto Press, 63–85.

Slater, J. (1989) Where there is dogma, let us sow doubt. In J. White (ed.) *The Aims of School History: The National Curriculum and beyond*. London: University of London Institute of Education (Bedford Way Papers), 45–53.

Tosh, J. (2008) *Why History Matters*. Basingstoke: Palgrave Macmillan.

White, J. (1994) The aims of school history. *Teaching History*, 74, 7–9.

Young, M. (2008) *Bringing Knowledge Back In: From social constructivism to social realism in the sociology of education*. London: Routledge.

The 'knowledge' debate

Whenever curricular reforms are proposed, history is almost invariably the subject that gives rise to the most heated controversy. Although the debates tend to reflect diverse views about the purposes of history education (see Chapter 1), they are often perceived as disputes about the historical knowledge that young people should acquire. One focus for debate is obviously the selection of the substantive content that they should study. The other main focus, all too easily and crudely caricatured as 'knowledge versus skills', is essentially concerned with the importance assigned to understanding history as a particular *form* of knowledge, rather than mastering it as a *body* of knowledge. In England the curriculum developed by the Schools Council 13–16 History Project (SHP 1976) challenged 'traditional' history teaching in relation *both* to the type of substantive knowledge taught *and* to the role of epistemology within it. New kinds of units (with a stronger focus on local history, for example) structured in different ways (long-term studies in development contrasting with short-term depth studies) were taught using an enquiry-based approach, intended to help children understand how historical knowledge was constructed. That approach, which came to be known as the 'new history', was both widely adopted and widely criticised, especially when elements of the enquiry-based approach were incorporated into a new national examination at 16+ (with the introduction of GCSEs in 1985). The kind of debates that raged then, and later as a national curriculum was introduced (and subsequently revised), not only echo much earlier debates between 'traditional' and 'progressive' views of education but are also reflected in similar national debates in many other countries.

Extract 1

Source

Rogers, P. (1987) The past as a frame of reference. In C. Portal (ed.) *The History Curriculum for Teachers*. Lewes: The Falmer Press, 3–21.

Introduction

In the chapter from which this extract is taken, Peter Rogers, essentially an advocate of the 'new history', argues that an enquiry-based approach to history education, understood as the construction of *all* facts from historical sources, is entirely inadequate. Not only is it far too time-consuming, but it also ignores the role of interpretation in establishing historical 'facts' – which are generally judgements about historical significance, and therefore depend on an extensive grasp of the historical context. Students therefore need a 'judicious blend of source-based enquiry and the study of scholarly work' (p. 9). Moreover, since the primary benefit that Rogers ascribes to history education is its contribution to young people's understanding of the world in which they live, the process of enquiry must be applied to genuine historical questions of real importance, thus providing students with a 'frame of reference' within which to make sense of their present experience.

Key words & phrases

'New history'; enquiry; epistemology; frame of reference; analogy; modern history; economics; familiarity; contrast

---

Extract

Perhaps the main feature of the 'new' history is a marked shift away from mere mastery of factual material towards a stress upon enquiry skills and problem-solving. It would be a caricature of traditional history teaching to suggest that it always consisted of the dreary, conning and regurgitation of dictated notes and dates from which enquiry, discussion and even thought were absent; but like most caricatures, this one contains enough truth to make stress upon the importance of enquiry thoroughly justified. Not only were many pupils bored by history, and many adults sceptical as to the point of their studying it, but all too often the teaching seriously misrepresented the nature of history itself. In philosophical terms 'know how' was grossly neglected in the interests of 'know that'... This neglect is not only psychologically damaging but logically absurd, since if the pupils acquire no acquaintance with the sort of ground and procedure upon which valid claims may rest, they are devoid of any means of appraising the truth of what they learn and, so far from being able to establish further knowledge, they lack 'the right to be sure' about even the information they have been given.

The neglect of 'know-how', then, is destructive of the subject, and renders it educationally sterile. But the contrary danger must also be guarded against – namely the tendency for the 'new' history to put *all* stress upon enquiry skills ('detective work') which can colloquially be summed up in the slogan 'content doesn't matter'; provided only that the children are 'interested' in what is chosen for study, and that something which may be described as 'enquiry' is promoted by it, all, apparently is well. Again, epistemology exposes the error. Just as there can be no 'know that' except as the outcome of 'know how', so there is no material upon which historical 'know how' can be exercised or developed except that of genuinely historical questions ...

And there is a second danger. If 'content doesn't matter' then attention may be concentrated upon questions which, while genuinely historical in that they are concerned with justly establishing true propositions about the past, are intrinsically trivial and are chosen because they happen (allegedly) to be interesting ... No matter how sophisticated and ingenious the enquiry procedures the children are inducted into may be, history will neither command nor deserve respect if the outcome of its enquiries is never more than mildly interesting triviality.

These seem to be the main weaknesses of the 'new' history as it is often practised – the *undue* stress upon enquiry, and the wider epistemological ignorance of which it is part and consequence, may result in a failure to discriminate enquiries which are genuinely historical, or may concentrate upon those which, while genuinely historical, are of little account because of the indifference to content. All these dangers must be guarded against if history is to be taken seriously in the curriculum.

... The study of history provides us, *inter alia*, with a stock or repertoire, so to speak, of analogies which together constitute a framework of reference, a 'way of looking' in terms of which alone many contemporary events may be *appropriately* classified and understood. And to fail to understand them is not only in some sense to fail as an educated person; it is always unfortunate, and may be disastrous, because of the practical misjudgements it may produce ...

In so far as 'understanding the world' is the reason for making history compulsory, it would seem to follow that *modern* history must be the chosen content. And this argument is perhaps strengthened by the self-evident need for a knowledge of economics if the world is to be understood; it is scarcely an exaggeration to say that the more modern the period studied the more economics is required to understand the course of events, and the more its acquisition is part and parcel of historical education ...

But as against this modernist 'tilt' it must be remembered that an important objective of studying history is to give pupils the experience of *contrast* ... The assumptions of our own society need critical review, and this cannot but be facilitated by the study of other societies where the assumptions were significantly different ... Amid the manifold and manifest differences between other societies and our own world, run strands of familiarity which make it possible to take those differences seriously, as relevant to our own experience and action ... To have penetrated the rationale of 'If you want peace, prepare for war' through the record of many conflicts between societies more or less different from our own is to have grasped not only the structural similarity of state conflicts, which preserves the cogency of the analogy, but the differences, and reasons *for* the differences, among them, which force relevant modifications of it to be made.

Summary

While Rogers insists that students cannot make any confident claim to historical knowledge if they do not understand the process by which it has been constructed, and thus how it could be validated, he is equally adamant that it is not enough simply for students to understand the nature of this process. Indeed they cannot truly understand it without also undertaking extensive study of historical narratives. The substantive content of those narratives and the enquiry questions that young people are encouraged to answer matter profoundly because of history's explanatory power. This derives from the stock of analogies that history can offer, which should encompass not only relatively recent parallels, but also examples from much earlier societies that can illuminate salient features precisely because of the attention they focus on differences over time and the reasons why those differences have arisen.

Questions to consider

1. Rogers argues that *neither* 'know how' *nor* 'know that' can be achieved independently of the other. Why do you think debates about the history curriculum are often presented in polarised terms that tend to pit one against the other?
2. Rogers is adamant that substantive content choices should not be based on students' interests alone. What part, if any, do you think such considerations should play in curriculum design?
3. Rogers' view that students need knowledge both of modern history and of more distant periods leads him to argue for a 'patch' approach to the history curriculum, enabling students to study a range of different historical periods. What are the benefits and drawbacks of such an approach? What kind of 'frame of reference' do you think would prove most useful to young people?

Extract 2

Source

Hirsch, E.D. (1987) *Cultural Literacy: What every American needs to know*. Boston: Houghton Mifflin. See pp. 19, 113, 127–8, 132–3.

Introduction

Cultural literacy is defined by E.D. Hirsch as possession of the 'basic information needed to thrive in the modern world'. The central argument of Hirsh's manifesto, originally outlined in the 1980s when he was Professor of English at the University of Virginia, and subsequently developed and promoted across the US by his Core Knowledge Foundation, is that all young people should be taught a basic core of information – the kind of 'common knowledge' that the creators of news reports assume they already possess. Without such knowledge (which extends across all 'the major domains of human activity from sports to science'), further learning is impossible, Hirsh argues, and thus the educational disadvantage of those from poor and illiterate homes is perpetuated. To begin to combat this problem, Hirsh and two colleagues (a historian and a physicist) compiled a preliminary alphabetical list of 'what literate Americans know', which was subsequently developed into a graded series of content lists for every year of schooling, each to be taught in a tightly structured, systematic fashion.

Key words & phrases

Cultural literacy; information; facts; associations; cultural memory; fragmentation; incoherence; curriculum coherence; core curriculum; critical thinking

---

Extract

The decline of teaching cultural literacy

Almost everybody knows what is meant by *dollar* and that cars must travel on the right-hand side of the road. But this elementary level of information is not sufficient for a modern democracy. It isn't sufficient to read newspapers (a sin against Jeffersonian democracy), and it isn't sufficient to achieve economic fairness and high productivity. Cultural literacy lies *above* the everyday levels of knowledge that everyone possesses and *below* the expert level known only to specialists. It is that middle ground of cultural knowledge possessed by the 'common reader'. It includes information that we have traditionally expected our children to receive in school, but which they no longer do …

The rise of the fragmented curriculum

To miss the opportunity of teaching young (and older) children the traditional materials of literate culture is a tragically wasteful mistake that deprives them of information they would continue to find useful in later life. The inevitable effect of this fundamental educational mistake has been a gradual disintegration of cultural memory, causing a gradual decline in our ability to communicate …

Principles of reform

One can think of the school curriculum as consisting of two complementary parts, which might be called the extensive curriculum and the intensive curriculum. The content of the extensive curriculum is traditional literate knowledge, the information, attitudes and assumptions that literate Americans share – cultural literacy. Of course, this curriculum should be taught not just as a shared series of items, or lists of words, but as a vivid system of shared associations. The name John Brown should evoke in children's minds not just a simple identifying definition but a whole network of lively traits, the traditionally known facts and values.

The nature of this world knowledge as it exists in the minds of literate adults is typically elementary and incomplete. People reliably share just a few associations about canaries such as yellow, sing, kept in cages, but not much more. Literate people know who Falstaff is, that he is fat, likes to eat and drink, but they can't reliably name the Shakespeare plays in which he appears. They know who Eisenhower was, and might recognize 'military-industrial complex', but they can't be counted on to state anything else about Eisenhower's Farewell Address. In short, the information that literate people dependably share is extensive but limited – a characteristic central to this discussion.

Yet students' possession of that limited information is a necessary preliminary to their acquiring more detailed information. To understand the full text of Dwight D. Eisenhower's Farewell Address and historical circumstances that gave rise to it, they have to know who Eisenhower was and what a farewell address is in the American tradition. The extensive curriculum would be designed to ensure that all our high school graduates are given the traditional information shared by other literate Americans. This extensive network of associations constitutes the part of the curriculum that has to be known by every child and must be common to all the schools of the nation …

The intensive curriculum, though different, is equally essential. Intensive study encourages a fully developed understanding of a subject, making one's knowledge of it integrated and coherent. It coincides with Dewey's recommendation that children should be deeply engaged with a small number of typical concrete instances. It is also that part of the total curriculum in which great flexibility in contents and methods can prevail. The intensive curriculum is the more pluralistic element of my proposal, because it ensures that individual students, teachers and schools can work intensively with materials that are appropriate for their diverse temperaments and aims …

At later levels of education, where teaching is done according to subject divisions, the national vocabulary needs continued systematic attention. We should incorporate the elements of cultural literacy into the structure of textbooks, courses and school requirements. We should teach more surveys that cover large movements of human thought and experience. Yet even now the goal of teaching shared information is under attack by the latest version of educational formalism, the 'critical thinking' movement. This well-meaning educational program aims to take children beyond the minimal skills mandated by state guidelines and to encourage the teaching of 'higher order' skills. Admirable, as these goals are, the denigration of 'mere facts' by the movement's proponents is a dangerous repetition of the mistakes of 1918.

Any educational movement that avoids coming to terms with the specific contents of literate education or evades the responsibility of conveying them to all citizens is committing a fundamental error. However noble its aims, any movement that deprecates facts as antiquated or irrelevant injures the cause of higher national literacy. The old prejudice that facts deaden the minds of children has a long history in the nineteenth and twentieth centuries and includes not just the disciples of Rousseau and Dewey but also Charles Dickens who, in the figure of Mr. Gradgrind in *Hard Times*, satirized the teaching of mere facts. But it isn't facts that deaden the minds of young children, who are storing facts in their minds everyday with astonishing voracity. It is incoherence – our failure to ensure that a pattern of shared, vividly taught, and socially enabling knowledge will emerge from our instruction.

Summary

Hirsch's interest in *cultural* literacy is rooted in his awareness of the role that cultural referents play within texts, and of the extent to which literacy itself – an appreciation of the meaning of texts – depends upon them. Unless every child learns about those reference points within the core curriculum, those students who lack access to them within their family contexts will remain excluded from literate culture. Although the list is an extensive one, and needs to be taught systematically, there is no need to examine each fact in depth. Effective use can be made of wide-ranging survey courses, allowing time for more intensive study of a few specific instances, chosen to meet the needs and interests of different groups of students. He condemns any early attempts to teach 'critical' or 'higher-order' thinking skills, arguing that they will prove utterly vacuous unless students have first mastered the essential facts that provide the foundations for future learning.

Questions to consider

1. How far do you agree with Hirsch's view that there are certain historical facts that should be taught to all young people? If you accept the idea of a 'common core', how extensive do you think it should be, and who should determine its content?
2. Although Hirsch calls for both breadth and depth of learning, he suggests that surveys will be effective for teaching the core curriculum. How can historical overviews be taught in ways that create a 'vivid network of shared associations'?
3. Hirsch insists that the development of an extensive core of factual knowledge has to *precede* the development of 'higher-order' thinking skills, such as analysis and evaluation. How do you see the relationship between the mastery of facts and the development of critical thinking, and what are the implications of this relationship for curriculum design?

Extract 3

Source

Counsell, C. (2000) Historical knowledge and historical skills: A distracting dichotomy. In J. Arthur and R. Phillips (eds) *Issues in History Teaching*. London: Routledge, 54–71.

Introduction

As the title of this chapter makes clear, the history educator Christine Counsell fundamentally rejects any assumed duality between 'knowledge' and 'skill'. While it is helpful to acknowledge the conceptual distinction between substantive content and historical process, she argues that the two are inevitably intertwined in learning history, and that neither can be meaningfully assessed without consideration of the other. In this particular extract, she seeks to address three arguments that have sometimes been advanced by history teachers who perceive the prescription of curriculum content as problematic. The first is the danger inherent in prescribing *any* body of historical knowledge, particularly within a multicultural society in which there are risks both of alienating some pupils or condemning others to a 'damningly limited cultural outlook' (p. 61) – the latter being the argument advanced by Hirsch in Extract 2 above. The second is the view (also challenged by Rogers) that specific content is somehow unimportant and serves only as the domain in which to practise things. The third is the condemnation of (particular kinds of) content for making history too difficult or unnecessarily boring.

Key words & phrases

Prescribed curriculum; indoctrination; interpretations of history; historical content; cumulative knowledge acquisition

---

Extract

It is not that these judgments deserve censure but rather that professionals need to analyse both the rationale for and the consequences of such judgments. The first warning of 'dangerous' is one to which curriculum policy-makers and teachers must forever be alert. To feed children a view of the past, uncritically (and even a choice of content for the purposes of a prescribed curriculum amounts to a 'view') is to close down other possibilities, other stories and other ways of telling them. Yet to try to solve this by opting for a criterion-based history curriculum seeking the ultimate balance in all cultural, ethnic, gender and social aspects is not to protect that pupil from indoctrination. It is just creating another kind of story reflecting and assumed consensus in contemporary accounts. It is arguably just as dangerous for any teacher to seek the holy grail of an ethnically, culturally, socially neutral history curriculum, however redemptive of past imbalances.

If the answer cannot lie in a perfectly balanced or politically-acceptable-to-all-parties-curriculum, then where does it lie? One answer to this particular difficulty was created by the first National Curriculum of 1991. Attainment Target 2, as it was then called, or 'Interpretations of History' was an astonishing innovation whose significance has been hugely underestimated. What this new curriculum device did was to make the danger of history the object of study itself. Here was the perfect solution: the way in which history reaches us, through textbook, teacher, film, family folklore or heritage tea-towel becomes the focus for our critical attention. The aim was not to judge its reliability, but simply to examine how it came to be. The Working Group's final report asserted that 'historical theories and interpretations are there to be constantly re-examined ... there are no monopolies of the truth' (DES 1990: 11). To teach interpretations well is to show pupils that history *is* dangerous.

What, then, of the charge that choice of historical content is unimportant? When the content of the curriculum is viewed in the context of learning process rather than outcome, when its function in children's learning is explored it becomes impossible to see content choice as unimportant. Much of our ability to make meaning from historical sources and accounts comes from the ability to spot analogy. As study continues, analogies multiply. This supplies a frame of reference without which most passages of history are unintelligible. The acquisition of historical knowledge is cumulative in its impact:

> We see the world in terms of our picture of it, and that picture is note a mere agglomeration of random sensory chaos but the outcome of a classificatory process which has grouped and separated experiences according to a sense of like/unlike. (Rogers 1987: 11)

... Rather than despair, [for example] that the bottom 40 per cent of the ability range cannot handle the religious concepts of the Reformation, it makes sense to build understanding of key religious mentalities very systematically [for example by first studying the German Reformation] so that during the subsequent study of the Reformation in England, Wales and Scotland, all pupils will be comfortable with the religious significance of innovations in theology. The more pupils know the more they are in a position to learn. To say that the learning of content is unimportant is to ignore its subtle role in future learning.

This brings us to the third and final charge – that an emphasis on knowledge acquisition will tend to boredom and difficulty. I deal with these two problems together because they are exactly the same thing. Pupils get bored when they get stuck. They persevere with the most impossible of questions when they are fired up and excited. To suggest that a particular detail or fact is not 'relevant' to a pupil is to indulge in slightly careless curricular thinking. All history is potentially relevant to adolescent and adult living: it is about the behaviour of men and women in society. What we really mean when we say that something is irrelevant is that either the information overload, or the unfamiliarity of the material, or the sheer banality of its presentation make the pupil switch off. It is either too strange or too familiar! If we are to overcome the kinds of difficulties that the majority of pupils still present, we need both to construct and to analyse short and long-term journeys into the difficulties themselves. Somehow the strange must be made familiar and the familiar strange. The critical question is how do (or might) teachers ensure that the virtuous circle of cumulative knowledge acquisition replaces the vicious cycle of boredom and difficulty?

Summary

The genuine and complex problems inherent in prescribing any particular body of historical content (and thereby excluding others) can be effectively addressed by teaching students explicitly about the power of history. Including 'interpretations of history' as a focus of the curriculum ensures that students learn how and why particular versions of the past come to be accepted (or challenged) by particular groups in society and why this makes history so dangerous. The cumulative nature of historical knowledge, which means that subsequent learning builds on students' understanding of previous topics, makes the choice of substantive content extremely important, especially in planning for progression. The difficulties that students often experience in learning about particular historical content should not be ascribed to the content itself, allowing it to be dismissed as inappropriate. They reflect problems in the way that the content is presented, and call for careful analysis and attention to how the curriculum is structured.

Questions to consider

1. How effectively can the inclusion of 'historical interpretations' as an explicit curriculum focus guard against the dangers of indoctrination inherent in any prescribed curriculum?
2. Counsell suggests that careful planning about when to teach particular substantive content is extremely important in securing progression. How effectively do you think this kind of planning could be done on a national scale? How much discretion about the sequence of topics should be left to teachers?
3. Counsell suggests that when students encounter difficulties, teachers are misguided in blaming the particular content of the curriculum. How far do you accept the argument that students' boredom or problems with certain substantive content can *always* be overcome by better curriculum planning or closer attention to the nature of the students' difficulties?

Investigations

Exam question analysis: Analyse a sample of the public examination questions that your students undertake, particularly the source-based questions. What kind of knowledge – and how much – do students need in order to tackle them effectively?

Review the structure of your history curriculum: Examine how effectively your current curriculum is structured to support cumulative knowledge acquisition. What are the substantive aspects of content knowledge that you think it is particularly important to revisit and develop? To what extent does the way in which topics are sequenced (within each school year – and over the course of several years) allow students to build on earlier understandings? How can students be helped to make useful connections from one year (or stage of learning) to another?

Use an action research approach to explore new approaches to teaching particularly challenging content: Identify one substantive element of your current curriculum that students tend to find particularly complex or dismiss as irrelevant. Find out what they think makes it so difficult and experiment with different approaches to overcoming the challenge. Could it be addressed by developing certain kinds of prior knowledge or by creating a more genuine and engaging puzzle?

Think deeper

The assumption that substantive content and historical process are inextricably combined, which underpins Counsell's argument in Extract 3 above, also means that she is as dissatisfied with assessment schemes that rely exclusively on concept or skill-based models of progression, as she is with those schemes that treat progression as the mere accumulation of more items of factual knowledge. Her argument that greater attention should be paid to the function of knowledge in progression is therefore explored more fully in Chapter 18.

In a call to rethink history education in American schools, Bruce VanSledright (2011), who shares the view that historical thinking requires an enquiry-based approach and an understanding of history as a form of knowledge, seeks to illustrate his arguments through the practice of an 'invented history-teacher-protagonist', Thomas Becker. Becker, he explains, operates with a 'three-dimensional model' of subject matter knowledge: (1) first-order knowledge – of what happened in the past, when, involving whom and with what results – is certainly required, but it develops as consequence of also knowing about (2) the kinds of organising ideas that can be used to order and construct that knowledge (such as change and continuity, or causation) and (3) the practices and strategies for getting there (the use of evidence). Modelling his understanding of the relationship between these three types of subject–matter knowledge on the practices of historians (the experts who best epitomise depth of understanding of the American past), Becker encourages his students to ask questions. But recognising that, unlike historians, his students start without much knowledge of what has already been written about the event they are investigating, he begins by immersing them in 'first questions': 'What happened here? Why? How do we know?' These questions, which necessitate investigation of original sources, serve to build up the students' prior knowledge (of substantive content, organising concepts *and* historical processes) and so equip them to develop the 'deep content knowledge' that comes from thinking and analysing. The examples that VanSledright presents of Becker's curriculum planning, specific teaching episodes and test papers serve to suggest how the three different dimensions might be effectively developed, successfully integrated and meaningfully assessed.

The process of combining 'knowing' and 'doing' history is frequently described as 'historical contextualisation': situating information about the past in its own time and space, and in relationship to long-term developments or other particular events in order to give meaning to it (Wineburg 1998). The creation of meaning by locating unique events within what appear (at least with hindsight) to be coherent sequences of phenomena was originally described by William Walsh (1967) as the process of 'colligation', a term examined in some detail by the Canadian history educator Stéphane Lévesque (2008) in defining what it means to think historically. Walsh claimed that to study a period in history and develop a coherent understanding of its events, historians must create or reveal common themes intrinsic to the changes that occurred within it. In so doing, they both sum up the individual events and tell the reader how to interpret them. Colligatory concepts, according to Walsh, must meet three key principles. The first is that they should be 'well-founded in the facts', effectively emerging from the sources. The second is that they should genuinely serve to illuminate those facts, rendering the past 'real and intelligible' to those in the present. The third is that they should be 'thought of as concrete and universal' – allowing the particular to be understood as an instance of a recurring phenomenon. As Lévesque explains, this final principle has since been questioned, allowing for a broader conception of colligatory concepts, including those such as 'revolution', which can serve to describe more than one historical series of events, and others, such as 'The Industrial Revolution', which are far more restrictive in their application, constituting 'a unique historical whole'. Since colligations play a central role in the organisation of historical knowledge, particularly encapsulating historians' ideas about the nature of change, students' must be able to use them appropriately if their knowledge of the past is genuinely to serve as a frame of reference.

In his wider discussion of *Why History Matters* the academic historian John Tosh (2008) considers the question of the knowledge that young people should acquire from school history. He fully recognises that much of what they learn will quickly become obsolete (just as it does in information technology or science), and that no amount of forethought could enable curriculum planners to predict the particular topics that will be most relevant to students' future political lives. This does not, however, mean that history's main contribution must therefore lie in developing generic skills of argument and analysis: instead it is the ability that it promotes to apply historical perspectives to current issues, informed by an appreciation of the 'historically literate' questions that it is important to ask. Using the example of the invasion of Iraq in 2003, and the caution that might have been advised in light of careful study of Britain's previous occupation of Basra in 1914 and the fate of the original British Mandate (rather than crude comparisons between Saddam Hussein and Adolf Hitler), Tosh argues that an informed citizen is one who recognises that history is an 'indisputable basis for understanding an unfamiliar society'. Such a citizen would have enough historical knowledge to recognise the 'centrality of change and development in accounting for the world around them' and to 'grasp the merits – and the drawbacks – of historical comparison' in considering possible future outcomes. Tosh echoes Rogers in calling both for substantial attention to be paid to modern history (post-1945) and for sufficient study of a more distant past, but is more wary of the 'patch' approach that Rogers endorses because of its tendency to break historical knowledge into disconnected fragments. In arguments that resonate with some of those discussed in Chapters 7 and 11, Tosh claims that a chronological framework extending across several centuries is necessary to develop an understanding of the processes of change and development, but he sees no reason why the focus of that extended narrative should be the nation state.

Think wider

Hirsch's argument (in Extract 2 above) about the importance of cultural literacy – valued for the access that it gives to political life – has a certain resonance with the arguments of the French sociologist, Pierre Bourdieu, about the importance of 'cultural capital'. Indeed, Hirsch subsequently cited Bourdieu (1973), claiming that he had 'shown that those who possess a larger share of "cultural capital" tend to acquire much more wealth and status, and to gain more abilities, than those who start out with very little of this precious resource' (Hirsch 1996: 225). However, critics such as Feinberg (1997) have been quick to challenge Hirsch's attempt to 'appropriate' Bourdieu. The latter's argument is fundamentally a critical one: not that cultural capital adds value to our world that is then recognised and rightly rewarded, but that it merely serves to *legitimise* wealth and status. Indeed Hirsch's systematic lists of facts might be seen as the epitome of what Bourdieu described as the commodification of knowledge to serve class reproduction. As Feinberg argues, what Hirsch takes as cultural capital – his lists of 'core knowledge' – form only a small component in what is, for Bourdieu, a larger, more arbitrary social and political scheme. It is not the mere possession of information that determines access to power, but the ways in which one pursues and displays this knowledge: 'it is not what one knows that provides capital. Rather it is how one knows it that establishes its worth as capital. How knowledge is carried is a sign of membership in a certain class' (Feinberg 1997: 30).

Debates about the specific substantive content of the history curriculum and about the relationship between substantive and procedural knowledge have occurred in a wide variety of contexts. Indeed the cases explored in Taylor and Guyver's (2012) *History Wars and the Classroom* detail experiences of tensions over the past 30 years drawn from six continents and ten democratic nations. Although they acknowledge that the term 'history wars' was deliberately adopted (first in Australia) as a publisher's device to ignite debate and has not been used so freely elsewhere, Taylor and Guyver regard the cases presented in their book as illustrative of two kinds of political attack on the teaching of history. The first, in which arguments are advanced in favour of presenting historical knowledge as a single national story, they characterise as an attempt to 'usurp the critical, reflective, reflexive and multi-perspectival nature of the discipline' in favour of a 'politically expedient, self-serving mono-culturalism' (2012: xii). The second form of attack, marketed politically and educationally as 'a progressive act', according to Taylor and Guyver, undermines any endeavour to teach students about the nature of history as a form of knowledge by attacking it as 'regressive, narrow and elitist' (2012: xii) and calling for more cross-curricular or integrated forms of education in social studies.

Nakou and Barca (2010) offer a similarly wide-ranging survey of *Contemporary Public Debates over History Education*, in which the 14 examples they present are categorised both in terms of the degree of passion that the debates have aroused and the extent to which they have been conducted in educational rather than political or national terms. The editors conclude that the content of history education – the specific knowledge to be developed – remains problematic, whatever approach is adopted, although it is conceived differently within different approaches. Within 'elaborated disciplinary approaches' (concerned with the cultivation of historical thinking), the content of history education is debated in relation to the development of a 'flexible frame of reference which would enable young people to understand the present and the future in historical terms' (2010: 2). Where approaches have focused less on the nature of history as a form of knowledge, but have sought to become more inclusive, the problem of content mainly refers to the geographical and social focus of history education, seeking ways in which to cover both national and world history. In traditional educational environments in which history education is conceived of as the reproduction of a closed national 'historical' narrative, the substance of that narrative is 'passionately protected from any potential alterations and interpretations' (2010: 8).

The first of these approaches (and the limitation of the second) is also richly illustrated by Grever and Stuurman's (2007) collection of examples from diverse national contexts. All of the contributors accept the need for twenty-first century history curricula to go 'beyond the canon' and none of them assumes that it will be enough simply to replace national canons by 'counter-canons' such as 'history from below' or the historical voice of 'the others' (2007: 15). While they all certainly propose to reconfigure national histories by linking them to transnational processes and global connections, they also insist on the importance of plurality. Teachers, they argue, should be free to experiment with different types and formats of history, and pupils and students should be taught to understand and judge competing historical perspectives.

Debates about the role and relative importance of knowledge within the school curriculum have not been confined to history. In an early response to the British government's announcement in 2010 of plans to reform the National Curriculum, Michael Young (2011) discussed what he called the 'return to subjects' in terms of three possible futures for schooling, each based on different curricular assumptions about the role and nature of knowledge. Future 1 (of which Hirsch is a leading proponent) treats access to knowledge as the core purpose of the curriculum and assumes that the range of subjects and the boundaries that define that knowledge are largely given. In contrast, Future 2 rejects the 'givenness' of knowledge, treating it purely as a 'social construct' that is therefore a product of, and responsive to, changing social and economic demands. Driven by the goals of expanding access to education and securing economic benefits, Future 2 dismisses the idea that the boundaries between subjects and those between school and everyday knowledge might express epistemological realities. From this perspective, arguments in favour of school subjects and the boundaries between them come to be seen as conservative or backward looking – as Taylor and Guyver (2012) claim happened to history – and are increasingly treated as little more than masks to perpetuate privilege. Whereas Future 1 denies the social and historical basis of knowledge and its organisation into subjects and disciplines, Future 2 treats the ways that knowledge is organised as historically arbitrary and in some forms as little more than expressions of power. Both are wrong, Young claims, in the assumptions that they make about knowledge. The third option that he offers, Future 3, treats knowledge as *both* social in origin *and* objective. Indeed its objectivity derives from its social origins, in the practice of specialist communities of researchers in different fields. This 'social realist' view of knowledge has been interpreted as an important defence of teaching history as a form of knowledge (Harris and Burn 2011). It also has strong parallels with Seixas' (1993) discussion of the relationship between school and academic 'communities of inquiry' and is therefore examined in more detail in Chapter 3.

References

Bourdieu, P. (1973) Cultural reproduction and social reproduction. In R. Brown (ed.) *Knowledge, Education and Cultural Change*. London: Tavistock, 71–112.

DES (1990) *The Final Report of the History Working Group History for Ages 5 to 16*. London: HMSO.

Feinberg, W. (1997) Educational manifestos and the new fundamentalism. *Educational Researcher*, 26, 27–35.

Grever, M. and Stuurman, S. (2007) *Beyond the Canon: History for the twenty-first century*. Basingstoke: Palgrave Macmillan.

Harris, R. and Burn, K. (2011) Curriculum theory, curriculum policy and the problem of ill-disciplined thinking. *Journal of Education Policy*, 26 (2), 245–61.

Hirsch, E.D. (1996) *The Schools We Need and Why We Don't Have Them*. New York: Doubleday.

Lévesque, S. (2008) *Thinking Historically: Educating students for the twenty-first century*. Toronto: University of Toronto Press.

Nakou, I. and Barca, I. (2010) *Contemporary Debates over History Education*. Charlotte, NC: Information Age Publishing.

Rogers, P. (1987) The past as a frame of reference. In C. Portal (ed.) *The History Curriculum for Teachers*. Lewes: The Falmer Press, 3–21.

Seixas, P. (1993) The community of inquiry as a basis for knowledge and learning: The case of history. *American Educational Research Journal*, 30 (2), 305–24.

SHP (1976) *A New Look at History: School History 13–16 Project*. Edinburgh: Holmes McDougall.

Taylor, T. and Guyver, R. (2012) *History Wars and the Classroom: Global perspectives*. Charlotte, NC: Information Age Publishing.

Tosh, J. (2008) *Why History Matters*. Basingstoke: Palgrave Macmillan.

VanSledright, B. (2011) *The Challenge of Re-thinking History Education: On practices, theories and policy*. New York and London: Routledge.

Walsh, W. (1967) Colligatory concepts in history. In W. Burston and D. Thompson (eds) *Studies in the Nature and Teaching of History*. London: Routledge and Kegan Paul, 65–84.

Wineburg, S. (1998) Reading Abraham Lincoln: An expert/expert study in the interpretation of historical texts. *Cognitive Science*, 22 (3), 319–46.

Young, M. (2011) The return to subjects: a sociological perspective on the UK Coalition Government's approach to the 14–19 curriculum. *The Curriculum Journal*, 22 (2), 265–78.

The relationship between school history and academic history

Some history teachers confidently conceive of their students as 'mini-historians' capable of engaging directly in the processes of constructing historical knowledge. Indeed they regard such engagement as essential if their students are to develop a secure understanding of the nature of historical knowledge. Others reject the idea of basing school history on the academic discipline, generally arguing either that such an approach is far too difficult for school-children (a claim famously advanced by the Tudor historian Geoffrey Elton) or that it is too time-consuming when what young people really need is sufficient substantive knowledge to give them a mental map of the past. This chapter examines the position that history teachers occupy between the academy and their students, and the kinds of relationship that they can forge between the two communities. It explores the arguments that have been advanced for modelling school history closely on academic practice and illustrates the variety of ways in which teachers have brought historians' work into the classroom and the impact that this can have on students' motivation and historical writing.

Extract 1

Source

Seixas, P. (1993) The community of inquiry as a basis for knowledge and learning: The case of history. *American Educational Research Journal*, 30 (2), 305–24.

Introduction

In this article Canadian history educator Peter Seixas first explores the diverse routes by which scholarly research within the disciplines and classroom practice have both come to depend on the notion of a community of enquiry. Over the past 40 years, challenges to confident assumptions about the objectivity of knowledge have led to a pragmatic emphasis on the power of the processes of enquiry and rigorous critique within each discipline to generate *provisional* claims (the best that is currently known). In an entirely separate process, psychosocial theories and empirical research (most obviously associated with the work of Vygotsky and Bruner) have led to an understanding of learning in the classroom as a communal activity in which knowledge and understanding are socially constructed. Seixas then uses the subject of history as a case-study to compare the two different communities of enquiry and examine the role of the school teacher in negotiating the knowledge that is generated in each. He not only rejects a hierarchical relationship in which teachers merely pass on the products of scholarly research but also any attempt to conflate the two systems.

Key words & phrases

Community of enquiry; academic community; historian; historical scholarship; contingency of historical interpretations; dialogue

---

Extract

History teachers occupy a key position between two communities organized around history knowledge and learning. They have a difficult job in both directions. To the extent that they are actively engaged in historical research or writing, they can participate in the construction of historical knowledge with the community of historians. But institutionally, there are few supports for and, in fact, massive constraints on history teachers undertaking these activities. Their distance from the academic community makes them tend to see historical knowledge as being created by others. To the extent that they receive history as inert, opaque information, it is not surprising that they reproduce those presentations when they turn to face the students in the classroom. Thus, their exclusion from the academic community of inquiry reinforces other structural tendencies in the schools (McNeil, 1986). Enough distance from the academic community of historians may, in fact, make history teachers unable to construct a classroom community around historical problems (Wilson and Wineburg, 1988).

On the other hand, there are surely ways, short of writing monographs and scholarly history articles, for history teachers to approach the community of historians. The central professional task they face is the construction of historical presentations for students. Sufficient contact with the historians' community (through seminars, journal reading, and conferences) and sufficient opportunity to work with each other would constitute the foundations of their own community of inquiry as a basis for a specialized historical knowledge (which Shulman, Wineburg, and Wilson might call pedagogical historical knowledge). What differentiates this historical knowledge from that of historians is its more central concern with the problems of presentation to members of a community beyond itself. These concerns might, if addressed by teachers well versed in the new historical scholarship, be of great interest, in turn, to historians hoping to extend their reach beyond their own community.

Students in a classroom, of course, can only constitute a community of inquiry for studying history under the skilful direction of a teacher. Given too much interpretive leeway, students may construct and reinforce untenable views of the past and of their place in historical time. On the other hand, if students are given too little opportunity for active, interpretive participation in a classroom community of inquiry, their formal history lessons may not connect at all with their informal and naive sense of the past, in which case their history education is entirely ineffective (Gardner, 1991). Although the analysis presented here denies a central role for the teacher as the presenter of authoritative historical 'facts', it does not preclude the teacher's acting in other epistemologically authoritative ways in constructing a community of inquiry in the classroom: establishing criteria for historical evidence, methods of determining historical significance, and limits on interpretive license.

The potential benefits of a community of inquiry that includes teachers and historians emerge from this analysis. History teachers might find in historians' emerging questions, in their shifting discourse, interrogations of the past more pertinent to current conditions than any other, simply because the community of historians builds its intellectual life around such questions. The recognition of the contingency of any particular construction of history, that is, the recognition of the historicity of historical dialogue itself, brings along with it an obligation of an ongoing engagement with the dialogue. History teachers' failure to participate in the dialogue may well leave them with residual history (constructions that were framed for some other present), whereas historians' failure to invite a broader group (particularly teachers and students) to participate in history-making restricts their constructions to a narrow audience within the present …

Social studies educators' concern about too much participation by historians in the shaping of school curriculum (e.g. Nelson, 1992) is ironic in view of the potential value of teachers' contact with the historians' community of inquiry. It is precisely the lack of ongoing contact that leads to the lifeless and irrelevant history that these social studies educators fear. Conversely, teachers' participation in the historians' community of inquiry would provide an entry into the most sophisticated historical contextualizations of current issues. Social studies educators might alternatively see themselves as intermediaries who generate the mechanisms to transcend the gaps between the languages and cultures of disciplinary specialist and teacher.

Within the limits of time and resources, the more teachers are integrated into the scholarly community, the better the chances that they will understand the nature of historiographic investigation, interpretation, and debate. For their part, historians need to sustain their confrontation with the problem of historical understanding beyond the historical community. The contingency and interpretive fluidity of historical knowledge based in the community of inquiry are not compatible with the institutions that have grown for the dissemination of 'history' beyond that community. Historians, like educators, need to join in an active search for new forms. History teachers are arguably their best allies. Whether teachers and scholars in other disciplines are similarly poised I leave as a question for them to answer.

Summary

Despite the difficulties of engaging in historical research and writing, teachers who are too distant from the academic community are more likely to offer their students inert information about the past rather than engage them in tackling historical problems. History teachers' own community of enquiry is most obviously focused on the creation of teaching materials and appropriate scaffolds for learning, in order to guide their students' enquiry and induct them into appropriate strategies for evaluating and interpreting evidence and establishing of criteria for determining historical significance. Greater interaction between historians and history teachers in a single community of enquiry would benefit both, enabling teachers to see how historians' questions and interpretations are responding to current concerns (recognising history as an ever-changing dialogue between the present and the past) and ensuring that historians' accounts and explanations not only reach a much wider audience but also are genuinely responsive to that audience.

Questions to consider

1. How far do you agree with Seixas that it is a problem if teachers become too distant from the academic community of historians?
2. What opportunities, if any, are open to you to engage with historians as well as with other teachers in a community of enquiry?
3. Seixas presents history as a case-study of the kind of relationship between academic and classroom communities of enquiry that he thinks should also exist in other subjects. Do you think history teachers tend to be better or worse connected to the academic community than teachers of other subjects? Are there examples of liaison within other subjects from which you think historians and history teachers could learn?

Extract 2

Source

Bellinger, L. (2008) Cultivating curiosity about complexity: What happens when Year 12 start to read Orlando Figes' *The Whisperers? Teaching History*, 132, 5–13.

Introduction

As a trainee teacher, Laura Bellinger introduced the work of historian Orlando Figes into her classroom with a number of very specific purposes. The exam specification that she was teaching tended to take a top-down perspective that risked reducing the victims of Stalin's purges to little more than dry statistics. Her hope was that a recent account, rooted in detailed archival research, would illuminate for them both the reality and the diversity of individual human experience. She chose a series of extracts with considerable care and constructed specific tasks to provoke discussion as students introduced each other to different individuals' experiences and drew on their particular case-studies to challenge a series of deliberately provocative claims. To examine the effects of this approach, she collected and analysed a range of observation and video data as well as examples of the students' work, looking not only at the passion behind their argument but also at the incisiveness of their analysis.

Key words & phrases

Curiosity; student engagement; personal stories; analytic writing; complexity

---

Extract

Students' initial responses to reading the first extract about the Piatnitsky family were fascinating. A key theme that made meaning out of their learning was curiosity. The process at work was a kind of cumulative curiosity as one student's questions or comments provoked curiosity and questioning in others. For example, after a hands-up vote on how they felt about the reading, all were positive except Kay, who said, 'Well this didn't happen to everyone in Russia, did it?' This prompted James to ask how typical this was of people's feelings about the party. One student then asked if only men had been purged. And so on. The curiosity intensified cumulatively.

In their written work, student engagement and judgement concerning central issues could be discerned through a range of patterns in the note-taking styles such as use of capital letters and choice of quotes from the text … [In discussion] students were animated and showed attachment to the individuals about whom they had read as they challenged each other. The process of selecting information for their exhibitions seems somewhat random in places, but this in itself was analytically useful to me. It seemed to reflect the fact that certain students in the group were determined to include particular examples and areas of personal reading.

Of 17 essays, nine explicitly referred to Figes at some point. Students varied widely in how well they qualified and contextualised their examples and how successfully they located these within the structure and framework of their argument. In some cases, however, the use of personal stories seemed to make analysis more manageable: they were able to pick up on particular issues and concepts as these were borne out in the stories of individuals …

In several places students took on particular language used by Figes. Their writing also became tighter, more passionate and more nuanced as they became involved with describing personal stories. I also noted that some students wrote with a new fluency as they described the atmosphere of fear created by the purges …

Asked how they found reading Figes, the most common questionnaire responses were: interesting (10), useful/helpful (7), shocking (4) and moving/inspiring (3). Three felt that it had been unnecessary, one of these saying that it would be interesting for leisure reading, and two students found it 'hard' or 'confusing'. One of these said that this was because there had been too many people in the extract that they had read but that, overall, reading the accounts had been helpful. When asked in what ways the extracts had affected their understanding, ten students said it had made it more personal and three explicitly linked this to helping them understand …

According to the questionnaires, the majority of students had found AS history interesting anyway, so I had probably not created any new passionate historians. Nonetheless, the data as a whole suggests that their perspective was broadened by this study. One student told me several weeks later that she had bought her own copy of *The Whisperers* [Figes, 2007] as she had enjoyed it so much. All of the students used examples from personal accounts in their museum exhibitions and some students formed some attachment to the particular stories that they had read …

Asking students to read different extracts and to discuss them seems to have supported analytic thinking in some students. As they were set up with different perspectives from contrasting readings, they immediately had to engage critically with each other, questioning and challenging. This produced a sharper analytical focus in oral discussion than I had witnessed before. Moreover, devoting an entire lesson to using Figes seemed to allow for sustained reflection, supporting more probing analysis of issues.

I had hoped that all this oral analysis would provide a stepping stone between the reading and the level of analysis expected in an essay. However, for most students, it would have been beneficial to spend more time setting up the essay. I concentrated so much on the value of reading Figes that I neglected to focus on the practice of argument and how to weave in examples …

On the other hand, there was evidence that using Figes helped students to write in a way that was more exploratory, reflective and interesting, particularly in relation to the atmosphere that the purges created in society. Studying personal stories that highlight a variety of perspectives seemed to help them to embrace complexity and to discuss it more readily.

Summary

The specific focus for which Bellinger had selected the work of Figes was the level of personal detail that it provided about a variety of individuals. The stories served to provoke students' curiosity and, for many, a sense of personal engagement and commitment to the lives about which they were learning. While the diversity of these cases made some students' writing more nuanced and tentative, a few resented the additional complexity and the additional time that it took to build this picture (although this awareness of how history has to be constructed might be seen as an important enrichment of their understanding). While students' writing was perhaps more passionate and fluent, they had not learned simply from reading an academic text how to handle the additional detail within an analytical structure and this would need more attention.

Questions to consider

1. In this case the value of the historian's work seemed to lie in the direct access that it gave to individual stories to which he had accessed through archival research. Does this seem to you to be an argument for more engagement with the work of historians or merely for more direct engagement with original sources?
2. Engagement with historical scholarship clearly created an additional level of complexity for these history students. How appropriate do you think it is for teachers to create this kind of additional challenge (if exam specifications do not formally require it), and thereby run the risk of confusing or frustrating students? How could teachers help students to handle the complexity?
4. Is it reasonable to expect that reading the work of academic historians will lead to improvements in the quality of students' writing in history? What potential benefits do you think it might have and how could they be maximised?

Extract 3

Source

Foster, R. (2011) Using academic history in the classroom. In I. Davies (ed.) *Debates in History Teaching*. London: Routledge, 199–211.

Introduction

In the chapter from which this extract is taken, Rachel Foster reviews the range of purposes for which teachers use academic history in the classroom, before explaining her own rationale and outlining the planning that she undertook to enable 13–14 year-olds to engage with an argumentative text, *Hitler's Willing Executioners* (Goldhagen 1996). Foster first highlights the different kinds of extrinsic purpose that have prompted the use of academic texts, all underpinned by notions of progression, and based on the assumption that exposure to academic history will help students to get better at 'doing' history, or understanding it as a discipline, or communicating their own historical knowledge. Less 'tangible' or more intrinsic purposes, she suggests, rest on belief in the *transformative* power of historical texts: making students more independent, inspiring them with a love of reading, or bringing them closer to the heart of the discipline. Foster acknowledges that underlying her own consciously held justifications was a deep conviction that only by getting students *reading* could she really get them to understand and enjoy history as a discipline.

Key words & phrases

Historian; academic debate; independent reading; engagement; literacy

---

Extract

Choosing historians to use in the classroom

I knew that to engage Key Stage 3 students with the work of an academic historian in a meaningful way I would need to find a book that had a compelling subject matter and a clear line of argument couched in an argumentative style. I was familiar with *Hitler's Willing Executioners* (Goldhagen 1996) from my undergraduate studies and on re-reading it felt confident that it fully met those criteria. Goldhagen's book addresses the motivations of the perpetrators of the Holocaust, interweaving powerful narrative and strong argument in a style that is provocative and engaging.

Goldhagen's book also held a distinct advantage: it had been written as a direct response to the work of another historian, Christopher Browning's *Ordinary Men* (1992), criticizing his thesis in what Birn (1998, p. 57) has described as 'unusually strong language'. Browning had responded in turn (Browning 1998) making the two historians' arguments obviously dialogic. Both historians had researched the same case study, German Reserve Police Battalion 101, yet had drawn very different conclusions from the evidence. This meant it would be possible to examine both the claims made by the historians and the evidential basis on which they made them …

Scaffolding

Given that the goal of the enquiry was for students to encounter the processes and products of an academic debate, students needed to engage not just with the historians' claims and evidence but also with its end product, a text. While it would have been possible to construct an enquiry that addressed Goldhagen's and Browning's claims without asking students to read the texts, I wanted students to independently read extended sections for themselves. Both books had a profound effect on me when I first read them. Much of this was to do with the immediacy and power of the story itself, but also with the authors' skills as story tellers and historians. Anger, outrage and conviction burns out of Goldhagen's book in particular: he demands to be heard and compels a response. The intensity and immediacy of the prose inescapably draws the reader into their argument. If I stripped this out of the enquiry – if students never had the chance to hear directly from the authors themselves – it would make the teaching challenge harder by depriving me of a vital way of making it interesting.

Indeed, as my goal of supporting students into independent reading of academic history was less to do with equipping students with the vocabulary and concepts they needed and more to do with giving them the confidence and desire to read, both these things – confidence and motivation – needed to be cumulatively developed over the duration of the enquiry. The planning challenge was therefore to scaffold both individual activities and students' learning *across* the enquiry in order to gradually move them towards independent reading.

The scaffolding strategies I used had three key variables: the nature of the text used, the form in which students encountered it and the process by which they encountered it (i.e. what the students were asked to *do* with the text). Scaffolding students into extended reading began with the selection of the text. My main criteria for choosing an extract was that it should be fascinating in its detail, its storytelling, its argument or its language. If I could find a text that gripped students then their motivation to read would help them to overcome the challenge the text posed …

Conclusion

From Year 7 I may teach students to support their points with evidence, to consider how far the evidence supports their arguments and to modify their language to make it appropriate to the strength of their claims, but I struggle to help them see why it really matters that they do this. By focusing on the processes of history while neglecting the primary product of history – a text – they fail to see the purpose of the process or to enjoy its outcome. Asking students to consciously reflect on what history is and how it is written therefore gave them an opportunity to engage with history in a far more holistic way than a focus on a single concept normally allows. This was particularly true of the concept of evidential thinking, because students were doing it within the context of a real historical debate that gave their thinking purpose and meaning.

Although my goals were explicitly focused on helping students to get better at history, this necessarily meant helping students get better at literacy. Literacy skills were inherent in activities whose acknowledged purpose was to help students think historically – reading for different purposes, identifying and extracting different types of information within a text (for example, claims and evidence), evaluating the effects of tone and language, selecting appropriate vocabulary in their writing, modelling their writing on the style of another writer – students did all this and more through the different activities of the enquiry.

… Finally, I hope that at least some of them will be inspired to carry on reading and engaging with history beyond their formal education. Young people will surely be more likely to pick up a history book if they have the confidence to know that they can read it, and an expectation that they will find it a rewarding experience. Where will they acquire this hope and confidence if not from their history lessons?

Summary

At the heart of Foster's determination to get her students reading academic history is the conviction that direct engagement with historians' arguments will inspire genuine interest and an understanding of why history lessons matter. Her choice of historical texts is therefore based on the clarity and power of their argument and all her skill as a teacher is invested in helping students to 'hear' that argument, essentially unmediated by her own voice. The full chapter describes in detail the range of strategies that she employs to help students access the different texts, through carefully planned forms of scaffolding that serve not only to develop students' literacy skills but also to boost their confidence. Acquiring such confidence in history lessons, she hopes, will inspire them to keep on – or later return to – reading history.

Questions to consider

1. How far do you agree with Foster's view that teachers' attempts to help students to write effectively in history are likely to be limited in their effectiveness if students do not see examples of professional historians' writing?

2. Foster focuses particularly on the power of historical argument as a means of engaging students' interest in an academic text. Are there other kinds of historical writing – or particular features of it – that you think it would be valuable to get students reading?

3. Foster invested considerable time and care in selecting extracts and finding ways to make them accessible to Year 9 students (aged 13–14) because she thought it important to give all students a rewarding experience with a real historical text before some chose to give up the subject. How important do you think it is to use academic texts with lower school students? What other ways are there in which younger students could engage productively with historians' work?

Investigations

Explore the impact on your teaching of closer engagement with academic history: Choose one or two specific ways in which you could engage more directly with academic scholarship in relation to topics that you are teaching. This could simply involve reading one or two items, or attendance at a specialist lecture or seminar. Explore whether and, if so, in what ways, this connection impacts on your planning or teaching.

Evaluate the impact of working with historians' accounts on students' own writing: Plan and evaluate the impact of a unit of work focused on carefully selected extracts from an academic history text, chosen to model particular features of historical writing.

Conduct a survey of students' expectations of learning history at university: Develop a questionnaire survey to find out about the perspective of students studying history at an advanced level, exploring their views of their current experiences and their assumptions about what degree-level history might involve. How realistic are their assumptions, and how might you challenge misconceptions or better prepare them to tackle particular demands?

Think deeper

The extent to which learning history in school should reflect the processes in which historians themselves engage has been extensively and often passionately debated. In most cases, the argument has focused specifically on the use of sources, and the importance or feasibility of asking students to evaluate evidence critically in order to construct their own accounts or explanations of the past. That particular debate is explored within Chapter 8, which is specifically concerned with 'evidence'. Seixas and Morton (2013), however, have gone further, developing a collection of curriculum materials for Canadian teachers, in which their introduction of *each* of their 'big six' historical thinking concepts is explored and analysed in the practice of leading Canadian historians. This is a very deliberate attempt to illuminate for teachers and their students the 'rules' that operate within the academic community of historical enquiry, and the historians were chosen both for the strength of their academic reputations, but also for their popular appeal. Their discussion of the concept of continuity and change, for example, is rooted in Margaret MacMillan's (2003) award-winning *Paris 1919: Six months that changed the world* (published in the UK as *Peacemakers*) that juxtaposes the small-scale close range details of the daily life of the individuals assembled to negotiate the terms of the peace treaties with the large-scale long-range impact of the decisions that they made. Despite the claim of its title, perhaps the most fascinating dimension of the book, as Seixas and Morton illustrate, is the interplay that MacMillan's narrative actually weaves between continuities and change.

Diana Laffin (2012), who teaches 16–19 year olds in a sixth-form college setting, is firmly convinced that her students are themselves 'fledgling historians'. If their own writing is to move beyond the banal and repetitive, they need to need to engage with the 'fluent, logical and expressive' writing of a wide variety of professionals historians. Inspired by Foster's work, Laffin has experimented with a series of activities intended to promote students' wider reading and their effective use of that reading in developing their own historical writing. An online book club, to which teachers as well as students are invited to contribute reviews, helps to demonstrate teachers' own engagement with scholarship, thereby raising student aspirations and helping them to appreciate that different kinds of texts may serve different purposes. The analytical tasks that Laffin devises include classifying a series of books along a continuum from 'popular' to 'academic' and inferring the 'habits' of historians (which they themselves should seek to cultivate) from the language that they commonly use. Extending the ornithological metaphor, Laffin seeks to equip students both to identify the common characteristics of the genus 'historian' and to discriminate between the particular approaches of individual practitioners. Thus, Andrew Marr, for example, is seen more as 'magpie' than 'marsh-harrier' for his wide-ranging, top-down approach.

Although Laffin's work was conducted with A-level students, the idea of using historians' writing as a model with which to inspire and guide students' own writing has certainly not been confined to older students. Christine Counsell, whose work on developing literacy in history is discussed in more detail in Chapter 17, provides a detailed example of how such approaches can be used successfully with students as young as 11 or 12, using the work of distinguished medieval historian, Eileen Power (1975). Like Foster, Counsell (2004) deliberately chose a historian who was presenting a clear line of argument, seeking in this case to engage students not merely with Power's skilful use of limited evidence, but also with her *attitude* and the highly effective ways in which she conveyed it.

Other than using historians' accounts as models for students' own writing, the most common reason for introducing students to the work of academic historians is to help them engage with the concept of historical interpretation – developing an understanding of how and why the accounts that historians construct differ from one another. This became a specific feature of the National Curriculum for England when it was first introduced in 1991, meaning that engagement with 'historiography' could no longer be seen as the preserve of A-level students. Chapter 10, which deals with the concept of 'historical interpretations', therefore offers many more examples of teachers' experimentation with academic history in the classroom. Arthur Chapman (2012) has a particular interest in how students account for differences between historians' accounts and has been experimenting for a number of years in a series of collaborations between school teachers and practising historians to examine whether online discussion between students and academic historians can enrich young people's understanding of the nature of historians' work. The most successful iterations of the project have suggested that direct engagement with historians (responding online to students' original explanations of the reasons for differences between two historians' accounts) can indeed enhance students' sense of the agency of historians as active interpreters of the past (rather than essentially passive products of the time and circumstances in which they happen to be working), and alert them to the importance of considering historians' research questions and their theoretical and methodological assumptions, rather than merely the nature of the sources to which they have access.

Think wider

The appeal that Seixas (1993) made in his article (see Extract 1) to the practices of the academic community of enquiry resonates both with what the American historian Alan Megill (2007) has called 'disciplinary objectivity' and with the arguments of the sociologist, Michael Young (2008). The latter claims that that the power of the knowledge to which young people ought to be introduced in school derives essentially from its endorsement by an 'expert' community, which uses rigorous forms of peer review not merely to judge the quality of specific products that academics create, but also to critique, evaluate and gradually refine the processes by which new knowledge is created within different disciplines. Young's 'social realist' theory of knowledge ('social' in that it derives from the warrant of the community; 'realist' in terms of its internal coherence and explanatory power beyond that community) has been articulated in opposition to vocational or competency-based curricula, driven by the immediate practical concerns of employers and focused on generic 'key skills'. Such approaches, Young argues, will fail to move students beyond the 'everyday' understandings they already hold, denying them access to genuinely powerful knowledge, shared by specialist teachers, university researchers and professional associations.

Claims that school history should *not* seek to imitate the practices of historians have come from historians themselves, most obviously perhaps in Elton's (1970) declaration that suggestions that children can usefully analyse or evaluate the nature of the evidence are 'seriously mistaken'. Such challenges often rest on arguments about the difficulty of history or the time that it takes for students to engage in the processes of constructing or co-constructing knowledge. Somewhat surprisingly, however, appeals to the authority of the academic community have also been challenged even by those who advocate an enquiry-based approach to teaching history. Keith Barton (2009) is concerned that references to 'disciplinary history', which imply a sharp demarcation between legitimate historical scholarship and the variety of ways in which history is used in wider society, may lead young people to dismiss the subject as one that has little relevance to their own lives. While Seixas argues that history teachers' direct engagement with the scholarly community can help to ensure that historical scholarship does not become 'lifeless' and 'irrelevant', Barton counters that teachers should actually be forging connections for their students with history as it is *experienced*: as a social phenomenon, in the work of genealogists, film-makers, politicians and the lives of their family members. Appealing to the authority of the academic community, he fears, risks alienating students, asking them to deny their own interests and perspectives rather than deepening and enriching their ability to use history in a variety of contexts and for multiple purposes.

Recent calls in England for universities to play a greater part in setting public examinations at 18+ have helped to focus attention on the transition from school to university. Barbara Hibbert (2002), a school teacher whose doctoral research involved comparisons of history students' experience at school and university, discovered how difficult the transition was for many of them and urged teachers to focus on developing greater independence among A-level students. Effective preparation for university, she argued, could actually best be achieved by making much more extensive use of the kinds of active – but rigorous – learning strategies that teachers tended to employ much lower down the school. Exploring the issue from a university perspective, Alan Booth (1997) undertook an annual survey of first-year history undergraduates at Nottingham University. Although his specific findings have been overtaken by changes to A-level specifications and innovations in curriculum, pedagogy and assessment within higher education, the principles that underpin his recommendations, rooted in the need to understand students' rationale for pursuing the subject, and the way in which their conceptions of learning and expectations of their tutors have been shaped by their prior experiences, have an enduring significance. Marcus Collins (2011: 34), Director of the history degree programme at Loughborough University, recognised the value of encouraging students to reflect on those prior experiences by writing a 'historiographical analysis of the history that [they] studied at school'. This was preceded by series of classes examining the politicisation of the discipline and the tensions between 'artistic' and 'scientific', 'new' and 'traditional' approaches to history. They were thus equipped with a series of binary categories to apply to their previous experiences:

Rankean/Annales, positivism/idealism, political/social, history from above/people's history, inductive/deductive, historicist/presentist. Most respondents tended to portray themselves as having progressed (especially at A level) from perceiving history in a 'traditional', 'scientific' and Eurocentric fashion to one which emphasised its 'new', 'artistic' and global aspects. They often criticised the former for its biased subject matter and simple (even simplistic) methodology in comparison with the more holistic and democratic approach of the latter. The teaching of British history was sometimes condemned for its traditionalism and parochialism, and while most students accepted the idea that the curriculum should include a moral or civic dimension, they were quick to condemn its political bias. Some students felt that the values it seemed to embody were at odds with their own, and Collins was concerned that so many students felt dissatisfied and even 'cheated' by their experience of school history.

References

Barton, K. (2009) The denial of desire: How to make history education meaningless. In L. Symcox and A. Wilschut (eds) *National History Standards: The problem of the canon and the future of teaching history*. Charlotte, NC: Information Age Publishing, 265–82.

Birn, R. (1998) Historiographical review: Revising the Holocaust. In R. Birn and N. Frankelstein (eds) *A Nation on Trial: The Goldhagen thesis and historical truth*. New York: Metropolitan Books.

Booth, A. (1997) Listening to students: Experiences and expectations in the transition to a history degree. *Studies in Higher Education*, 22 (2), 205–20.

Browning, C. (1992, 1998 2nd edn) *Ordinary Men*. London: Penguin.

Chapman, A. (2012) 'They have come to differing opinions because of their differing interpretations': Developing 16–19 year-old English students' understandings of historical interpretation through on-line inter-institutional discussion. *International Journal of Historical Learning Teaching and Research*, 11 (1), 188–214.

Collins, M. (2011) Historiography from below: How undergraduates remember learning history at school. *Teaching History*, 142, 34–8.

Counsell, C. (2004) *History and Literacy in Year 7: Building the lesson around the text*. London: John Murray. (See chapter 5 'Hearing the style and power of an argument: Eileen Power surprises us about medieval women'.)

Elton, G. (1970) What sort of history should we teach? In M. Ballard (ed.) *New Movements in the Study and Teaching of History*. London: Temple Smith, 221–30.

Figes, O. (2007) *The Whisperers: Private life in Stalin's Russia*. London: Penguin/Allen Lane.

Gardner, H. (1991) *The Unschooled Mind: How children think and how schools should teach*. New York: Basic Books.

Goldhagen, D. (1996) *Hitler's Willing Executioners: Ordinary Germans and the Holocaust*. London: Abacus.

Hibbert, B. (2002) 'It's a lot harder than politics' … students' experience of history at Advanced Level. *Teaching History*, 109, 39–43.

Laffin, D. (2012) Marr: magpie or marsh harrier? The quest for the common characteristics of the genus 'historian' with 16- to 19-year-olds. *Teaching History*, 149, 18–25.

MacMillan, M. (2003) *Paris 1919: Six months that changed the world*. Toronto: Random House.

McNeil, L. (1986) *Contradictions of Control*. New York: Routledge and Kegan Paul.

Megill, A. (2007) *Historical Knowledge, Historical Error: A contemporary guide to practice*. Chicago: University of Chicago Press.

Nelson, J. (1992) Reaction to Michael Whelan: 'History and the social studies'. *Theory and Research in Social Education*, 20 (3), 318–24.

Power, E. (1975) *Medieval Women* (M. Postan, ed.). Cambridge: Cambridge University Press.

Seixas, P. and Morton, T. (2013) *The Big Six Historical Thinking Concepts*. Toronto: Nelson Education.

Wilson, S. and Wineburg, S. (1988) Peering at history through different lenses: The role of disciplinary perspectives in teaching history. *Teachers' College Record*, 89 (4), 525–39.

Young, M. (2008). *Bringing Knowledge Back in: From social constructivism to social realism in the sociology of education*. London: Routledge.

Pupil perspectives on history education

It is very easy to overlook the perspective of pupils when considering the teaching of history. There have been numerous books and articles written, both professional and academic, that discuss a range of issues associated with history pedagogy, the purposes of teaching history, what should be taught and so forth. Many of these debates are held between the 'grown ups', but what do pupils make of studying the past and do they make sense of it in ways that teachers and educationalists want? This chapter provides insights into the ways that pupils engage with history in schools.

Extract 1

Source

Haydn, T. and Harris, R. (2010) Pupil perspectives on the purposes and benefits of studying history in high school: A view from the UK. *Journal of Curriculum Studies*, 42 (2), 241–61.

Introduction

In this study the authors draw upon data from 1,740 pupil questionnaires and 160 pupils in focus-group interviews. The pupils were aged from 11 to 14. The study focused on British pupils' ideas about why they study history at school. The data suggest that many pupils have very vague ideas about the purposes of school history, although there are variations among schools, which suggests that there are things that teachers can do better to explain the purposes and benefits of school history. It is suggested that were teachers to devote more time and thought to helping pupils understand the purposes and benefits of studying their subject in secondary school, this would help improve the motivation and engagement of their pupils.

Key words & phrases

Purpose of history; pupil perspective; student attitudes; pupil voice; usefulness

Extract

Overall the survey suggests that in terms of pupil perceptions of history as a school subject, more pupils believe that history is useful than in previous UK surveys (with the caveats and qualifications which one would normally add when comparing different surveys over time). However, although a majority of pupils reported that they regarded school history as useful, there were large numbers of pupils who could not say why it was useful, or who gave reasons which bore little relation to the stated curriculum justifications for the subject (DfEE/QCA 1999, QCA 2007). The survey suggests that there may be many history classrooms where there is very limited shared understanding between teacher and pupils about why they are studying the past.

It seems possible that, to at least some degree, there has been an extensive debate between 'the grown-ups' about the purpose and nature of a historical education for young people, which has been conducted largely over the heads of those for whom the curriculum was designed. It would appear that the rationale for school history has not percolated meaningfully into the consciousness of many of those for whom the curriculum was designed, or been explained effectively to all learners of history.

In spite of recent changes to the ways in which history is taught in the UK over the past quarter of a century, with more emphasis on history as a form of knowledge as against (primarily) the transmission of a 'body of knowledge' (Lee and Ashby 2000), the majority of responses made little mention of ideas about history as a form of knowledge – with its own procedures and conventions for handling information and assessing the validity of claims – and the ways in which these might be of use or relevance in their lives outside school and when they leave school. There is a degree of irony or paradox about this situation given that it is common practice in the UK for teachers to write up the aims and objectives for the lesson on the board at the start of the lesson. Hackman (2007) suggests that this might be explained by teachers identifying aims and objectives at the micro-level, while neglecting to address more holistic and macro-level reasons for studying particular morsels of the past, and history in general. The following extract from her interview (Hackman 2007) with a Key Stage 3 pupil supports this point:

SH: Don't the teachers put the lesson objectives on the board, I thought everyone put the lesson objectives on the board now?

Pupil: Oh yes … they do that.

SH: Well what do you mean then 'You don't get it'?

Pupil: Well, I don't get the whole of it.

SH: Well, give me an example …

Pupil: Well, what's the point of doing the Stuarts?

There did appear to be a school (or departmental) effect in the pattern of responses … In one school, there were virtually no comments that went beyond tautological or very vague responses, whereas in another school, a substantial number of pupils could put forward reasons for studying history which bore some relation to the stated aims of the National Curriculum for History (DfEE/QCA 1999, QCA 2007).

… It seems possible that some history departments are taking more time than others to try to make the purposes and possible benefits of school history explicit to pupils. Yan Pong and Morris (2002) argue that how teachers make available 'the object of learning' to their pupils has been a neglected element of subject pedagogy – with many teachers focusing on content coverage and teaching approaches at the expense of explaining to pupils why they are learning about something. Initial analysis of the second phase of the research, which focused on history teachers and advisors, suggests that, although history teachers put a great deal of thought into making their lessons interesting and enjoyable for pupils, they may be devoting less time and thought to getting across to pupils the reasons for studying the past, both as a whole, and in terms of the salience and value of particular topics.

It is also possible that the absence of a clear understanding of why they are studying a subject might impact negatively on pupil effort and attainment in subjects other than history. In the words of Hackman (2007):

There are some kids who just don't get it …. [T]hey just don't get what school is for. They come to school and are pretty well behaved but they come for us … for their parents, for the teachers. They come because that's what you do … you come to school. But they don't go for themselves, they don't understand that learning is something for them, they see it as something that is done to them.

Sadler (1994) argued that often teachers simply take for granted many aspects of pupil understanding, and thus fail to teach effectively. Our study lends some support to this hypothesis and suggests that it is important that teachers do not make assumptions about pupils' understanding of the purposes and benefits of studying the subject that they teach.

Summary

Although pupils generally enjoy being taught history and feel it is useful, the findings suggest that pupils on the whole have little clear understanding as to why they study history in schools. The most common reasons presented were related to naive assumptions about employability. However, the variation of pupil responses between schools suggests that teachers can make a positive impact here. It is also argued that a clearer understanding of the value and purpose of a subject will help pupils' motivation and achievement.

Questions to consider

1. Why should pupils study history?
2. How might teachers better convey the reasons for studying history (or any other subject)?
3. If there was a greater emphasis on pupils understanding the value and purpose of a subject, what do you anticipate the impact of this might be?

Extract 2

Source

Traille, E.K.A. (2007) 'You should be proud about your history. They made me feel ashamed': Teaching history hurts. *Teaching History*, 127, 31–7.

Introduction

There is evidence to show that the history curriculum usually reflects the history of the dominant groups in society and that those from minority ethnic groups are often excluded or overlooked. Attempts to bring greater diversity into the curriculum are to be welcomed but teachers need to be aware of the issues this can present. This article draws upon a PhD study by Kay Traille, in which 124 students of African-Caribbean descent and non-African-Caribbean descent aged 13 to 17 were surveyed about their ideas of the past and attitudes towards their history lessons in a postal survey. A further group of 12 students, six of African-Caribbean and six of non-African-Caribbean heritage between the ages of 12 and 17, and their mothers were subsequently interviewed. The findings show that students of African-Caribbean descent see the value of history, but the way in which it is presented often fails to acknowledge the emotional impact topics can have on students, and that this can result in serious unintended consequences such as hurt and alienation.

Key words & phrases

Purpose of history; pupil perspective; student attitudes; pupil voice; minority ethnic groups; diversity; emotional impact

---

Extract

My work began with the belief that it was important to understand how a particular subject, history, made students of African-Caribbean descent think and feel about themselves. We know a lot about the academic performance of students of African-Caribbean descent from the point of view of educators. However, we know not nearly enough from the point of view of the students. Exploring whether the pictures of the past those students received about black people in history attracted, engaged or constrained was a necessary aspect of the study …

Students of African-Caribbean heritage referred to content in history lessons where teachers or peers imposed identities on black people in the past that they rejected. They brought up instances when they felt implicitly and explicitly negatively stereotyped by teachers and peers because of their black heritage. The imposed identity often reflected a value judgement of a particular 'out group' in direct contrast to the positive attributes of an 'in group'.

In both questionnaire and interview the students of African- Caribbean descent stated that they felt more linked to a particular history topic because of a direct family or ancestral link. It seemed that being able to make tangible connections with an ethnic group or family members in the past gave an added sense of connection and ownership within history lessons. Thus, perhaps not unsurprisingly, having being taught or having it implied by peers or teachers that black people were inferior or victims did not increase feelings of involvement in a positive way for some of these students …

Ideas expressed by the respondents in my study indicate that some students of African-Caribbean descent thought of negative attitudes of peers and teachers about black people in history as personal attacks on their identity. Their responses indicate that the resulting hurt, anger, bewilderment and feelings of temporary exclusion could impact adversely on their learning experience. Researchers have argued that the experience of school must present students with learning experiences which hold their attentions not only briefly, but also can command their loyalties and passions …

Negative portrayals of people of colour are ingrained in society. Black people are seen, more often than not, as associated with societal problems. Such negative misconceptions and preconceptions need at least to be challenged within the history curriculum and pedagogy. We cannot afford to ignore the way we make our students feel. When teaching, at times there is a need to tread softly. This is not political correctness, it is common sense. As previously mentioned Shannon, a student of African-Caribbean descent (interview), said 'As long as they are teaching it well, then there is no reason why that shouldn't be shown. It's the truth'. 'Teaching it well' is key. Certain topics are more sensitive than others, and that does not preclude them from being taught, but they need to be taught 'well' with foresight and some sensitivity. Some teachers are still making careless comments about black people in history. They are apparently ignorant of the damage they may be inflicting on young minds. This is a problem that must be addressed and recognised as a priority for teacher training.

Summary

Traille highlights the need for teachers to be sensitive to the needs of their pupils when teaching topics that have a potentially personal connection. This study highlights the unintended consequences for pupils where teachers are either insensitive to the emotional reactions of pupils or lack an in-depth knowledge of the topics they teach. Traille also highlights concerns that teachers may avoid or be uncomfortable dealing with topics that may be seen as controversial and/or sensitive. Although teachers may be trying to create a more inclusive curriculum by bringing in more black figures into the history curriculum, there is a danger that an emphasis on the negative or a derogatory portrayal of the black experience in the past can alienate young people from African-Caribbean descent.

Questions to consider

1. Why is it important to introduce greater diversity of subject content in history?
2. Where in the curriculum is the diversity of people's lives and experiences represented?
3. Consider what images and language are used to portray this diversity and whether this creates a negative impression of different people/groups in the past.

Extract 3

Source

Grever, M., Haydn, T. and Ribbens, K. (2008) Identity and school history: The perspectives of young people from the Netherlands and England. *British Journal of Educational Studies*, 56 (1), 76–94.

Introduction

This study, by Maria Grever, Terry Haydn and Kees Ribbens, draws on findings from a survey of over 400 students in England and the Netherlands. Although it touched on their understanding of why history should be taught, the survey also asked about what history the students felt should be taught, and how history impacted on their sense of identity. The researchers were able to identify responses by gender and minority ethnic group, and it was this latter variable that revealed the strongest differences.

Key words & phrases

Content selection; pupil perspective; student attitudes; pupil voice; minority ethnic groups; diversity

---

Extract

Probably the question which revealed the biggest difference between indigenous and ethnic minority background pupils was 'What kinds of history are important to you?' Respondents were asked to make a 'top 5' of the kinds of history which they considered most important to them out of a list of ten items …

There were some facets of history which were thought to be important by both indigenous and ethnic minority background respondents. One example of this was 'the history of my family', which was identified as in the top three 'types' of history (out of ten options) by most groups. There were also areas where the historical 'priorities' of differing ethnic minority background groups differed.

One example of this was the importance accorded to knowing about 'the history of the country my parents come from', which came top of the list of priorities for respondents from a Turkish background, but only seventh in importance for those from a 'mixed' and 'non-Western' background. Whereas the 'history of the Netherlands' was felt to be most important for indigenous pupils, it was low in the priorities of many allochthonous groups. The area which elicited the greatest polarisation was in the field of religion. Thus, whereas for indigenous Dutch respondents, religion was judged the form of history which was least important to them, for some allochthonous groups, it was deemed to be the most important.

[The responses from English students showed that] [n]ational history was seen as more important to the indigenous pupils, and more importance was attached to religious history by ethnic minority background pupils, but the importance attached to religion by differing sub-sets of allochthonous groups varied considerably. The importance attached to 'the History of Europe' also fluctuated across groups. It is, moreover, interesting to note that 'World history' emerged as more important than national history compared to Dutch responses, in several cases emerging as the form of history which respondents saw as most important overall …

One question asking respondents to consider a 'top 5' of how they would see themselves in terms of identity revealed striking differences between indigenous and ethnic minority background pupils, with indigenous pupils identifying themselves primarily by their country of residence identity, and those from ethnic minority backgrounds identifying themselves primarily by country of origin of their parents or religious identity. Out of 88 indigenous Dutch respondents, 58 per cent chose their national identity as the one that was most important to them. The choice of a national identity as 'prime' identity fell to 19.4 per cent with (44) Surinamese and Antillean respondents, and to under 3 per cent of (85) Moroccan and Turkish respondents.

A majority of Turkish and Moroccan background pupils gave their religion as their 'prime' identity, as against 33 per cent of Surinamese and Antillean pupils.

Only 1 per cent of indigenous Dutch pupils cited religion as their prime identity.

It was interesting to note that a significant minority of pupils from all groups gave a 'supranational' choice for their prime identity (either 'world citizen' or 'European'). This was around 5 per cent overall, but rose to over 11 per cent with Surinamese/Antillean pupils.

Similar patterns could be observed from studying the responses of the pupils in the English school system. Out of 72 indigenous pupils, 67.7 per cent cited national identity as their prime identity ('I see myself as ...'). This fell to between 15 and 20 per cent for the different groups from ethnic minority backgrounds. Over 70 per cent of pupils from 'British-India' backgrounds (Bangladesh, India and Pakistan) cited their religion as their prime identity, as against 37.5 per cent of those from a background outside former British colonies, and 3.2 per cent of indigenous pupils (three times the Dutch figure).

It was interesting to note that whereas only 3.2 per cent of indigenous English pupils gave a 'supranational' choice as their prime identity, this rose to over 10 per cent of ethnic minority background pupils.

Summary

This study is interesting in comparing the views of students in two countries, but also identifies clear differences between the views of those who are termed 'indigenous' and those who are first- or second-generation minority ethnic groups. Generally speaking, indigenous students placed a greater emphasis on studying national history, and were more likely to link their sense of identity to the nation than students from minority ethnic groups, who were more inclined to study the history of their religion or the region where they lived or came from.

Questions to consider

1. How important is it to study the history of the country in which you live?
2. What role does history play in shaping someone's sense of identity?
3. Is the purpose of history to foster a sense of national/regional/personal identity? If so, what should be the balance of topics taught?

Investigations

Pupil attitudes to the history curriculum: Conduct a survey using the questionnaire devised by Haydn and Harris (or something similar) to investigate pupil attitudes towards history. Identify the key issues that emerge. Find out what pupils believe are the benefits of studying history (and how closely this relates to your views). Ask pupils to identify which topics they enjoy and feel are the most relevant to them and which ones are not. Analyse the results to see whether responses differ via minority ethnic group, or another variable, such as gender. Try to analyse why pupils prefer particular topics and dislike others.

Review teacher understanding of history and the history curriculum: What do teachers within a department see as the value of history and what do they think should be studied. To what extent is there a shared sense of value, purpose and content? How far do these ideas reflect those of the pupils? How far are the teachers' ideas represented in the curriculum taught in the school (and how might they be better realised)?

Developing the history curriculum: Work with pupils to plan and enhance your history curriculum. You could look at approaches to teaching, introducing different content or types of history (e.g. more social history or family history) and/or content that present a more inclusive and diverse history curriculum. Explore ways in which you could help students understand why history is a valuable subject. Evaluate the impact that teaching approaches, content selection and understanding the value of history have on pupil motivation and achievement.

Think deeper

The work by Terry Haydn and Richard Harris (e.g. Harris and Haydn 2006 and other papers) builds on earlier studies by Ken Adey and Mary Biddulph (2001) and Biddulph and Adey (2003, 2004), which looked at pupil understanding of history and geography, as well as their expectation and actual experience of studying these subjects at GCSE (examination level for 16 year olds in the UK). Collectively these studies therefore combine pupils' understanding and experience of being taught history from the ages of 11 to 16. Adey and Biddulph's work suggests that pupils have a limited understanding of the value and purpose of history (and geography), and they had unrealistic (negative) ideas about what it would be like to study these subjects at GCSE.

Bruce VanSledright (1997) did a similar study in the USA, and it is useful to consider how students in different contexts perceive these issues. VanSledright's study showed that in his sample of primary and secondary school pupils, the purpose of studying history was overwhelmingly associated with avoiding the mistakes of the past and employment related. Students were also puzzled by the questions asked as they had never been required to consider them before. This has implications for teachers in terms of how they share their vision of history and why it merits a place in the curriculum.

Barton and Levstik (2004) offer an interesting perspective on the various reasons history may be taught. They identify four general 'stances', which they call the identification, analytical, moral response and exhibition stances. Each stance covers a range of purposes, e.g. the identification stance covers personal identity, the value of studying the national past (and the different forms this might take) and studying a diverse past. Barton and Levstik are concerned that many teachers are too preoccupied with content coverage and classroom control, and as a consequence developing genuine historical understanding as a goal of teaching is often relegated. They argue that teachers need a strong sense of the purpose of teaching history in order to improve the quality of their practice and as such improve students' understanding of the subject.

Think wider

The studies cited here focus, understandably, on history education, but there are useful studies that explore pupil perspectives more generally, which also provide important insights for the history teacher.

Paul Cooper and Donald McIntyre (1994) offer an insight into how teachers and pupils view various classroom activities and which they see as being fun and worthwhile. Cooper and McIntyre identify an important issue: both teachers and pupils are aware of teaching approaches that are enjoyable and enable pupils to engage with and understand what is being taught. However, it is clear that such approaches are not universally adopted, nor are they regularly employed by those teachers who are inclined to use them. Contextual factors such as the time available, the nature of the class and concerns about classroom management often influence teacher choice of activity more readily than what are seen to be effective teaching strategies. There appears to be an important distinction to make here, identified by Cooper and McIntyre: the type of fun, 'hands-on' teaching approaches that pupils enjoy are perceived by teachers to be a means of engaging pupils, while pupils see them as integral to effective learning.

Donald McIntyre, David Pedder and Jean Rudduck (2005) report on six teachers and how feedback from pupils affected how they taught. Pupils identified the ways in which they enjoyed being taught; pupils enjoyed lessons that were interactive and could clearly identify approaches that aided learning. The teachers were encouraged to use the feedback to modify their teaching; some were able to do this successfully, some were only able to maintain this for a short period of time and others did not change their approaches.

More recently, Stephen Gorard and Beng Huat See (2011) report on a large-scale survey, involving some 3,000 14–16 year old students, about their enjoyment of formal education. They identify factors such as successful social relationships, small classes, variation in learning and students having some control of their learning as being important in promoting enjoyment. They identify perceived lack of respect or concern by teaching staff and passive pedagogy as major factors in lack of enjoyment. For some disengaged students, a work or college environment with more adult relationships appears to restore enjoyment and enthusiasm. Interestingly, unlike attainment where there are close correlations between factors such as class, ethnicity and gender, enjoyment does not seem to be particularly stratified by such variables, nor do the authors identify any clear evidence of school effect.

References

Adey, K. and Biddulph, M. (2001) The influence of pupil perceptions on subject choice at 14+ in geography and history. *Educational Studies*, 27 (4), 439–47.

Barton, K. and Levstik, L. (2004) *Teaching History for the Common Good*. Mahwah, NJ: Lawrence Erlbaum Associates.

Biddulph, M. and Adey, K. (2003) Perceptions v. reality: Pupils' experiences of learning in history and geography at Key Stage 4. *Curriculum Journal*, 14 (3), 291–303.

Biddulph, M. and Adey, K. (2004) Pupil perceptions of effective teaching and subject relevance in history and geography at Key Stage 3. *Research in Education*, 71 (1), 1–8.

Cooper, P. and McIntyre, D. (1994) Teachers' and pupils' perceptions of effective classroom learning: Conflicts and commonalities. In M. Hughes (ed.) *Perceptions of Teaching and Learning*. Clevedon: Multilingual Matters, 66–95.

Department for Education and Employment (DfEE)/Qualifications and Curriculum Authority (QCA) (1999) *History: The National Curriculum for England*. London: DfES/QCA.

Gorard, S. and See, B.H. (2011) How can we enhance enjoyment of secondary school? The student view. *British Educational Research Journal*, 37 (4), 671–90.

Hackman, S. (2007) *Personalising Progress* [Teachers TV broadcast]. Available at: www.teachers.tv/video/17832 (accessed 4 September 2009).

Harris, R. and Haydn, T. (2006) Pupils' enjoyment of history: What lessons can teachers learn from their pupils? *Curriculum Journal*, 17 (4), 315–33.

Lee, P. and Ashby, R. (2000) Progression in historical understanding amongst students aged 7–14. In P. Stearns, P. Seixas and S. Wineburg (eds) *Knowing, Teaching, and Learning History: National and international perspectives*. New York: New York University Press, 199–222.

McIntyre, D., Pedder, D. and Rudduck, J. (2005) Pupil voice: Comfortable and uncomfortable learnings for teachers. *Research Papers in Education*, 20 (2), 149–68.

QCA (2007) History: Programme of study for Key Stage 3 and attainment target. Available at: http://media.education.gov.uk/assets/files/pdf/h/history%202007%20programme%20of%20study%20for%20key%20stage%203.pdf (accessed 6 June 2013).

Sadler, P. (1994) *Simple Minds. QED*. BBC2, 19 September.

VanSledright, B. (1997) And Santayana lives on: Students' views on the purposes for studying American history. *Journal of Curriculum Studies*, 29 (5), 529–57.

Yan Pong, W. and Morris, P. (2002) Accounting for differences in achievement. In F. Marton and P. Morris (eds) *What Matters? Discovering critical conditions of classroom learning*. Göteborg Studies in Educational Sciences 181. Gothenburg, Sweden: Acta Universitatis Gothoburgensis, 9–18.

History and identity

The relationship between history and identity is complex and often controversial. One of the key debates focuses on what should be taught. If history has a role to play in shaping a sense of national, regional and/or personal identity, then it appears logical to assume that the choice of content will affect the sense of identity being developed. To an extent this explains why the history curriculum is contentious in so many countries and why 'history wars' have been fought in so many different places to promote particular ways of looking at the national past. It is also important to recognise that identity is not fixed and that people have multiple identities, which makes the issue about what to teach more complex. The interplay between history and identity is also dynamic because our sense of who we are may shape how we interpret the history we are taught, but at the same time the history we are taught may shape who we are. The extracts in this chapter focus on the ways in which history does or could shape a young person's view of themselves and the world in which they live.

Extract 1

Source

Barton, K. and McCully, A. (2005) History, identity, and the school curriculum in Northern Ireland: An empirical study of secondary students' ideas and perspectives. *Journal of Curriculum Studies*, 37 (1), 85–116.

Introduction

This extract is based upon a study by Ken Barton and Alan McCully of secondary students' conceptions of history and identity in Northern Ireland. Drawing on interviews with 253 students from a variety of backgrounds, the study explores the relationship between the formal curriculum students are taught and how this interacts with their developing identification with the history of their own political/religious communities. The stimulus material in the interviews used a range of images; students had to select those with which they identified most readily and explain their reasoning. The study explores the tensions students face when they encounter a school history that is at odds with a community history that has shaped their sense of identity, and it reveals the complexity of their responses.

The study reached two main conclusions. The first, which is presented in the extract, focused on the influence of the students' community on their sense of identification with the past; the second focused on the range of students' responses, which varied considerably by school type, gender and geographic region, illustrating for example that '[i]dentification with national history and culture, for example, was more common among boys, at secondary schools, and in areas of conflict' (p. 109).

Key words & phrases

Secondary school; identity; community cohesion; Northern Ireland

---

Extract

[C]ommunity conflict in Northern Ireland is a strong influence – although not the only one – on students' perceptions of who they are and what is important to them. Readers familiar with Northern Ireland will hardly be surprised that students were most likely to identify with pictures that related to their national, religious, and cultural backgrounds, or that they consciously explained their choices in these terms. After all, such issues are a constant feature of public discourse and play an important role in the division between the two communities. However, students' responses contradict any simplistic generalizations about their historical identifications. Although items related to their national, religious, and cultural backgrounds were the most common sources of historical identification, fewer than 30% of students' responses involved such choices, and only 25% of their explanations were phrased in these terms. In other words, 70% or more of the responses involved identification with events other than those related to Protestant/Unionist or Catholic/Nationalist history.

Most notably, nearly as many responses indicated a general identification with Northern Ireland's Troubles: at all three types of schools [Protestant (Controlled schools), Catholic (Maintained) and mixed (Integrated)], a large portion of students chose pictures that suggested identification with the community conflict that surrounded them rather than (or in addition to) any of the specific parties to that conflict. And nearly 50% of students' choices had nothing whatever to do with the conflict but related instead to the World Wars, local heritage, leaders, or other historical items. Their explanations, meanwhile, indicated the importance of physical proximity, family connections and ancestors, a concern with rights and justice (beyond their own community), the effect of the past on the present, and a range of other factors. As our theoretical framework suggests, students were not passively absorbing established historical narratives but actively constructing their historical identifications from a range of sources. Among the students in this study, at least, we must conclude that, although national, political, and religious issues were important, they did not dominate their conceptualization of their connection to history.

However, such issues increasingly moved toward such dominance over the 3 years during which students studied national history. After just 1 year of study, students had a wide range of historical identifications (including archaeological sites, the Titanic, the World Wars, and castles and other old buildings) and they explained those identifications in a variety of ways – noting personal knowledge and interest, physical proximity, and school study. After the third year of study, however, their choices and explanations had narrowed considerably, and they were much more likely to focus on pictures related to their own national, religious, and cultural backgrounds. Moreover, their responses became much more specific as they used the content they had learned at school to add detail and context to their identifications: first-year students at a Controlled school might identify with Edward Carson because they saw a Union flag in the picture, but those in the third year identified with him because he fought against home rule and formed the UVF (pp. 107–8).

Summary

The extract highlights the complex way in which students make sense of the world around them and how this is (or is not) used to support their own developing sense of self. The findings suggest that the process is sophisticated, although the impact of the community is a major factor in how young people understand themselves, and this appears to become stronger as the students grow up. There are important implications from this research, one of which relates to pedagogy. If students draw upon the way in which their community understands the past, they are likely to develop a partisan view of the past; in such a scenario, the mediating role of the teacher in making links between the past and the present is crucial in helping young people to develop an alternative, contextualised view of the past. The study also highlights the importance of the curriculum and choice of content.

Questions to consider

1. What are the different sources from which students draw their knowledge of the past?
2. Which of these sources of knowledge do you consider to be the most influential in shaping how young people view themselves and society, and why?
3. How, and to what extent, do you feel it is possible for history taught in school to shape a young person's understanding of their sense of self?

Extract 2

Source

Epstein, T. (2009) *Interpreting National History: Race, identity, and pedagogy in classrooms and communities*. New York: Routledge; see pp. 86–8.

Introduction

This book is based upon a long-term ethnographic study of history teaching in an American school district. The data is drawn from observations of six teachers over a period of five years and interviews with over 100 children and adolescents, plus additional interviews with parents and teachers. The book explores the ways in which racial identity interacts with the way young people make sense of the past, both within and beyond the classroom. It therefore looks at how personal identity, in this case racial identity, mediates an understanding of the past. The author advocates a social justice approach to teaching history, whereby a study of the past is used to explore and shape understanding of the contemporary world. The book explores history teaching from the perspective of teachers, students and the wider community; the extract presented here focuses on the experience of the students and how their understanding of history is shaped by their own identity.

Key words & phrases

American history; identity, race; whiteness; student perceptions

---

Extract

White and black students began and ended the year with different explanations and interpretations about the role of race and rights in national formation and development. They also constructed different ideas about the meaning and significance of a national identity. White students began the year with concepts of Europeans or white Americans as heroes and nation builders throughout the course of national history, Native Americans and blacks appeared intermittently, primarily as victims and occasionally as isolated and exotic people (Native Americans) or civil rights leaders (blacks). They held unwavering beliefs in the ubiquity of rights and saw the oppression of people of color or women as exceptions to the nation's legacy of expanding democracy and power. They equated national history and contemporary society with democratic rule at home and abroad and a majority believed that equality existed in contemporary society. The few who believed that racism still existed saw it as individual rather than institutional in nature.

Black students began the year with a different interpretive framework. They thought of Europeans or white Americans as nation builders and oppressors of blacks and other people of color, blacks as historical subjects as well as victims who struggled against oppression throughout national history, and Native Americans as having had 'friendly' or conflict-ridden relations with whites or the government. A large majority of black adolescents and some children saw racism and exclusion from democratic principles of promises as ongoing, institutional, and inevitable aspects of national history and identity.

Teachers' pedagogies tended to amplify rather than alter students' pre-instructional explanations and interpretations and had greater effects on students' explanations of individual actors and events than it had on students' underlying interpretive frameworks …

Overall, most of the white teachers and students constructed ideas or narratives of national formation, development and identity in positive and progressive terms. They constructed explanations and themes about diverse social groups having gained greater freedom, rights over time and racial inequality as a thing of the past or a matter of individual prejudice. Black students, on the other hand, at the end of the year still constructed the nation in less positive terms, as one marked by racial violence and conflict which continued to exclude marginalized social groups.

Summary

This study, although confined to a specific area of America, highlights the impact that personal identity has in mediating the past. In this case the history that is taught resonates with the majority of white students and reinforces their sense of self, while the black students generally tend to find there is a conflict between their view of the past and the one they are taught. The book explores the issue more widely, for example examining the approaches teachers adopt to teaching about the past and the issue of race relations. Although teachers saw the need to teach a diverse past, their pedagogic practice tended to reinforce particular views of the past rather than challenging them, and so contributed to the different ways that white and black students interpreted the past.

Questions to consider

1. To what extent, and in what ways, do you think the background of students will affect the way they interpret the past?
2. How does your own background influence how you understand the past and therefore how you approach teaching it?
3. How do you take into account the backgrounds of students when teaching the past to ensure you teach a diverse and inclusive view of history?

Extract 3

Source

Barton, K. (2009) The denial of desire: How to make history education meaningless. In L. Symcox and A. Wilschut (eds) *National History Standards: The problem of the canon and the future of teaching history.* Charlotte, NC: Information Age Publishing, 265–82.

Introduction

One of the debates about history education regards the extent to which it should deliberately focus on developing a particular sense of identity. In some countries, such as the US, there is a strong focus on teaching about national heroes and milestones in the past. According to Keith Barton, it is successful in fostering a sense of identity linked to the nation, but can create a mythologised past, where things are omitted or distorted to fit into the national story. Often the national story reflects the views of the dominant social group and can marginalise the history of 'others'. To counter this, some countries, such as the UK, adopt a more disciplinary approach to history teaching, but Barton argues that this can be highly disengaging for students. Instead he argues that students will find history more engaging and meaningful if it is focused on identity formation. This extract presents part of his rationale for this position.

Key words & phrases

Identity; national identity; dominant group; other; distortion; identity formation

---

Extract

Young people seem determined to use history as a source of identification, whether we promote such efforts in school or not. Teachers in settings with large numbers of new immigrants – whose culture, religion, and ethnicity may differ from those that have previously predominated – often report that their students react to historical topics in ways they had not expected. Thus they may find that some Muslim students cheer for victories by the Ottoman Empire (or, more disturbingly, for the actions of Hitler or bin Laden), or that they show a sense of pride when contributions of the Muslim world to Western Europe are mentioned; even something as simple as importing tulips from the Ottoman Empire to Holland can be gratifying for Muslim students in the Netherlands. And one teacher in Australia told me that after a unit in which he taught about the Battle of Gallipoli from both British and Ottoman perspectives, two of his Turkish students told him, 'This is the first time we've studied World War I without feeling like the enemy.' Whether history educators consider current social identities to be relevant to the curriculum or not, students certainly do, and we ignore their perspectives at our peril. Students are not going to give up using history for a sense of identity simply because they do not encounter such approaches in school; rather, they will rely on more restricted and potentially divisive sources and dismiss school history as meaningless.

Moreover, the case could be made that schools *should* promote shared identity, and that this may be one of their most important functions, particularly in multi-cultural democracies. In a democracy, commitment to the well-being of our fellow citizens is necessary for the effective functioning of society ... Democratic nation-states and supranational entities (such as the European Union) depend on a shared identity, but where does that identity come from when there is no single religion or ethnicity? One of the most time-honored sources is history – stories of shared ancestors and experiences that we can all look back on as part of a past that we feel connected to .... History will become more meaningful if it strives to develop identities that are complex, diverse, and inclusive – rather than simple, monolithic, and exclusive, such as those found in traditional national histories.

Summary

Barton is aware of the dangers of creating a simple monolithic view of the past, so he emphasises the value of teaching about a past that is pluralistic and inclusive, with a view to developing a multi-faceted identity. This does, however, open up debate about what should be taught to young people, which in turn is linked to wider debates about the purpose of teaching history. Barton is clear that learning about the past has a social purpose, and this is what makes it engaging.

Questions to consider

1. To what extent do you agree with the view that the purpose of teaching history is to develop a stronger sense of identity?
2. What do you understand by the term 'national identity'?
3. How do you create a sense of national identity in a pluralistic society?

Investigations

Examining the department curriculum: Carry out an analysis of a history department's curriculum. What balance is there in the topics taught between personal, local, national and global history? What is the rationale for this balance of topics and what is the likely impact of these on students' sense of identity?

Exploring teachers' views on identity: Working with a group of history teach-ers, explore the extent to which they feel history has a role in shaping someone's sense of identity. To what extent are their views made explicit in the classroom, and how do they appear to influence their practice?

Exploring students' sense of identity in history: The research instrument that Barton and McCully used in Extract 1 was a collection of visual images of historical characters and events, from which they asked students to select those with which they most readily associated. Create a set of visual images appropriate to your context and explore the different ways in which students identify with the past. Examine the implications of what you find for what you think should be taught.

Think deeper

The extracts above deal with a number of complex issues, including the purpose of history and its relationship to identity formation, the challenge of choosing what to teach and the difficulties pupils face when they confront histories that do not fit into their view of the world.

These issues are explored further in a range of publications. Keith Barton and Linda Levstik have collaborated on a number of projects that address such points. Much of their book *Teaching History for the Common Good* is devoted to discussing the reasons for studying history, with a particular emphasis on what they term the 'identification stance' (see also Chapter 1 'The purposes of history teaching'). They explore the different ways in which young people can identify with the past, including at a personal, family, local and national level, but recognise that this process may be a double-edged sword. While people may naturally use the past to identify with a certain community or nation, their sense of connection and inclusion is often achieved by identifying others as being outside that particular group. Such exclusion can create additional problems within society.

When considering issues of identity, choosing what to teach becomes a central issue. Although somewhat dated, Rozina Visram's (1994) chapter still raises very important questions; indeed the fact that the issues discussed remain pertinent suggests that little progress has been made in this area. Visram argues that too much of what is seen as 'British' history represents a narrow view of the past, which excludes a host of different social groups and treats British history in isolation. She goes on to argue that British history is inextricably linked to the history of other parts of the world and cannot be studied without reference to the presence of minority groups such as the black peoples of Britain.

A more recent book edited by Maria Grever and Siep Stuurman (2007) deals with the idea of teaching an historical canon, exploring the tensions evident in debates from across Europe. As they explain (2007: 3),

> replacing the received national canon of history with a multicultural or feminist counter-canon does not work, if only because it comes down to the addition of new voices to the same grand narrative. On the other hand, anxiously clinging to the old canon will be of no avail. In a globalizing world an inward-looking national canon will become less and less convincing.

The contributors to the book present a range of perspectives, which unpack the issues surrounding this fundamental debate.

Such a debate becomes more important in light of the challenges young people face in making sense of the past. As the extracts illustrate, some young people, who are looking for affirmation of their identity within the curriculum, struggle to reconcile the history they are taught with what they have learned informally within their families and communities. Even where students are able to 'buy into' the history they are taught, some events remain problematic. Barton and Levstik (2008) show how students who saw American history as being characterised by the progressive expansion of rights, opportunities and freedoms, struggled to locate events such as the Vietnam War within such a view.

Think wider

Many of the issues explored in this chapter are not unique to history, and address broader questions about the nature and purpose of the curriculum. Curriculum debates are not new, but in an increasingly complex and interconnected world, they appear to be even more important. If a curriculum is to play a role in creating a sense of identity or identities, then students should be able to see the different components on which they could draw in defining their identity. What is important is that teachers are aware of how curriculum decisions expand or restrict the resources and perspectives on which young people can draw.

Geneva Gay (2004: 41) presents an analysis of different curriculum theories, but argues in practice a curriculum is too frequently 'loaded' against pupils from minority ethnic backgrounds:

> Knowledge taught in schools is a form of cultural capital and is a social construction that reflects the values, perspectives, and experiences of the dominant ethnic group. It systematically ignores or diminishes the validity and significance of the life experiences and contributions of ethnic and cultural groups that historically have been vanquished, marginalized, and silenced.

It is this perception of the mismatch between the curriculum as experienced in schools and students' lived experiences that is seen to be one of the contributing factors to the low attainment of many pupils. As Jagdish Gundara (2000) explains, the exclusion of cultural and ethnic groups from the curriculum can create a sense of exclusion and marginalisation. As a consequence pupils' self-esteem may be adversely affected, they may feel alienated from school, and may eventually perform poorly in high-stakes tests with potential knock-on effects for employment and subsequent life opportunities. This is highlighted in a range of studies. For example, Sonia Nieto (2004: 181) uses case-studies of individual pupils to illustrate 'a profound mismatch between students' cultures and the content of the curriculum'. The result is that students feel excluded and are more likely to drop out of schools, and so in the long term find themselves on the margins of society.

References

Barton, K. and Levstik, L. (2008) 'It wasn't a good part of history': National identity and students' explanations of historical significance. In L. Levstik and K. Barton (eds) *Researching History Education: Theory, method and context*. New York: Routledge, 240–72.

Gay, G. (2004) Curriculum theory and multicultural education. In J. Banks and C. McGee Banks (eds) *Handbook of Research on Multicultural Education*. San Francisco: Jossey-Bass, 30–49.

Grever, M. and Stuurman, S. (2007) *Beyond the Canon: History for the twenty-first century*. Basingstoke: Palgrave Macmillan.

Gundara, J.S. (2000) *Intercultural Education and Inclusion*. London: Paul Chapman Publishing.

Nieto, S. (2004) Critical multicultural education and students' perspectives. In G. Ladson-Billings and D. Gillborn (eds) *The RoutledgeFalmer Reader in Multicultural Education*. London: RoutledgeFalmer, 179–200.

Visram, R. (1994) British history: Whose history? Black perspectives on British history. In H. Bourdillon (ed.) *Teaching History*. London: Routledge, 53–61.

Teaching controversial, emotional and moral issues in history

When teaching history it is difficult to avoid topics that could be perceived as emotionally difficult, where injustice or brutality are part of what happened, or to avoid topics to which some pupils, due to their social backgrounds or personal experience, are deeply attached. Such topics raise a number of issues for teachers – what slant on the past should they adopt (if any), what is the most appropriate pedagogical approach to adopt, should emotional and moralistic issues be side-stepped, how might pupils react and how should this be taken into account, and so forth. Although there is a range of topics that could be considered 'difficult', the emphasis within this chapter is on teaching the Holocaust, not only because it is commonly taught, but also because the issues associated with teaching it are those that apply to a range of historical topics.

Extract 1

Source

Kinloch, N. (2001) Parallel catastrophes? Uniqueness, redemption and the Shoah. *Teaching History*, 104, 8–14.

Introduction

Teaching difficult issues in history is complex. Part of that complexity rests with the question of purpose – what is the point of teaching such topics in history? The debate around purpose has been particularly fierce around the topic of the Holocaust. In 1998 Nicholas Kinloch stirred the debate by stating that in history classrooms the Holocaust ought to be taught purely as a piece of history, rather than for any social, moral or spiritual purpose. In this extract from an article in 2001, Kinloch expands on these initial ideas and presents a more fully rounded defence of his position.

Extract

Apart from the most general lessons, however, the Shoah probably has no more to teach British students than any other genocide of modern – or for that matter, medieval – times. There may be good reason to teach children that killing other human beings is generally undesirable. Whether the history class is really the place for such lessons, however, remains debatable. There is less of a consensus here than most of those called upon to teach it might realise. The Freiburg professor Ulrich Herbert [2000] suggests that:

> Historical research into National Socialist mass extermination policy has brought to light a process that was so complex, so multi-layered in terms of the perpetrators, so characterised by competitions, ambition, private interests, banality, lust for murder and petit-bourgeois hypocrisy, as well as by political utopianism and ostensibly scientific systems for interpreting the world, that this extraordinarily multifaceted image is ill-suited as a metaphor for political education and, in a sense, cannot easily be identified with. And yet the didactic challenge of the history of the Holocaust lies precisely in the fact that it does not lend itself to explanations involving pithy formulations and simple, readily-digested concepts or theories... The Holocaust possesses no theory or redemptive formula.

Peter Novick [1999] also concludes that the Shoah may not be useful as a bearer of lessons. One reason he puts forward is its very extremity, which renders doubtful its applicability to everyday life. Like Herbert, he also concludes that the Shoah is simply too complex for the kind of easy didacticism for which it is often employed. He continues:

> If there are lessons to be extracted from encountering the past, that encounter has to be with the past in all its messiness; they're not likely to come from an encounter with a past that's been shaped and shaded so that inspiring lessons will emerge ... The desire to find and teach lessons of the Holocaust has various sources – different sources for different people, one assumes. Probably one of its principal sources is the hope of extracting from the Holocaust something that is, if not redemptive, at least useful. I doubt it can be done.

Some writers for students also accept that the Shoah is more complex, and the lessons less obvious, than is often assumed. In the conclusion to the Imperial War

Museum's student guide to the Holocaust Exhibition, Paul Salmons [2000] agrees that the cry of 'Never again' has a hollow ring to it: there have been too many genocides before and since for this slogan to have real meaning. Alain Destexhe [1995] asks how many of those who wept whilst watching Spielberg's 1994 film *Schindler's List* wept for the victims of the Rwandan genocide who were being slaughtered that same year. And in a recent article on the significance of the Holocaust Memorial Day, journalist Polly Toynbee [2001] went still further:

> I want my children and their children's children to know in detail what happened under the Nazis, but I want it taught as hard-headed history with cause and effect, with parallels drawn, with meaning. I do not want it turned into a pseudo-religion, weepily implying that there is something holy about this disgusting thing.

Similarly, whilst Britain's Chief Rabbi was positive in his welcome of Holocaust memory as a means of redefining the moral and political values of modern Britain, seeing 27 January as a day of 'universal reflection on what it (is) to be human', others were less certain. Rabbis Jonathan Romain and Ed Kessler believe that what they term the 'Holocaust fixation' risks the Jewish community's seeing itself primarily in terms of victimhood, and thus ceding a posthumous victory to Nazism.

To conclude: where the Shoah is concerned, perhaps a certain amount of what Steve Illingworth [2000] derided as 'pessimism and lack of ambition' is well in order. Some acceptance of the complexity of the topic, and the difficulty in extracting from it more than the most banal of moral conclusions, would do the profession no harm. History itself, and the history of that history, might well induce a certain propensity to pessimism, and a more realistic acceptance of what the classroom teacher is likely to be able to achieve. I repeat my original claim: that what history teachers can best do is to help their students become better historians. And I shall continue to believe that this is a difficult task.

Summary

For Kinloch the ultimate point of teaching history is to teach history. Therefore events such as the Shoah need to be taught from an historical perspective, with a focus on the disciplinary nature of history; in this case an exploration of causation, use of evidence and so forth are perfectly acceptable foci for teaching the Holocaust. Kinloch is concerned that any attempt to adopt a moralistic position leads to bland generalisations and simplistic platitudes, which ignore the complexity of the event(s) being studied.

Questions to consider

1. To what extent do you agree that the main point of teaching history is to promote historical thinking, rather than adopting any moralistic purpose?

2. Is it possible to approach a topic such as the Holocaust without prompting questions about morality and social responsibility? If not, how should these be dealt with in the context of teaching about the past?

Extract 2

Source

Short, G. (2003) Lessons of the Holocaust: A response to the critics. *Educational Review*, 55 (3), 277–87.

Introduction

Geoffrey Short argues that there are very important reasons for teaching the Holocaust, and in this article he confronts what he sees as the short-sightedness of people such as Nicholas Kinloch. According to Short, the persistence of crimes against humanity is not a justifiable reason for ignoring the teaching of the Holocaust as a form of social and moral education. He argues that there is a range of important reasons that forces individuals and society to examine their social and moral beliefs and actions.

Key words & phrases

Purpose; moral education; Holocaust education; anti-racist education; citizenship education; commemoration; remembrance

Extract

While it is indisputable that a knowledge of the Holocaust has not brought an end to genocide, it is a non-sequitur to argue, from this fact alone, that the Holocaust has no useful lessons to impart. The critics fail to distinguish between a historical event containing lessons and those lessons being learnt (that is, understood and applied). Yet it is precisely this distinction that leaves open the possibility of the Holocaust providing significant lessons despite the occurrence of subsequent genocides. The same possibility also arises as a result of the critics' apparent failure to appreciate that lessons drawn from the Holocaust can be of value even though they do no more than diminish the likelihood of genocide. It is unnecessary, as well as unrealistic, to demand that they lead to a complete cessation. Having thus limited the scope of what can be learnt from the Holocaust, it is important to note that the lessons themselves apply not just to individual students but to the educational system as a whole. I shall deal with each in turn beginning with the latter.

Commemoration

Arguably, one of the main lessons to derive from the Holocaust is the importance of commemoration and particularly the need for schools to teach and explain what happened to future generations. Historians who fail to locate cautionary tales in the destruction of European Jewry tend to overlook the possibility that Hitler was prompted to give vent to his apocalyptic fantasies by a belief that the international community had forgotten about an earlier attempt at genocide. In a speech delivered to high-ranking army officers on the eve of Germany's invasion of Poland, Hitler is reputed to have said:

> Ghengis Khan had millions of women and men killed by his own will and with a gay heart. History sees in him only a great state builder … and I have sent to the east … my 'Death's Head Units', with the order to kill without mercy men, women and children of Polish race or language. Only in such a way will we win the 'Lebensraum' that we need. Who, after all, talks nowadays of the extermination of the Armenians? (Fein, 1979, p. 4)

The well-known final sentence of this quotation suggests that a sine qua non of reducing the chances of a second Holocaust (or its equivalent) is that time be devoted to the subject in the school curriculum. George Santayana (1905) might have overstated the case when he wrote that those who do not remember the past are condemned to repeat it, but there is surely a greater probability of replicating a mistake if that mistake is subsequently forgotten.

Antiracist and Multicultural Education

In 1953, the philosopher Karl Jaspers wrote of the Holocaust: 'It was possible for this to happen, and it remains possible for it to happen again at any minute. Only in knowledge can it be prevented' (Jaspers, 1953, p. 149). With this aim in mind, a knowledge of racism would seem self-evidently helpful. To be protected against its seductive 'logic', students should be able to recognise and appreciate the limitations of stereotypes, and understand the flawed nature of the scapegoating process. According to the final report of the Advisory Group on Citizenship (Qualifications and Curriculum Authority, 1998) they should 'also understand the meaning of terms such as *prejudice, xenophobia, discrimination (and) pluralism*' (p. 49: original emphasis). They need to know that any group, if sufficiently vulnerable, can suffer the effects of racism and if sufficiently powerful, can perpetrate it. And they should know too that racists themselves are not inclined to restrict their pathological hatred to a single group.

Moral Education

One lesson thrown into particularly sharp relief by the Holocaust is the importance of schools prioritising their pupils' moral development. An educational system that fails in this respect risks turning out academically well-qualified barbarians, an embodiment of evil much in evidence during the Holocaust. For example, in January 1942 half of the Nazi functionaries who gathered at Wansee to organise the murder of European Jewry, possessed doctorates, as, of course, did a number of leading Nazis such as Joseph Goebbels, Hitler's chief propagandist. Other beneficiaries of a 'good education' included Hans Frank, governor general of occupied Poland and Ernst Kaltenbrunner, Head of the Reich Main Security Office, both of whom were university trained lawyers. Pace Socrates, academic knowledge is clearly not synonymous with virtue. The latter must be taught as part of the formal and the hidden curriculum and the central focus has to be the encouragement of prosocial behaviour.

Summary

For Short, teaching about the Holocaust has clear objectives that are not necessarily related simply to the teaching of history. Whereas Kinloch argues for a focus on achieving a better understanding of history, Short stresses the clear social and moral lessons that need to be derived from this topic, both at an individual and societal level. Educated people carried out the atrocities of the Holocaust and so it follows that educated people without a properly developed sense of social and moral sensibilities can carry out similar actions in the future. In this sense, teaching the Holocaust has to go beyond simply teaching students history, and so history has to serve a broader educational and societal purpose.

Questions to consider

1. There is a clear 'citizenship' agenda in Short's argument. To what extent do you feel history should serve the needs of citizenship?
2. To what extent does a focus on the social and moral lessons of the Holocaust distort the study of the history of the Holocaust?
3. Short argues that studying the Holocaust 'leaves students in no doubt as to where racism can lead' and they 'can hardly fail to realise the perils of turning a blind eye to evil'. There is an emphasis here on the actions of the individual, which may leave many students feeling a sense of powerlessness, when events such as the Holocaust occur at a wider, societal level. How can students be helped to overcome any sense of powerlessness?

Extract 3

Source

Salmons, P. (2010) Universal meaning or historical understanding? The Holocaust in history and history in the curriculum. *Teaching History*, 141, 57–63.

Introduction

Paul Salmons presents an argument for the importance of studying the Holocaust in its historical context and the important and distinctive contribution this can make to young people's understanding of the world. Using data from a national survey he highlights that most teachers approach the Holocaust from a moral perspective, attempting to combat prejudice and to prevent such events happening again. Although laudable, Salmons raises the question about what is the distinctive contribution of history to an understanding of the Holocaust. He argues a focus on generating emotional responses to events and an emphasis on universal moral lessons risk distorting the past. Here he offers an argument that requires students to see the unsettling complexity of the past, and to examine the questions this raises for us as a society, by focusing on the question of remembrance and what a society chooses to remember or how it remembers.

Key words & phrases

Purpose; moral education; Holocaust education; anti-racist education; citizenship education; commemoration; remembrance

Extract

Each day on my way between St Pancras railway station and my office at the Institute of Education, I take a short cut through the courtyard of the British Library, and walk past a small tree … that was planted there in 1998. A plaque nearby reads: 'To commemorate Anne Frank and all the children killed in wars and conflict in this century.'

Few would argue with the importance of public acts of remembrance for the innocent victims of war. But what does such a memorial tell us about the child in whose name it was dedicated? Anne Frank was killed during wartime, of course, but not as a casualty of either war or conflict. Anne Frank was a victim of genocide: she was not one of the 'collateral' deaths of modern warfare – but rather she was specifically targeted for death because she was a Jew, in an unprecedented programme to murder all people of this group everywhere that the perpetrators could reach them. The universal message contained in this dedication includes no mention of this historical reality and conveys a quite different understanding of the circumstances of her death. As such it could be said that it has become another of Cole's 'Holocaust' myths. To reiterate, the term myth is not used here to imply that the story told on the plaque is false, but rather that it is employed as 'a story that evokes strong sentiments, and transmits and reinforces basic societal values'.

The problem, of course, is not with the 'basic societal values' themselves, but that in the pursuit of such universal meanings we risk distorting the past. After all, why stop with the deaths of children in wartime? If we choose to universalise even further, Anne Frank died of typhus in Bergen-Belsen, so on this reckoning those remembered on this plaque could be extended to include 'all children who have died of disease': an equal tragedy surely, and a tragedy not only of greater number than children killed in war but arguably one that is more preventable. The cause in both cases – drawing attention to the tragedy of young lives cut short by war or by disease – is unmistakeably and unreservedly good; but the 'lessons' in each case have little to do with Anne Frank or the Holocaust.

If the cause is good, why does this matter? By universalising this young girl's murder, we dissolve it of meaning. By decontextualising Anne Frank's death, we fail to confront the historical reality that 90% of all Jewish children in German occupied Europe were intentionally murdered. Not 'killed in war and conflict' but sought out and murdered as part of a state-led plan to kill every Jewish man, woman and child everywhere that the Nazis and their collaborators could reach them. Surely, this difference matters. But whatever 'lessons' this may hold for our society, they are 'pre-empted' (in Langer's phrase) by a rendering of the past that makes the Holocaust itself more manageable, more palatable, more comfortable: locating it within a frame of reference – 'war is bad', 'racism is wrong', 'evil should be confronted' – upon which there is already broad consensus (p. 59).

… The presence of the Holocaust in our collective memory, in mass media and public discourse, and the use of Holocaust imagery and motifs in the service of diverse political and social agendas, make it essential for young people's educational literacy that they understand this central event of our time and are able to evaluate critically the diverse claims made about it. The many sources and forms of information about the past to which young people are exposed, and the meanings and messages they are used to convey, raise the question of whether all opinions, all interpretations, all representations of the past are equally valid. If not, how do we distinguish between them? These are important ideas for young people to grapple with. What is the status of knowledge? How do we know what we know? How do we weigh different truth claims? They are also essential questions for the history classroom.

Summary

Salmons argues that the Holocaust makes little sense without an understanding of the historical context. For him, teaching the Holocaust in history means there must be a historical perspective rather than a simply moralistic one. Thus when teaching the Holocaust in history there are two key aspects that need to be present, namely seeing the complexity of the past and the way in which the memory of the Holocaust has been created and commemorated. The complexity comes through a more detailed approach to teaching the topic, drawing on a range of evidence and perspectives, which raise uncomfortable questions about human behaviours. In addition, a historical approach to teaching the Holocaust requires students to engage with ideas about how the past has been represented and remembered, and to ask critical questions of these representations and memories.

Questions to consider

1. Kinloch, Short and Salmons adopt different positions towards the reasons for teaching the Holocaust. Which position do you feel is the most appropriate and why?
2. What do you feel young people should understand and know about the Holocaust?
3. What specific content should pupils study when learning about the Holocaust?

Investigations

Examine teachers' perspectives on teaching the Holocaust: Gather the views of a group of history teachers. What do they see as the main reason(s) for teaching the Holocaust, and to what extent is this different to teaching other historical topics?

Explore pupils' perspectives: Carry out a survey of pupils' views and identify what they feel they gain by studying this topic? Get pupils to create mind–maps of their knowledge about the Holocaust. Examine what misconceptions or stereotypes they have prior to starting the topic. Identify ways you could address these issues. Get them to redo the mind–maps at the end of the topic. To what extent have their misconceptions and stereotypes been challenged after studying the topic?

Other curriculum areas: Talk to other teachers outside history and find out how they address difficult topics such as the Holocaust, and how do these differ to the rationale and approaches adopted in history classrooms. What benefits for students might there be if there was more 'joined-up' thinking in tackling the Holocaust across the curriculum.

Difficult issues in the history curriculum: Examine the history curriculum you teach. What other topics might be considered difficult? What makes them difficult? How might the issues associated with teaching the Holocaust apply to other difficult issues, and therefore how you approach teaching them?

Think deeper

The Historical Association's journal, *Teaching History*, has dedicated two editions (numbers 104 and 141) to the issue of teaching the Holocaust. Both contain articles that explore the rational for teaching this topic and practical approaches to fulfil these aims. In *Teaching History* 104, Kate Hammond (2001) cleverly examines the relationship between moral questions and historical questions that the Holocaust raises and explores ways students can move between these, while also considering the historical significance of the Holocaust. In the same edition, Alison Kitson (2001) addresses questions about tackling stereotypes that students often have when studying the Holocaust. Using mini case-studies to illustrate the range of responses from the German people towards the Jews, Kitson reveals the complexity of people's actions in the past.

There are also some books that address the issues of teaching the Holocaust. *Teaching the Holocaust* (Davies 2000) explores some of the background knowledge to the topic, as well as providing reviews of teaching about the Holocaust from different countries, and examples of teaching approaches in different subject areas. Richard Harris, Simon Harrison and Richard McFahn (2012), in chapter 6 of their book, consider the benefits of adopting a cross-curricular approach to teaching the Holocaust within the humanities subjects. By focusing on the different ways of thinking each subject encourages and the differing perspectives they provide on human activity and society, Harris et al. explore how students' understanding of the Holocaust can be enhanced. Geoffrey Short and Carole Ann Reed (2004) examine a wide range of issues, including the development of teaching about the Holocaust and the issues that have been encountered during this process. For example they explore the relationship between Holocaust education and anti-racist education and citizenship education, they discuss the curricular, organisational and ethical issues teachers may need to consider. They also report on research into teachers' attitudes and practices, compare different curricula approaches and the value of how museums approach the Holocaust.

Think wider

Clearly the Holocaust is not the only 'difficult' issue that will be taught in the history classroom. The Historical Association's *Teaching Emotive and Controversial History* (2007) report looks at the issue more broadly, and identifies the challenges facing teachers and students across the primary and secondary school age range, and examines the factors that inhibit the effective teaching of emotive and controversial history, and provides examples of effective practice. Some of the barriers are logistical, relating to a lack of curriculum time, restricted access to training and paucity of quality resources, whereas others are to do with the teachers, for example subject knowledge, concerns about what they are trying to achieve, worries about how pupils will respond and a lack of incentive to take risks by teaching potentially difficult topics. Although there are examples of effective and inspiring practice, more needs to be done to encourage teachers to address such topics.

Hilary Claire and Cathie Holden (2007) address a broad range of controversial issues in their book, including war and peace, education for sustainability, the controversial nature of democracies and dealing with religious controversy, and how these may be dealt with through the curriculum. They also examine the promotion of whole-school values and action as a means of addressing controversial topics, for example how schools might address racism.

Elizabeth Cole (2007) addresses a specific aspect of history, which raises particular issues. In *Teaching the Violent Past*, Cole examines the difficulties of the role of history in a process of reconciliation. In many societies where different groups have variously been involved in suppression of other groups or have been victims of violence or systematic repression themselves, or where societies are emerging from conflict, how the past is taught and what is taught become extraordinarily important. This book draws on case-studies from around the world, and looks at what has been done to address the issue of reconciliation in the history classroom. The book raises fascinating questions about the role of history, issues over what history is/should be taught, how the past is/should be remembered and how it is/should be taught.

Additionally, a study in Northern Ireland by Alison Kitson and Alan McCully (2005) talks about the different positions teachers adopt towards sensitive topics. Clearly history teaching in Northern Ireland where events in the past have been interpreted differently and where different social groups promote partisan histories, it is easy to see why teachers may be concerned about teaching Ireland's past. Kitson and McCully (2005) categorise teachers as risk-takers, containers or avoiders. This refers to the willingness of teachers to engage with the controversial nature of many of the history topics, but raises fundamental questions about teachers, the positions they adopt and the reasons for these, as well as thinking about how to move teachers forward in their practice. Richard Harris and Gill Clarke (2011) also explore this issue further, through a focus on teaching a more culturally and ethnically diverse past. They present a 'confidence continuum' that categorises teachers by their understanding of the issues associated with teaching a diverse past and their willingness to do so. Again it raises fundamental questions about teachers, their ideas, attitudes, beliefs and practices, and how to move them forward.

References

Claire, H. and Holden, C. (2007) *The Challenge of Teaching Controversial Issues*. Stoke-on-Trent: Trentham Books.

Cole, E. (ed.) (2007) *Teaching the Violent Past*. Plymouth: Rowan and Littlefield.

Davies, I. (ed.) (2000) *Teaching the Holocaust*. London: Continuum.

Destexhe, A. (1995) *Rwanda and Genocide in the Twentieth Century*. London: Pluto Press.

Fein, H. (1979) *Accounting for Genocide: National responses and Jewish victimization during the Holocaust*. London: The Free Press.

Hammond, K. (2001) From horror to history: Teaching pupils to reflect on significance. *Teaching History*, 104, 15–23.

Harris, R. and Clarke, G. (2011) Embracing diversity in the history curriculum: A study of the challenges facing trainee teachers. *Cambridge Journal of Education*, 41 (2), 159–75.

Harris, R., Harrison, S. and McFahn, R. (2012) *Cross-curricular Teaching and Learning in the Secondary School: Humanities*. London: Routledge.

Herbert, U. (2000) Extermination policy: New answers and questions about the history of the 'Holocaust' in German historiography. In U. Herbert (ed.) *National Socialist Extermination Policies: Contemporary German perspectives and controversies*. New York: Berghahn, 1–52.

Historical Association (2007) *Teaching Emotive and Controversial History 3–19*. London: Historical Association.

Illingworth, S. (2000) Hearts, minds and souls: Exploring values through history. *Teaching History*, 100, 20–24.

Jaspers, K. (1953) *The Origin and Goal of History*. New Haven, CT: Yale University Press.

Kitson, A. (2001) Challenging stereotypes and avoiding the superficial: A suggested approach to teaching the Holocaust. *Teaching History*, 104, 41–8.

Kitson, A. and McCully (2005) 'You hear about it for real in school.' Avoiding, containing and risk-taking in the classroom. *Teaching History*, 120, 32–7.

Novick, P. (1999) *The Holocaust and Collective Memory*. London: Bloomsbury.

Qualifications and Curriculum Authority (1998) *Education for Citizenship and the Teaching of Democracy in Schools*. London: Qualifications and Curriculum Authority.

Salmons, P. (2000) *Torn Apart: A student's guide to the Holocaust exhibition*. London: Imperial War Museum.

Santayana, G. (1905) *The Life of Reason*, vol. 1. New York: Charles Scribner's Sons.

Short, G. and Reed, C. (2004) *Issues in Holocaust Education*. Aldershot: Ashgate.

Toynbee, P. (2001) Opinion. *Radio Times,* 27 January, p. 16.

Historical consciousness

Although the notion of 'historical consciousness' was established as a key concept within German history education as far back as the 1970s, use of the term has only spread slowly through the Nordic countries to inform European and North American educational discourse. The Centre for the Study of Historical Consciousness, established in Canada in 2002, defines historical consciousness as 'individual and collective understandings of the past, the cognitive and cultural factors which shape those understandings, as well as the relations of historical understandings to those of the present and the future' (http://www.cshc.ubc.ca/about/). It thus extends far beyond school history to embrace all the cultural resources that inform people's views of the past (including, for example, popular films, documentaries and novels, heritage sites, public monuments and commemorations, as well as more intimate family photos), and to consider how that understanding is brought to bear on their understanding of the present and their assumptions about the future. This notion of 'orientation in time' – the way in which people conceive of the relationship between past, present and future, and thus draw on history to extrapolate likely future trajectories and inform their decisions about how to act in the present – is therefore central to the study of historical consciousness. Although Rüsen has claimed that 'history is the mirror of past actuality into which the present peers in order to learn something about its future' (2006: 67), some research has suggested that young people pay little (if any) attention to this rear-view mirror, not least because the view it currently offers is too fragmented to be of any use.

Extract 1

Source

Rüsen, J. (2006) Historical consciousness: Narrative structure, moral function and ontogenetic development. In P. Seixas (ed.) *Theorizing Historical Consciousness*. Toronto: University of Toronto Press; see pp. 70–8.

Introduction

The German philosopher of history Jörn Rüsen has been developing a theory of historical consciousness over many decades. In the article from which this extract is taken, he explains his conception of four different types of historical consciousness by referring to an ancient inscription and the story associated with it in Samuel Johnson's *Journey to the Western Isles of Scotland*. On a wall of the castle of Col, ancestral home of the Macleans, is engraved a promise of safety and protection to any member of the Maclonich clan who appeals for it, whatever the circumstances. The promise acknowledges a debt of gratitude for a cunning subterfuge once employed by the Maclonichs to save the heir of the Maclean clan. Rüsen recounts the circumstances in which the promise was made and invites his readers to imagine what they would actually do, as descendants of the Macleans, should Ian Maclonich arrive in the middle of the night, pursued by the police for a crime he has allegedly committed, and begging for help. The four lines of reasoning that Rüsen suggests the reader might pursue illustrate his view of the relationship between historical consciousness, identity formation and moral reasoning. The particular way in which we view the past and our relationship to it influence our interpretation of the present situation and the decisions that we take in response to it.

Key words & phrases

Historical consciousness; moral reasoning; orientation in time; traditional; exemplary; critical and genetic types

---

Extract

1. You can hide Ian Maclonich because you feel there is a binding obligation on your part to honour the ancient Highland agreement …

2. You can hide Ian Maclonich because in the past a Maclonich once aided a member of the Maclean clan and you now feel obliged to reciprocate on the basis of a *general principle* of reciprocity of favours …

3. You can present a series or combination of *critical historical arguments* to relieve you of the obligation to keep the ancient treaty …

4. You still feel obliged to help someone from the Maclonich clan, but wish to do so in a way based on *modern considerations,* and not as the ancient treaty prescribes …

The traditional type

When historical consciousness furnishes us with traditions, it reminds us of origins and the repetition of obligations, doing so in the form of concrete, factual past occurrences that demonstrate the validity and binding quality of values and value systems. Such is the case when, in our role as a member of the [Maclean] clan, we feel an obligating link to an ancient treaty. In such an approach, both our interpretation of what occurred in the past and our justification for hiding Maclonich are 'traditional' …

Traditional orientations guide human life externally by means of an affirmation of obligations requiring consent. Such traditional orientations define the 'togetherness' of social groups or whole societies in the terms of maintenance of a sense of common origin.

The exemplary type

It is not traditions we utilize here as argument – but rather rules. The story of the struggles between the clans and the transposition of the two infants stands here for a general timeless rule: it teaches us what course of action to take, and what action to refrain from doing …

The mode of orientation realized by historical consciousness in this exemplary type is rule-focused: it entails the application of historically derived and proven rules to actual situations …

The critical type

The decisive argument in the critical version of our narrative is that as a member of the Maclean clan we feel no obligation whatsoever to its presumed 'binding' quality. For us it is an ancient tale that has lost any relevance for present action and actuality …

We can develop an ideological critique, stating that there was a ruse involved, a trick by the Maclonichs to trap the Macleans into a kind of moral dependence on them. We can argue that even in that ancient period, it was prohibited to murder infants, which is the pivotal motif on which the narrative turns. Such argumentation is based on offering elements of a 'counter-narrative' to the one behind the stone engraving. By means of such a counter-narrative we can unmask a given story as a betrayal, debunk it as misinformation. We can also argue critically in another way, contending that the treaty engraved on the stone has lost its current validity, because new forms of laws have since emerged. Then we can narrate a brief 'counter-story', that is, the story of how laws have changed over time …

The concept of an embracing temporal totality including past, present and future is transformed into something negative: the notion of a rupture in continuity still operative in consciousness. History functions as the tool by which such continuity is ruptured, 'deconstructed', decoded – so that it loses its power as a source for present–day orientation.

Narratives of this type formulate historical standpoints by demarcation, distinguishing them from the temporal orientation entertained by others. By means of such critical stories we say *no* to pre-given temporal orientations of our lives.

The genetic type

In this framework our argument is that 'times have changed': we thus deny both the option of hiding Ian owing to traditional or exemplary reasons and of critically negating the obligation to this old story as a reason for refusing to hide him. In contrast we accept the story, but place it in a framework of interpretation within which the type of obligation to past events has itself changed from a pre-modern to a modern form of morality. Here *change* is of the essence and is what gives history its sense. Thus, the old treaty has lost its former validity and taken on a new one; consequently, our behaviour necessarily differs now from what it would have been in the distant past. We understand it within a process of dynamic evolvement.

[This] type of historical consciousness imbues historical identity with an essential temporalization. We define ourselves as bring at a cross-point, an interface of time and events, permanently in transition. To remain what we are, not to change and evolve, appears to us as a mode of self-loss, a threat to identity. Our identity lies in our ceaseless changing.

Summary

Rüsen's typology offers four different ways in which individuals might orient themselves in time. The particular kind of relationship that they envisage between the present – traditional, exemplary, critical or genetic – will determine their moral values and sense of identity and thus determine their decisions about how to act. Although Rüsen is not explicitly concerned with history education, he claims that experience in schools indicates that traditional forms of thought are easiest to learn, and that the exemplary form dominates most history curricula. The development of a critical orientation, and even more so, a genetic one, he argues, require 'enormous amounts of effort by both teacher and pupil' (2006: 8). Although he does not elaborate on the nature of the effort required, this claim obviously has profound implications in thinking about how much attention should be given to teaching young people about how historical knowledge is constructed and to helping them understanding the nature of change as a process.

Questions to consider

1. The explicit appeal to an ancient promise in the story that Rüsen uses to illustrate his typology obviously encourages the decision-maker to reflect on the implications of the past for the present and future. Is it realistic to suggest that historical reasoning could, or should, naturally play a central role in young people's moral reasoning?
2. Rüsen claims that most school history curricula are dominated by an exemplary form of historical consciousness. How true do you think that is of the history curriculum, for students of different ages, in your own school?
3. How far should our thinking about curriculum planning and structure be influenced by a concern to help young people recognise the relationship between past, present and future?

Extract 2

Source

Lee, P. (2004) Walking backwards into tomorrow: Historical consciousness and understanding history. *International Journal of Historical Learning, Teaching and Research*, 4 (1), 69–114.

Introduction

Peter Lee examines the implications of Rüsen's theory of historical consciousness for those specifically concerned with history education. While he welcomes Rüsen's focus on 'the ways in which the past figures in youngsters' views of the world (to the extent that it figures at all)' (p. 70), he uses various examples of children's dialogue to highlight the theory's limitations. It is not enough to ask *how* young people use their knowledge of the past; we also need to examine their assumptions about the nature and status of that knowledge. *What kind* of past are they drawing on?

Key words & phrases

Historical consciousness; orientation; usable framework; disciplinary matrix

---

Extract

Rüsen's questions are about the way in which students see the past (the substantive past they can call upon) and how they relate to it. Do they see what they find in the past as having a fixed meaning and significance for us, as something that gives us obligations that must be fulfilled to the letter, as they were in the beginning? Or do they see the same events and processes as exemplifying regularities or rules of conduct? Do they see these past events as having meaning that must be criticized or rejected? Or finally, do they see what they encounter as part of a transformation, in which identity is preserved through change?

An alternative range of questions becomes germane if we ask … questions concerned with students' understanding of the discipline of history …. How is the past that is being invoked understood? Is it understood as something given (so that questions about how we know do not arise), as something handed down by witnesses, or as an inference from present evidence? Is it a past in which changes are just events, are differences between points in time, or are equally products of historians' choices of theme and scale? Is the past understood as a report of events, as far as possible copying them, or as a construction within selected parameters in answer to certain questions and interests?

… Let us assume for the moment that we can operationalize Rüsen's typology, and provide, for a given task, indicators for each type of historical consciousness. If a student's orientation, as evidenced by responses on particular tasks, seems to fall under the category of (say) 'exemplary', then we still do not know whether he or she is treating the claim about the past involved in this orientation as information, or as inferred from evidence. Knowing that a student is orientated 'critically' still does not imply that he or she understands the version of the past at stake as being based on evidence: the student may simply 'know' that it is 'wrong', or think the 'right' version is guaranteed by testimony. Even a student whose responses are categorized as 'genetic' may either be thinking of accounts of the past as copies of that past, or alternatively may conceive them as constructions more akin to theories than to copies .... [Within this category] some students see historical changes as given elements of the past, discovered by historians like caches of coins, while others see them as ways in which historians choose to conceptualize relations between phenomena at different points in time. And in the 'traditional', 'exemplary' and 'critical' categories it may still be possible to ask whether students conceive change simply as the random explosion of events, or as historically significant difference between points in time.

... If we take seriously Rüsen's emphasis on orientation against the background of his disciplinary matrix, we must try to understand better how to enable students to develop a more usable framework of the past in terms of which they can orientate their lives. One way of characterizing this task is to say that we need a history that allows students to orientate themselves in time genetically, but to understand the past to which they orientate as constructed historically.

Summary

Lee recognises the fundamental role that our conceptions of the past play in the way in which we understand our present position and the options open to us, and takes seriously the challenge of ensuring that young people find the history that they study genuinely useful as a means of orientation in time. Given the importance of their assumptions about the past, it is essential that the versions of the past with which they operate are informed by disciplinary principles (related to the use of evidence or the nature of change, for example), rather than resting on informal and often ahistorical assumptions encountered in everyday life.

Questions to consider

1. Lee acknowledges that the past may barely figure at all in young people's thinking about the future. Is he right to be sceptical about this?
2. When young people do draw on their understanding of the past to think about the future, do you think they are more likely to draw on common-sense, popular views of the past, on family-generated understandings or on their school history experiences?
3. What kinds of ideas about the nature of change do children need to develop to make effective use of their knowledge of the past in thinking about the future?

Extract 3

Source

Foster, S., Ashby, R., Lee, P. and Howson, J. (2008) *Usable Historical Pasts: A study of students' frameworks of the past: Non-technical summary* (research summary). ESRC End of Award Report, RES-000-22-1676. Swindon: ESRC.

Introduction

This study, conducted with 47 students from three London schools, set out to explore whether and how students actually accessed and referred to the past as means of orientating themselves in time. The students (some of whom were studying history at examination level for GCSE) were given a written task and interviewed in groups, once at the beginning of Year 10 (at the age of 15) and once again the following year. The questions invited them to speculate on the future of the USA and to construct an account of British history over the last 2,000 years.

Key words & phrases

Usable historical past; historical perspectives; connections across time; change as event; change as process; narratives of British history

---

Extract

Overall, five main conclusions were drawn from the study.

First, analysis of student responses from written tasks and interviews revealed that the majority of students did not instinctively use historical knowledge to inform contemporary and future perspectives. For example, when asked to consider such questions as: 'Will the USA always be the most powerful country in the world?' rarely did students draw on historical perspectives or information. Analysis of student responses consistently demonstrated that many students found it difficult to connect the past, present and future in any meaningful way.

Second, when asked to produce and discuss in interview a narrative of British history over 2,000 years student responses revealed a range of understandings which were broadly classified into four categories. First, some students appeared unable to tackle the task in any way. Other students listed topics often in an arbitrary and unconnected manner. The third category included those students who produced a narrative that attempted to make a story out of a curriculum that deals with history in fragments. Finally, a few students employed a different strategy that attempted to thematise narratives. Clearly the four categories cannot easily be delineated as a linear hierarchy and further larger scale research would be required to develop exemplary levels of sophistication. However, analysis suggests that the basis of a progression model may be visible, and that more research on this may prove very productive.

Third, in structural terms a clear distinction was apparent between those students who saw the past as consisting of a catalogue of arbitrary and disconnected events and those who viewed history (albeit at an elementary level) as an unfolding process of change and development. Further analysis of these two broader categories (classified as 'event like' and 'process like') revealed that only a small number of students moved beyond recounting discrete and unconnected events to offer a sense of important themes, trends or processes in the passage of British history. These students appeared to have a conceptual apparatus that enabled them to make connections across time, but did not necessarily have the substantive knowledge to produce a convincing account.

Fourth, preliminary findings suggested that those students who accounted for British history in a 'process like' manner appeared more inclined to invoke the past in thoughtful ways when addressing questions of future and present concern. The study indicated that students who used the language of developmental change in addressing contemporary issues tended to produce informed future projection. In contrast, however, those students who constructed an 'event like' British past tended to see the past as dead and gone. For these students the past held no usable or significant bearing on present or future issues and concerns.

Finally, although the issue is unquestionably complex and requires further research, this study demonstrated that typically students did not believe that history (beyond personal and family history) was a major factor in influencing their own identity.

Implications and dissemination

Overall, the preliminary findings of this study suggest that the challenge for history education appears to be three-fold. First, it demands that students are provided with an apparatus which allows them to see that studying a meaningful past has some value and relevance both to their own lives and to the world in which they live. Second, it requires developing practices to help students make sense of the past in a coherent way that links past, present, and future. Third, it necessitates the development of a history education and curriculum that does not depend on a fixed narrative story (or 'party history'), but provides opportunities for students to acquire a flexible and usable understanding of the past.

Summary

The findings of the Usable Historical Pasts (UHP) research project reveal how difficult it is for most 16 year olds to make meaningful connections between their study of the past and the present (or future); and how unlikely it is that they will draw on their formal study of the past in constructing their own identities. The problem seems to be linked to their fragmented view of the past and to a restricted conception of change as an event rather than a process. Foster and his colleagues suggest that creating usable understandings of the past will require significant changes in the way that the history curriculum is structured.

Questions to consider

1. Most students in this study did not naturally turn to history to help them speculate about likely future outcomes. Do you think that this means that they could not use their knowledge of the past to help them, or merely that they did not recognise its potential to do so? What different sorts of changes might be needed in the way history is taught to address each of these issues?
2. What are the dangers that could arise if we re-frame the history curriculum to try to strengthen students' awareness of the connections between the past and the present?
3. Does it matter if students' formal study of history (in school) has no bearing on their developing sense of their own identity?

Investigations

Exploring students' big pictures of the past: The task set by the UHP – telling the story of British history over 1,000 or 2,000 years – offers a very simple device for looking at whether and how students can create a connected narrative and how they conceive of the process of change over time. Using the same task with students of different ages (or the same students over time) will allow you to examine how additional knowledge affects the content and structure of their narratives.

Examining students' use of their knowledge of the past: Asking students to explain particular events in the present or to speculate about future developments can help you to understand whether and how they draw on their knowledge of their past in making sense of the present. By asking carefully sequenced questions, you can examine whether they turn to the past unprompted, as well as how they use their knowledge of the past when they are reminded of it.

Exploring the ways in which families relate to the past: Although this kind of research can be quite complex and potentially sensitive, you can seek to find out more about how children encounter history at home or within their community. You could simply ask the students about this, or actually set up interviews with parents/carers. Using photos or songs (as Wineburg does in the example in 'Think wider') as a way of discussing ideas about the past can ease some of the tensions.

Think deeper

Individual teachers have been prompted by Rüsen's typology and by the findings of the UHP project both to adapt their teaching to focus much more deliberately on the development of usable historical frameworks and to examine their own students' views about the value of what they have learned and how it has impacted on the understanding of the world today. Specific examples of teachers' adaptations, such as Rick Rogers' (2008) approach to teaching about Magna Carta as a 'temporally contextualised topic' are discussed in Chapter 11, which deals with chronological understanding and frameworks. In a large UK college for 16–19-year-old students that offered two contrasting A-level specifications, Arthur Chapman and Jane Facey (2004) conducted a survey of history students in their final year, first inviting them to reflect on the use of studying the particular units in their course, and then asking whether what they had learned had influenced their thinking about (1) world affairs, (2) Britain and (3) current news stories. Their findings not only echo Rüsen's claim that most school curricula seem to promote exemplary views of historical consciousness, they also reveal the importance of the particular content choices that curriculum planners, teachers and students make. Those students who were following a traditional course on 'Democracy and dictatorship' (focused on Europe in the interwar period) claimed that the course had greatly increased their understanding of politics and hence their ability to make sense of the world. Those following the less conventional 'People, power and protest' course – which included two units on protest movements in Britain (the Chartists and the Suffragettes), two on various forms of resistance within the British Empire (slavery and emancipation in the British Caribbean and Indian nationalism) and a study of the US Civil Rights movement – tended to focus very strongly on British identity. Thus students tended to see 'their' country in very negative terms (despite the range of perspectives to which their teachers had introduced them), and also conveyed a much stronger sense of how much 'their' past mattered to them. In relating their responses to Rüsen's typology, Chapman and Facey found that while many of the students were clearly thinking in a critical way and challenging an accepted past, almost all of them were 'firmly wedded' to exemplary thinking. They treated the past as 'a storehouse of examples and precepts that should guide us in the present' (2004: 39). Responses that used the past in a genetic way, or that actually historicised it, were much rarer. While a few of the students traced the roots of present problems back, and used the past as a tool for understanding development, there was generally very little sense that the past might help us 'to understand our present by showing how the things that the present finds natural could and possibly should be very, very different' (2004: 41).

Lee and Howson (2009) build on their findings from the UHP project with data drawn from an informal study of the attempts of graduate historians (embarking on a postgraduate initial teacher education programme) to provide an account of British history over the past 100 years. Even the graduates, they discover, find it hard to turn topic lists into narratives of change, prompting the researchers to reflect that 'schools are not alone in failing to provide students with the tools for orientation' (2009: 240). Drawing on the argument advanced above, that any attempt to provide a usable past must attend to disciplinary principles (and so resist what Oakeshott has labelled as a purely 'practical past'), they begin to outline the necessary characteristics of any framework that might be taught to students to help them develop a 'big picture' of the past. The principles that they outline are also discussed in Chapter 11.

Rather than asking young people hypothetical questions about the potential value to them of historical knowledge, the Swedish researcher and history educator Kenneth Nordgren (2011) sought to examine the concept of historical consciousness in action. He used the occasion of the terrorist attacks on the United States in September 2001 to explore the ways in which young people generate historical narratives in specific cultural contexts in order to give meaning to events. The event in question was one that they initially experienced as incomprehensible, but incidents soon afterwards showed the narratives that students from two different minority groups had begun to construct. On the morning afterwards, for example, a number of students with Assyrian and Syriac backgrounds were arguing that the terrorist attacks were a repetition of their own historical experience (subject to genocidal attacks under the Ottoman Empire). In another classroom two days later several pupils from Iraqi, Iranian and Lebanese backgrounds decided not to participate in a moment of silence held to honour the victims, regarding the ceremony as a confirmation of their own historical experience – that Muslim suffering and oppression are repeatedly overlooked in the Western world. Using data from interviews with students from the two different groups, Nordgren shows how they each came to contextualise the event, weaving whole series of influences into narratives which then serve to legitimise their (multifaceted) identities. Shocked by the school's lack of understanding of alternative perspectives, he highlights the challenge of opening up schools to different historical narratives and the need for schools to reflect on their own historical consciousness.

Think wider

The study of historical consciousness obviously raises profound questions about the interplay between popular culture, including historical sites and the public commemorations of past events, and the kind of history that is learned in school. Two substantial American research projects cast light on this interplay by examining the ways in which individuals engage with and seek to make sense of the past.

Roy Rosenzweig (2000) and his colleague Dave Thelen undertook a telephone survey to investigate 'How Americans actually use and think about the past'. The 808 respondents included three minority samples of African Americans, Mexican Americans and Sioux Indians (200 of each). Each 40-minute interview included a mix of open and closed questions, the latter focusing, for example, on the kinds of 'past-related activities' that they had engaged in during the past 12 months (activities ranging from looking at photographs with friends, through visiting museums or historic sites to membership of a study or campaigning group) and the strength of the sense of connection that they felt with the past (on a scale of 1–10). Rosenzweig concluded that 'almost every American engages deeply with the past and the past that engages them most deeply is that of their family' (2000: 266).

While gender and education had some impact on respondents' level of engagement, the most substantial demographic variation was related to judgements about the most important aspect of the past: the history of their family, of their race or ethnic group, of their locality or of their country. Black Americans were six times more likely than whites to select the history of their racial or ethnic group, while the Ogala Sioux were ten times more likely to do so. Each group also used rather different terms to connect the past of their own family to the past of their racial group. For white Americans the pronoun 'we' was used to denote their family, while for African Americans it tended to mean 'our race, our people', as it did for the Sioux, who referred to 'our tribe, our language, our traditions'.

When asked to focus on specific events or periods that had most affected them, the groups also drew from very distinctive timelines and constructed distinctive historical narratives, appealing to specific dates, sites and sources. While Black Americans constructed a story of progress, drawing on metaphors of the distance travelled – 'how far we've come' – most white respondents tended to describe change for the worst. Both the Black Americans and the Ogala Sioux were also much more likely to construct collective narratives that they then used to understand their lives in the present. For white Americans the 'usable past' tended to consist of the stories of their own families.

Although the study did not specifically focus on school history, the classroom was consistently ranked lowest as a place in which respondents had felt connected with history. While most respondents appeared to value their history teachers, they saw their own role in lessons as that of conscripts, forced to engage in processes of memorisation and regurgitation. Rosenzweig's concern is that if school history does not engage young people, when they do turn to the past (as this research suggests they will) many white Americans in particular will be writing their histories alone – using the past in ways that make them suspicious of outsiders.

Taking up the theme of family and community, the educational psychologist Sam Wineburg (2000), focuses on one interview from a longitudinal study of 15 adolescents that set out to explore how these teenagers understood their own pasts, by interviewing them and their parents and teachers several times over the course of two and a half years. In one particular interview, conducted with a student and his parents, the student appealed on several occasions to the authority of the feature film *Forrest Gump* – a film that had been viewed on at least three occasions as a family activity. As Wineburg reflects, the fictionalised past – now permanently available on DVD – has become his frame of reference for the present.

By taking the interviews into students' homes, and focusing in detail on the lives of individuals, Wineburg's aim was to ensure that theories of collective memory, which had tended to focus on the *production* of cultural products such as novels and films, as well as on sites of memory such as battlefields and monuments, directed as much attention on their *consumption*. His argument is that by paying close attention to the ways in which adolescents make sense of the past, we can learn better how to engage their historical beliefs, stretch them and call them into question when necessary. By understanding more about how popular culture shapes historical consciousness, teachers can perhaps use it more effectively to advance students' historical understanding.

References

Chapman, A. and Facey, J. (2004) Placing history: Territory, story, identity – and historical consciousness. *Teaching History*, 116, 36–41.

Lee, P. and Howson, J. (2009) 'Two out of five did not know that Henry VIII had six wives': History education, historical literacy and historical consciousness. In L. Symcox and A. Wilschut (eds) *National History Standard: The problem of the canon and the future of history teaching*. Charlotte, NC: Information Age Publishing, 211–61.

Nordgren, K. (2011) Historical consciousness and September 11, 2001. In K. Norgren, P. Eliasson and C. Rönnqvist (eds) *The Processes of History Teaching*. Karlstad: Karlstad University Press, 165–91.

Rogers, R. (2008) Raising the bar: Developing meaningful historical consciousness at Key Stage 3. *Teaching History*, 133, 24–31.

Rosenzweig, R. (2000) How Americans use and think about the past: Implications from a national survey for the teaching of history. In P. Stearns, P. Seixas and S. Wineburg (eds) *Knowing, Teaching and Learning History: National and international perspectives*. New York: New York University Press, 262–84.

Wineburg, S. (2000) Making historical sense. In P. Stearns, P. Seixas and S. Wineburg (eds) *Knowing, Teaching and Learning History: National and international perspectives*. New York: New York University Press, 306–25.

Constructing historical knowledge and understanding

Evidence

John Fines (1994) claimed that evidence is the 'basis of the discipline' of history. While there is little disputing this for academic history, it is only in the past 40 years that source material has come to be used more commonly in schools; in the UK, for example, it was given a prominent position in the GCSE examination for 16 year olds (from 1986) and the National Curriculum (from 1990). Now the use of a range of source material is widespread in history classrooms across the secondary age range. Yet evidential thinking does not necessarily come easily to many pupils. The first extract in this chapter sets out a justification for the place of evidential work in school history; the second suggests some approaches that might help overcome typical misconceptions pupils have when using evidence; the third explores the methods students use when they approach documentary sources.

Extract 1

Source

Fines, J. (1994) Evidence: The basis of the discipline. In H. Bourdillon (ed.) *Teaching History*. London: Routledge, 122–5.

Introduction

This chapter defines the processes involved in 'doing history'. It then goes on to justify the place of history in schools as an evidence-based discipline that involves knowing how the history we receive has been arrived at. Fines argues that history is not 'what happened in the past' as we simply cannot be sure about all of that happened in the past. History is therefore 'what we can do with what comes to us out of the past' (2004: 122).

Key words & phrases

Doing history; historian; children as historians; active learning; historical process; discipline of history; primary sources

---

Extract

The processes undertaken by anyone 'doing history' … may be pictured in a pattern or model. We start off with a stock of experience of human nature and activity, some skills of interpreting evidence, and some knowledge about the past as our base … Out of this we might generate a question about the past …

Having established a question (or many questions) we go back to the primary, or first-hand sources, that is the information which comes to us untreated from the period about which we are asking. From the sources we will select those pieces of information (that is, evidence) that will help us to answer our question, and we must try to understand the evidence, weigh it, and see how far it can take us towards an answer.

Usually what happens is that this process only raises new questions, but occasionally it helps us revise our view of history (or the view presented by the secondary sources we have read), and more rarely it provides us with new history, ideas and explanations that have not been presented before.

The point in the model where the experience, skills and knowledge are most required is at the stage of processing the evidence. To do this effectively with a document, for example, we need to know who wrote it, in what circumstances, with what intentions and for whom … We also need to know the context of the document in order to make meaning – we must be able to recognise the names he mentions, and know who the people were, for example. We need experience and skill in order to help our intuitive reading of the document to try to read between the lines, to ascertain the deeper meaning.

Children as historians?

But, you may be saying, this is all about historians, not about children, where is the connection? Many people have posed that question, notably Professor G.R. Elton. He, and those who take a similar view, claim that there is no point in treating children as if they were all training to become research historians, and in this they are obviously correct. I once calculated that, of the 4000 children in my peer group in my home town, only four of us studied history at university, and of that handful only I earn my living by it. So the proposition that children should be trained as historians is demonstrably unwise.

Yet let us remember the word common to both groups – professional historians and young children are said to be studying *history*, and unless what they do is substantially similar we should find a new name for one of the activities, possibly retitling history in school as 'Biogoheritage studies' or something equally mischievous.

More seriously, there are three reasons why children should study in similar ways to historians:

1. Without knowing how the history we receive has been arrived at, we can only take it as a series of mystery assertions, which can only be learnt in the sense of learning off by heart. Rote-learning history can serve only the interests of quiz contestants, it cannot be used, and is therefore useless.

2. Good learning is always active learning, in which the children, rather than the teacher, do the work. Learning to cope with the problems of evidence is challenging, mind-stretching, satisfying and it helps make sense of what is being studied. Active learning leads to understanding.

3. Using source-material and tackling the problems of evidence gives a feeling of reality which second-hand history can rarely give. To handle evidence from the time gives an insight into many aspects of that time, and helps us to feel for the topic we are studying. Material given at second-hand does not readily attach our emotions, our imagination or our commitment; first-hand, primary sources do, if they are handled with care.

Summary

Fines presents a powerful case for the use of sources in the history classroom, focusing in particular on what can be learnt from the explicit use of primary sources. He wants all students to tackle the problems of evidence as part of their study of history, seeing this as a right for all, rather than as part of the training of a professional historian. He suggests avoiding the retelling of simplistic narratives of the past, arguing that this encourages rote-learning, which is essentially useless. Although this chapter was written nearly 20 years ago, and use of evidence in the history classroom has become even more commonplace since then, it is important to revisit these arguments in the light of recent debates, which have tended to focus more on the substantive content to be included within the curriculum.

Questions to consider

1. To what extent are your pupils aware of the processes involved in 'doing history' as described by Fines? How might they benefit from these processes being made explicit to them? How might your explanation of the processes differ for 11-year-old or 18-year-old students?

2. Fines suggests that primary sources can engage our emotions, our imagination and our commitment. To what extent is this your experience of using evidence with your pupils? What changes could you make to your selection or use of primary sources to help strengthen pupil engagement?

3. What problems do your students face in learning to use evidence? What scaffolding systems need to be in place to support students' developing independence in dealing with such challenges?

Extract 2

Source

Ashby, R. (2011) Understanding historical evidence: Teaching and learning challenges. In I. Davis (ed.) *Debates in History Teaching*. London: Routledge, 137–47.

Introduction

This extract comes from a summary chapter in an edited book. It raises lots of questions about the way students' concept of evidence can be developed. Ashby is clear that evidence is a concept to be understood rather than a skill or process to be mastered and rehearsed, and that, as a concept, evidence should not be detached from knowledge goals in the classroom. She emphasises the distinction between sources, as raw materials, and evidence, as what is yielded by sources to support a claim or generate a hypothesis. Ashby goes on to suggest that rather than a 'jigsaw' version of the past, students might be encouraged to think about a 'Lego view of history,' where the evidence available can be put together in different but perfectly valid ways.

Key words & phrases

Historical source; enquiry; evidence; bias; student understanding

---

Extract

Students, however, do have a propensity to treat historical sources as face-value information. This is particularly true when using written sources, where the focus is on 'What does it say?' 'What is it about?' Activities designed to offer some cognitive challenge to this position encourage students to shift their focus to 'What is it?' through questions that ask 'Who wrote it?' 'Why did they write it?' 'Who was it written for?' … These questions can lead students to conclude that particular sources should be rejected for their bias and unreliability. Attempts to shift students away from naïve responses to testimony have been attempted through questions that ask whether a source, despite its problems, might nevertheless be useful for a specific enquiry.

Objects and artefacts can have some advantage over written sources. Not just because they avoid problems of literacy but also because students often respond to encounters with these sources with the question 'What is it?' rather than 'What does it say?' While problems of bias and reliability are less likely to get in the way of learning, other problems come to the fore. Teachers are often left without important contextual information that would allow this question to take student thinking forward …

The question or enquiry

The question or enquiry we are pursuing determines how we might use any given source as evidence. It is not possible to determine the value, usefulness, utility or reliability of a source, or its category as primary or secondary, independently of the use to which we want to put it as evidence. … The relationship between the material the past has left behind and the focus of our historical enquiry is central to an understanding of evidence. Developing students' understanding of this relationship can be approached through a focus on the nature of the question.

Questions or enquiries set parameters for what can count as evidence in answering them. Given the nature of the question what evidence is needed? What sources might generate this? How do the evidential implications of a particular kind of question relate to the likely status of the claim we then make? Some questions have less complex relationships with the evidence than others. For example, questions about what happened and questions about why something happened offer a clear distinction between what might count as evidence in the first and what counts in the second. A description of an action can be witnessed, whereas the intention behind the action has to be understood within the complexities of the context of that action, and inferred through the range of possibilities that might attach themselves to it in this context. Claims about intentions will be less certain than those about actions. An enquiry question asking for the intentions behind an action would need to be broken down further. What does this person have to gain by this action? What might this person be trying to prevent or defend? What might they be reacting to? Why react in this way and not another way? Further, the intentions behind an action might be difficult to ascertain if the outcome of that action is one that was not intended. Distinctions might need to be made about the stated intentions of the historical character and those the historian perceives.

Summary

Ashby sets out some key parameters within which the concept of evidence should be taught, emphasising the type of questions that should be asked of evidence, the enquiry question framework that evidence should be explored within and the relationships that might be teased out between types of question asked and the strength of the claim that might then be made from the evidence. This extract does not, however, provide specific examples of how this form of teaching might work in a history classroom without becoming dry and repetitive. Here, knowledge of particular topics and careful thought about rigorous, engaging enquiry questions that might sustain interest is crucial.

Questions to consider

1. How do you define the difference between sources and evidence? How do you help your students understand this difference and encourage correct use of such terminology?

2. What questions do your pupils ask about evidence? How might they be encouraged to move away from asking 'what does it say?' or 'what is it about?' to questions more focused on nature and purpose?

3.   Once this first step is achieved, how might you prevent students from asking only mechanistic questions about the nature and purpose of sources? How might they be encouraged to use the answers to their questions about the nature of the source to answer broader questions about the past? How might overarching enquiry questions be framed and used to encourage this broader approach?

Extract 3

Source

Pickles, E. (2010) How can students' use of historical evidence be enhanced? A research study of the role of knowledge in Year 8 to Year 13 students' interpretations of historical sources. *Teaching History*, 139, 41–51.

Introduction

This article is based on empirical research that Elisabeth Pickles carried out with 164 secondary school students across 19 schools. The students were given an evidence task dealing with Cromwell's motives for supporting the execution of Charles I. Half of the students were aged around 13 and half aged around 17; half had recently studied the topic to which the sources related and half had not. While 126 of the students provided written responses to the task, 38 used a 'think-aloud' method that was later transcribed. The article describes the responses of five students in detail. This extract goes on to analyse those responses.

Key words & phrases

Documentary evidence; historical source; historical methods; meta-cognition; interpretation; substantive knowledge

---

Extract

Students' ideas about methodology

Although there was considerable variety among these students' approaches, when asked explicitly about historical methods, their answers bore similarities. All seemed to think that historians' views brought to the task would play a bigger part in the conclusions they reached than the methods used or the types of understanding deployed. This perhaps suggests they were not sufficiently aware of the methods and understanding they were themselves using. If students were encouraged to reflect on how the types of understanding outlined below may affect their inferences, their use of sources could be enhanced and they would be in a better position to argue that one interpretation is more valid than another. This suggests the importance of meta-cognition in conjunction with clarity about the understandings that are important.

The effects of different types of understanding: substantive knowledge

Substantive knowledge enabled students such as Andrew and Jane to gain a much deeper understanding of the sources, especially in relation to Cromwell's perspective, and this affected their judgements about his motives. In the case of Jane, knowledge also alerted her to the fact that working out meaning can be problematic because her initial reading of Source E did not fit readily with the framework of knowledge she brought to the task.

The depth of conceptual understanding of substantive ideas would appear to have influenced the effectiveness of the use of knowledge. Katrina was aware of Divine Right but interpreted opposition to the King as necessarily implying a lack of belief in it. By contrast, Jane and Andrew's understanding of this idea and of Providence enabled them to explore Cromwell's professed belief that Charles I no longer had God's favour. A deeper understanding of substantive ideas thus led to more analysis of the meaning of the sources.

However, substantive knowledge did not necessarily lead to more effective use of sources. Andrew made the most references to knowledge but he used this to provide a commentary on the sources rather than to extend his knowledge. Annabelle made a number of references to period knowledge but made limited use of them in reaching her conclusion because of her belief that seventeenth-century beliefs were misguided. Katrina drew on contextual knowledge of the situation but used questionable assumptions to draw inferences about Cromwell's motives because she combined factual knowledge with everyday understandings of human behaviour. This would suggest the importance of second-order understandings to enable students to make most effective use of knowledge.

The effects of different types of understanding: ideas about evidence

Judgements about the reliability of the accounts of Cromwell's behaviour did not play a major part in the conclusions reached. Each of these students raised questions about the reliability of Source F and/or Source G (although on different grounds) but, partly as a result, they did not make use of these sources in reaching their conclusions. All but Annabelle made at least one comment on the nature of the sources in which Cromwell's words were reported but the chief difference between them appeared to lie in whether they drew firm inferences or considered possibilities and, if the latter, the nature of the reasoning employed to decide between them. This appeared to be affected by their empathetic understanding which is considered below.

All these students were using the sources to work things out that they were not intended to show and thus using the sources as evidence rather than as information, although Andrew was not consistent in this approach. They differed greatly, however, in the range of contextual knowledge they drew on. The Key Stage 5 students also showed some awareness of the need to establish meaning in a period context (Thomas by using other sources and Jane and Andrew by applying knowledge brought). The Key Stage 3 students gave no evidence that they considered the establishment of meaning in any way problematic.

Summary

Pickles questions the way external examinations in England have valued the 'skill' of establishing the reliability of a source over the 'skill' of interpreting a source. She considers the relationship between the knowledge that students brought to an evidence task and the ways in which they used the sources. The research suggested that students' conceptual understandings of substantive issues were as important as – and interacted with – their ideas relating to evidence and to empathy. Pickles argues that if students' attention was directed to the significance of this range of understandings in relation to sources, they could perhaps make more effective use of them.

Questions to consider

1. What might meta-cognition involve when using historical evidence in the classroom? How might you encourage such approaches among your own students?
2. Pickles suggests that students' conceptual understandings of substantive issues interacted with their ideas relating to evidence and to empathy. What might that mean for the way substantive issues and evidential understanding are approached in your classroom?
3. Where should the balance lie between teaching students to establish the reliability of a source and teaching students how to interpret sources? How should these 'skills' be taught?

Investigations

Research your students' understanding of evidence: Use Pickles' 'think-aloud' method to record the process of thinking some of your students go through when completing an evidence task. How do they approach the task? What use do they make of contextual knowledge? To what extent can they substantiate their claims?

Share departmental views on using sources: Discuss in a department meeting personal justifications for using primary evidence in the history classroom. Use the Fines extract (Extract 1) as stimulus material. Discuss how far you are able to carry out these aims within your current schemes of work. How might they benefit from changes to resources or enquiry questions in the future?

Progression in evidential understanding: Describe in detail the conceptual understanding of evidence you would like to see in a school-leaver going on to study history at university. How will your younger students need to develop if they are to achieve this level of understanding before they leave school? What activities and strategies could you put in place to ensure progression in evidential understanding across the time spent in your school?

Think deeper

Chris Husbands (1996) supports the view of Fines and others that historical evidence has a crucial place in the history classroom, but he draws a clear distinction between that and its place in the work of historians. Unlike historians, Husbands argues, 'school pupils will not claim to generate "new" public knowledge from the study of (selected) historical evidence; they will generate new private understandings'. He argues for the place of evidence in the classroom, 'not because it makes classroom history "authentic", nor because it "models" the activity of the historians, but because of the sorts of learning it makes possible' (1996: 26). Husbands goes on to discuss the types of thinking and questioning involved in using evidence.

Christine Counsell (2000) has suggested there is a need to plan for student progression in understanding evidence, particularly across the 11–14 age range. She advises teaching students to use the language of evidential understanding: making distinctions, dealing in layers of certainty, searching for useful labels and classifying. The focus is on the teacher knowing the particular difficulties individual students are facing in using sources effectively at particular stages, and then using a rigorous enquiry question and detailed planning to help those students make progress. Counsell goes on to make a tentative claim as to what such progress might look like in reality.

In reflecting on evidence arising from his evaluation of the Schools Council Project History 13–16, Denis Shemilt (1987) put forward a model of adolescent conceptualisations of the nature and uses of historical evidence. He posited four stages. In Stage 1 knowledge of the past is taken for granted. As Shemilt puts it, pupils 'frequently fall back upon the authority of teacher and textbook in order to explain why knowledge need not be questioned' (1987: 42). In Stage 2, 'Evidence = Privileged Information about the Past'. Here the student accepts 'how do we know?' as a sensible question and accepts that there may be more than one possible answer to questions of fact and interpretation. In Stage 3, 'Evidence is a Basis for Inference about the Past' and in Stage IV comes an 'Awareness of the Historicity of Evidence'. Here written history is beginning to be recognised as 'no more than a *reconstruction* of past events', but that this reconstruction 'makes visible connections and continuities, moralities and motives, that contemporaries would not have perceived' (1987: 56). In further research Shemilt and Lee generated a more developed model of progression that is summarised in the article 'A scaffold, not a cage' (Lee and Shemilt 2003). Their arguments about the value of such research-based models of progression are discussed in Chapter 18.

Think wider

Assessment requirements can lead to mechanistic teaching of approaches to short written sources, known to some as 'Death by Sources A to F' (LeCocq 2000). There have been many recent articles that show practice has moved away from this approach in trying to give students a deeper and richer understanding of a wider variety of source material.

Claire Riley (1999) develops a 'layers of inference' approach that helps pupils decipher the different levels of meaning it is possible to infer from a series of challenging sources. This learning is integrated with substantive knowledge and understanding of literacy to move pupils forward in a more comprehensive fashion. Heidi LeCocq (2000) builds on this work and shows how a series of lessons incorporating evidence over a six-month period can move pupils beyond trite, formulaic responses to a fuller understanding of the tentative nature of evidence.

Simon Butler (2003) provides a list of examples of twentieth-century rock and roll that he has used as source material in the history classroom. This ranges from Billie Holliday's powerful rendition of *Strange Fruit* to Paul Hardcastle's song *Nineteen* on soldiers of the Vietnam War. Butler suggests that music can be used as excellent 'Initial Stimulus Material' to excite and engage pupils, but is rigorous in his follow-up questions, asking pupils to engage with the mood and style of the music as well as the lyrics. This allows students to construct layers of meaning that might be missed in an analysis of the written word alone.

Chris Edwards (2006) describes an oral history project that moved students' thinking about evidence on substantially as they were expected to gather and evaluate evidence themselves in order to construct an account. Edwards says that his history department was struck by 'the effectiveness of oral history to convey to students … the main learning points of source evaluation' (2006: 25). As it was 'personal, immediate and concrete' teachers felt there was a good case for considering oral testimony as a starting point for source work in general.

Teachers' awareness of the highly specific demands of the source-based paper within the GCSE examination for 16 year olds has encouraged a tendency to concentrate on short extracts of source material. Mary Woolley (2003) argues that to cut down on length is to cut out context and to restrict severely the enjoyable experience of reading about the past. Woolley used a short story by Thomas Hardy as a source of evidence in the history classroom. Students were already familiar with the text and narrative from their English lessons, but through this series of lessons they learn how to interrogate a lengthy text as evidence, select appropriate material to answer enquiry questions and ask questions of their own based on the text.

References

Butler, S. (2003) 'What's that stuff you're listening to, Sir?' Rock and pop music as a rich source for historical enquiry. *Teaching History*, 111, 20–5.

Counsell, C. (2000) 'Didn't we do that in Year 7?' Planning for progress in evidential understanding. *Teaching History*, 99, 36–41.

Edwards, C. (2006) Putting life into history: How pupils can use oral history to become critical historians. *Teaching History*, 123, 21–5.

Husbands, C. (1996) *What Is History Teaching? Language, ideas and learning about the past.* Buckingham: Open University Press.

LeCocq, H. (2000) Beyond bias: Making source evaluation meaningful to Year 7. *Teaching History*, 99, 50–5.

Lee, P. and Shemilt, D. (2003) A scaffold, not a cage: Progression and progression models in history. *Teaching History*, 113, 13–23.

Riley, C. (1999) Evidential understanding, period knowledge and the development of literacy: A practical approach to 'layers of inference' for Key Stage 3. *Teaching History*, 97, 6–12.

Shemilt, D. (1987) Adolescent ideas about evidence and methodology in history. In C. Portal (ed.) *The History Curriculum for Teachers*. London: The Falmer Press, 39–61.

Woolley, M. (2003) 'Really weird and freaky': Using a Thomas Hardy short story as a source of evidence in the Year 8 classroom. *Teaching History*, 111, 6–11.

Historical significance

The design of any history curriculum depends on judgements about historical significance. Traditionally, children and young people have been presented with the outcomes of other people's judgements about historical significance: the selection of individuals, periods, events and developments that policy makers, textbook authors and/or teachers have determined it is most important for them to learn. Sometimes the criteria on which those judgments have been based are made explicit to the students. But where history is simply taught as a body of knowledge, students may not even be aware that there has been a process of selection. Teaching about historical significance means making that process explicit: helping students to understand the process by which subsequent ages decide what it is most important to learn about people in the past. As well as enabling young people to understand and critically evaluate judgements made by *others*, some have argued that it also means equipping them to make their *own* judgements about historical significance. The literature discussed in this chapter includes research into the ways in which children actually understand the concept of historical significance and examples of history educators' theorising about the key ideas that they would want young people to develop, particularly analysing how the concept of significance extends beyond simply assessing the consequences of events or determining their relevance to the present.

Extract 1

Source

Cercadillo, L. (2001) Significance in History: Students' ideas in England and Spain. In A. Dickinson, P. Gordon and P. Lee (eds) *Raising Standards in History Education: International review of history education, volume 3*. London: Woburn Press, 116–45.

Introduction

Lis Cercadillo's doctoral research explored students' understanding of the concept of historical significance by comparing the views of carefully selected samples of English and Spanish students (of different ages: 12–13, 14–15 and 16–17). Tasks were set on two different topics – the defeat of the Spanish Armada (commonly taught in both countries) and the conquests of Alexander the Great (a 'neutral' topic, unrelated to the secondary curriculum). Students read two competing accounts of each event selected to illustrate the fact that historians disagree with each other about the importance of particular historical events. They were then asked to give their own opinion as to how much each event mattered and why (or why not).

Key words & phrases

Intrinsic and contextual significance; fixed and variable significance; causal significance; contemporary significance; pattern significance; symbolic significance; significance for the present and the future

---

Extract

The main characteristics and pointers for the categorization of each type in students' responses are presented below.

Contemporary significance The event is seen as important by people at the time in the context of their perceptions, beliefs and view of the world … In the case of the Spanish Armada, we observe whether they are attentive to the different viewpoints of contemporaries such as the English and the Spanish, or whether their own nationality prevents them from perceiving the others' side.

Causal significance This situates a causal event or process in relation to its causal power; hence its significance is in part dependent on later events or consequences. An awareness of this type of always indicates a degree of contextuality … Hints for causal significance are verbs such as 'help', 'make', 'benefit', 'enable', 'change', 'achieve' … ; consequential links such as 'therefore', 'so', 'that is why'; or the use of counterfactuals and such like. The nature of causal significance may be defined in pupils answers by aspect (economic, social, political, religious, cultural), geographical space (England, Spain, Greece, Persia) and time-scale (immediate, short-term, long-term).

Pattern significance This indicates a higher level of sophistication in students' answers. It is always allied to contextuality, and usually refers to concrete models of emplotment, such as the concepts of progress and decline. Markers for data-coding within this category are those terms which allude to the event or process as a turning-point or a trend in a developmental account, such as words like 'milestone'; or … 'it marked the beginning', 'from then on', 'it was the start of' …

Symbolic significance This may operate from the perspective of people in the past and from the perspective of subsequent presents. Symbolic significance is attached specifically to notions of moral example (lessons from history) and mythical past. It implies a particular use of history related to issues of national identity and partisanship, but it can also be connected to more general or ahistorical concepts such as piety or transcendental moral ideas ... General expressions such as 'it showed', it gives an indication', 'it proved', 'it highlighted' usually indicate this type of attribution; it can also be expressed by more definitive terms such as 'teaches us', 'set a good example for others', 'he was an inspiration for', 'was a role model' and so on.

Significance for the present and the future Closely related to importance and causal weighting, it only operates in the long term, when the bond with the future is emphasized.

Analysis suggests that pattern and symbolic notions of significance and significance for the present and future may be considered as possible indicators of progression in historical understanding ... One-third of students from Year 8, almost half of students from Year 10 and the majority of those from Year 12 who mentioned pattern, symbolic or 'connection with the present' notions of significance did also suggest contemporary or causal notions in their responses. This could be interpreted as indicating that these students reached particular levels of understanding but went beyond those to achieve more sophisticated modes.

In the consideration of variety of types of significance, then, contemporary and causal alone were located at a lower level than other types even if internal variations in the former occurred. This led us to disregard internal variations in contemporary and causal attribution, that is, variations within types (such as differentiation of short- and long-term consequences in causal significance) in pursuit of variations across attributions. A second indicator of progression was the consideration of significance as variable within or between attributions of types of significance. Therefore, variable significance between accounts is always regarded as at a higher level than fixed significance, even if only the contemporary and the causal types are indicated.

Bearing those reasons in mind, the model of progression in types of significance was defined as follows:

Level 1: No allusion to any type of significance

Level 2: Intrinsic and single significance

Level 3: Fixed contextual significance: significance is fixed within/across attributions (contemporary and causal only)

Level 4: Fixed contextual significance: significance is fixed within/across attributions (besides or other than contemporary and causal)

Level 5: Variable contextual significance: significance varies within/across attributions
    5.1 contemporary and causal only
    5.2 besides or other than contemporary and causal

Summary

While Cercadillo accepts that consideration of the consequences of an event obviously forms one component within a judgement of its significance, she suggests that locating particular consequences within *patterns* of development indicates a more complex understanding of the nature of change. Responses that she suggests reveal higher levels of understanding within the concept of significance depend on an appreciation that significance is not a fixed or intrinsic property of any particular event, but an ascribed value that changes depending on subsequent developments and on the nature of the relationship between the person making the judgement (and their context) and the event being judged.

Questions to consider

1. What does this extract reveal about the processes and steps involved in analysing students' written answers to determine the nature of their understanding of particular concepts?
2. On what grounds does Cercadillo claim that certain kinds of response represent a higher level of understanding in relation to significance than others? How convinced are you by these claims?
3. Within the hierarchy that Cercadillo establishes, the shift from claims rooted in contemporary or causal conceptions of significance towards other kinds of conceptions (particularly 'symbolic' significance or 'connections with the present/future') seems to be an important advance. How do you think students could be helped to make that transition?

Extract 2

Source

Counsell, C. (2004) Looking through a Josephine-Butler-shaped window: Focusing pupils' thinking on historical significance. *Teaching History*, 114, 30–6.

Introduction

In 2002 Rob Phillips famously described 'historical significance' as the 'forgotten key element' in the National Curriculum for England. By that point, however, the situation was already changing, stimulated both by research – such as that by Cercadillo – and reconsideration of earlier theoretical ideas. In the article from which this extract comes, Christine Counsell reviews a range of criteria that Phillips and others had proposed might be used to assess historical significance, and then offers her own suggestions – intended as a stimulus for debate. Her first priority, however, is to identify and dismiss important *misconceptions* about what is meant by historical significance.

Key words & phrases

Historical significance; meta-concept; presentism; significance as an ascribed not a fixed property

Extract

Thinking about historical significance is everyone's business and it is every history teacher's right to contribute to the debate.

We want pupils to think about it

To start with, let us keep the focus on 'thinking about'. This immediately discounts a few red herrings and common distractions.

One red herring is the view that teaching historical significance is about teaching pupils the significance of a particular event (or person or situation) as though this were a matter of fixed consensus. 'They need to know why this event is so significant' I hear some history teachers say. Fine, such a view may well be defensible, and each of us selects content for study within the massive freedom of the National Curriculum and assorted specifications at GCSE and A Level on precisely that basis. But we should not confuse our own views, as teachers, about what is significant, with activities to secure pupils' reflection on the issue. This would suggest that the significance of an event is something uncontested, something about which we all agree. It also suggests that pupils just have to know why something is significant, rather than engage with the very idea of significance itself, which is surely the point of naming it as a Key Element of the current National Curriculum. Its position there suggests that we treat it as a process of reasoning, something that is up for grabs, not a given condition.

Historical significance is not a property of the event itself. It is something that others ascribe to that event, development or situation ...

Getting beyond 'relevance to today'

A second red herring is easy appeal to 'relevance to today'. Whilst pupils' grasp of an event's supposed link with today might be a useful realisation, it does not necessarily take pupils closer to thinking about historical significance.

Of course, the history teacher constantly helps pupils to make sense of why studying the past matters and, of course, they will often use the relevance of events to today or their impact on our own lives and values. This is a good way 'in' to a topic or a useful way of reflecting on it afterwards. But we lay ourselves open to charges of presentism if our conception of historical significance is intrinsically or necessarily related to this. Relevance to today is just one possible consideration in a judgement about the significance of an event ...

On its own, however, it would leave pupils with an incomplete picture of the idea of historical significance. It certainly does not explain why many events and developments are judged so significant that they live on in the history books, in scholarly debates, in TV history, in a theme park or in a heated, sensitive argument in a pub.

Getting beyond consequences

A third distraction occurs when we fail to get beyond 'consequences' or 'results'. Plenty of consequences, short-term and long-term, attach to the First World War, the Russian Revolution, the Glorious Revolution, the emergence of the railways. These easily explain their significance. But the few, negligible short-term results that might attach to the Tolpuddle Martyrs, to the Children's Crusade, to the poetry of Walt Whitman or to the Jarrow March do not explain the significance of these phenomena ...

Why did these things end up discussed in public domains long after the event? That is the issue. This is what needs to be examined by pupils. Perhaps these things are iconic, perhaps they reveal things about their age, perhaps they have personal significance for particular groups, perhaps they had indirect results, perhaps subsequent interpretation changed things more than the event itself. Whatever the reason, the simple idea of results or consequences being an equivalent of historical significance will not do. If it can simply be reduced to consequences, we do not need the concept of historical significance at all.

Martin Hunt (2003, p. 35) is clear about this: 'There is also a danger in what may be an apparent overlap with the "second order" concept of consequence. Greater understanding of historical significance is more likely to be achieved if there is a clear distinction between the two.' Hunt argues that significance is a 'wider concept' than consequence – a kind of meta-concept. When pupils work on significance, they are really standing outside all the usual concepts and could be drawing upon any of them. Whether cause or change or consequence or diversity – any could be functional in a judgement about what is historically 'significant'.

Summary

Both Hunt and Phillips had argued that a stronger focus on historical significance would significantly enhance students' awareness of the value of studying history. Counsell shares this conviction, but calls for a much more extensive role for students: not merely learning to recognise and apply standards generated by others, but also determining and debating those criteria for themselves. Looking simply at the relevance of an event or development to the present day risks distorting the way we look at the past; while simply focusing on its consequences makes the concept effectively redundant.

Questions to consider

1. Counsell thinks that *telling* students why a particular event is significant will give rise to profound misconceptions about historical significance. How far do you think her fears are justified?

2. What are the dangers of presentism (viewing the past through the lens of the present)? Is it possible to avoid them, without students dismissing history as irrelevant?
3. Counsell insists that historical significance rests on more than relevance to the present day, or consequences. What other criteria did Cercadillo discover being used? Are there others that you think students should be encouraged to consider?

Extract 3

Source

Brown, G. and Woodcock, J. (2009) Relevant, rigorous and revisited: Using local history to make meaning of historical significance. *Teaching History*, 134, 4–11.

Introduction

Geraint Brown and James Woodcock took up Counsell's challenge to theorise about the kinds of thinking students should be doing in relation to historical significance. As their department re-structured an enquiry on the local significance of the First World War, they 'discussed', 'reflected' and 'wrestled' over a range of questions, including the criteria that might be used to determine significance. Their conclusions are profoundly influenced by the '5Rs' – a selection of criteria first put forward by Counsell ('Remarkable', 'Remembered', 'Resonant', 'Resulting in change', 'Revealing') – but they have augmented and developed her ideas.

Key words & phrases

Criteria; commemoration; historical significance; relevance; remarkable; remembrance; resulting in change; resonance; revealing

---

Extract

What are the indicators that something is thought to be significant?

Remembered and referred to

If something has been commemorated, subsequently referred to, subsequently taught, subsequently talked about, subsequently written about, then this is an indication that someone believes that the event is significant in some way.

However, being remembered does not of itself indicate why something is thought significant, or what its significance is believed to be. For example, some might remember the Holocaust because they argue it is unique; others might remember it because they argue that it is not unique, being one of many appalling genocides. To understand the nature of the significance being asserted, we need to dig deeper, beyond the fact of its remembrance.

Remembrance might often be an indication that a community believes an event to be significant. However, one individual might refer to an event in order to assert that it ought to be remembered by others. Either way, the fact of, or desire for, remembrance reveals a belief in the significance of the event.

In what ways can something be thought to be significant?

Resulting in change

This is perhaps where many pupils begin (and end) their thinking about significance. An event can be seen to be significant because it 'changed history' or was a turning point. An event which is thought to have changed the course of other events, or had wide-reaching, long-lasting consequences will thus be considered significant.

Relevant

Educators, society at large, and curriculum designers will often decide that an event is significant because of its perceived relevance to their own time and world. Olaudah Equiano is referred to in the Key Stage 3 National Curriculum in part because of his perceived relevance to multicultural Britain and partly because telling his story is (un) wittingly part of a cathartic process being undergone by elements in British society with regards to Britain's past involvement in the transatlantic slave trade.

Revealing

Historians and other commentators will often choose an individual or a particular event and use it as an illustration of a bigger issue, as a window into a bigger story. Indeed, we as teachers will often use this strategy when deciding upon a focal point for a lesson sequence or activity. For example, an enquiry such as 'What can the story of Siegfried Sassoon tell us about the First World War?' asks pupils to consider, among other things, just how revealing Sassoon's story is of other soldiers' experiences in the war.

Remarkable

An event might be considered significant because it is (or was) unique, special, different, or unusual, compared with what came before and/or after it. Rosa Parks might be considered significant for this reason, but her significance could also be challenged on the same grounds, as Claudette Colvin had previously similarly refused to move seats on a segregated bus.

Remarked upon

Something which has been commented upon at the time might often lead people subsequently to see it as significant. Counsell cites the Children's Crusade as an example of this.

Resonates

Some events create echoes and ripples through later time. Their effects can be seen in later attitudes, actions, and beliefs. People might wittingly or unwittingly be influenced by such echoes, and might or might not explicitly refer to such events. If an observer sees similarities between a past event and a subsequent event, then they might well draw comparisons between the two. Events might become part of the culture, a reference point for a particular community. Some events' significance might fade with time; that of others' might grow, or re-emerge. The Vietnam War is perhaps the strongest of such examples, with the phrase 'The new Vietnam' being part of the culture and often used to describe the Iraq War or the war in Afghanistan. An example of an event whose significance has re-emerged and shifted is Pearl Harbor; while it never left American culture, the event was given higher prominence and was seen to have new resonances in the wake of the 11 September 2001 attacks.

Summary

Before presenting the fruits of their departmental deliberations, Brown and Woodcock acknowledge an enormous debt to Counsell, arguing that her 5Rs are not merely a 'useful stimulus' for teachers but that they also 'stand up to a great deal of analytic scrutiny' (p. 10). Their elaboration and embellishment of Counsell's ideas illustrate not only the range of criteria that might underpin judgements of historical significance, but also the importance of collaborative discussion and experimentation in the development of teachers' professional knowledge.

Questions to consider

1. Why have Brown and Woodcock thought it necessary to distinguish between the indications that an event is regarded as significant and the different ways in which (or the grounds on which) it might be regarded as significant?
2. How is the criterion of resonance different from that of relevance?
3. Which of the suggested criteria do you think students would find it easiest to engage with?

Investigations

Students' perceptions of historical significance: You can explore your students' existing ideas in a variety of ways. One is to ask them at the end of a particular topic, *why* they think this particular topic was included in the curriculum, or indeed *whether* they think it was worth including (and on what grounds). An alternative approach is to ask them to review the curriculum they have studied over that particular year or series of years and ask them which topics they regard as the most significant. Use probing questions about the selection they have made to uncover and encourage them to reflect on the criteria they have used.

The relationship between students' perceptions of historical significance and the value they ascribe to the study of history: Carry out an action research enquiry to explore whether and, if so, in what ways, encouraging students to evaluate the significance of historical events (or to explain why others have attributed significance to them) impacts positively on their personal views of the value of studying history.

Teachers' perceptions of historical significance: Interview teachers about their current curriculum and the topics that they have chosen to include. On what grounds do they justify the choices that they have made? How far do criteria of historical significance – and which particular criteria – seem to have determined their selection?

Think deeper

Martin Hunt (2000) is among those whose theoretical discussions of the purpose – and potential pitfalls – associated with teaching about historical significance helped to bring the concept to greater prominence. Working from the premise that focusing on significance would help students to appreciate for themselves the importance of studying the past, he enumerates the 'educational outcomes' that arise from it, including:

- Redressing the balance caused by a 'compartmentalised episodic approach' that can result from the inevitable process of breaking topics down into individual, manageable lessons. At the end of Key Stage 3 in particular, a focus on significance can encourage much more meaningful review of topics that were studied earlier, with students now sufficiently mature to appreciate the continuing connections between those past events and their own lives.
- Developing students' understanding of human conduct and motivation in specific historical contexts. While previous work on the role of the individual may have tended to highlight the moral example that they were assumed to have set (often understood in decontextualised, ahistorical terms), more recent considerations of historical significance focus on the interaction between the individual and his or her specific circumstances.
- Promoting the use of generalisations and thereby supporting the development of students' ability to engage and work effectively with a range of substantive – but essentially abstract – concepts, such as freedom, equality, class.
- Making an important contribution to citizenship, though the fundamental questions that judgements of significance raise about our own values.

Hunt's reflections also alert history teachers to four kinds of challenges that may arise for young people when studying historical significance: These are:

- *The negative:* this can range from the assumption held by many young people that the past is simply irrelevant to their lives, to a much more active rejection of the past in contexts where issues of past injustice or oppression may seem all too familiar therefore students would prefer something more escapist.
- *The sceptical:* studying history can be diminished in students' eyes if its significance is seen merely in the perpetuation of past conflicts, or where lessons from the past have not been learned. Such scepticism can also arise from a sense of frustration that there is no one unquestionable set of significant and true facts about a situation or event (Lomas 1990).
- *The psychological:* precisely because of its dependence on abstract concepts, teaching about significance requires teachers to go beyond the specific to the

general, to identify the wider and more enduring issues and to be able to make links and connections across time.

■ *The practical:* it is important to recognise just how profoundly judgements of significance depend upon breadth of knowledge and command of language. Teachers should not underestimate these very real demands, and work hard not only to develop the necessary literacy skills but also to generate sufficient interest in the subject to carry students thought the challenges they will face.

In offering practical guidance to new and experienced teachers – who are perhaps feeling overwhelmed by these potential problems as well as by the sheer variety of the criteria offered to students – Kitson et al. (2011) offer a helpful summary of four possible strategies:

1. Asking pupils 'to decide *why* something or someone is deemed to be significant. The challenge is not to decide whether a particular aspect of the past is significant but rather to explore why it is commonly agreed to be so. This might include trying to discern the kinds of criteria that have been used by others to ascribe significance to an aspect of the past' (p. 86).
2. Asking pupils 'to decide *whether* an event or person is significant, or to judge the extent of the significance' (p. 86).
3. Asking pupils 'to *compare* the significance of historical events, either events which are close in time or context, or events which require considerable breadth of knowledge' (p. 87). This might be done by asking students to select those events they regard as most worthy of study from a given period or range.
4. Asking pupils to suggest why and 'how judgements about significance have changed over time'. This might involve thinking about 'why no one appeared to bother much about a given event until recently, or why some historical events once considered important are now rarely studied' (p. 87).

The authors go on to outline two specific enquiry sequences in detail exploring how these different elements might be combined, while highlighting the critical role that they think work on significance should always play in alerting students to the value of studying the past.

Think wider

Hunt (2000) has argued that significance is a meta-concept that can be applied in relation to a number of other concepts – most obviously causation, but also to change and continuity or diversity. Robin Conway's (2006) small-scale research with a class of pupils aged 12–13 working on the Industrial Revolution reveals some of the ways in which ideas about significance interact with other assumptions that students hold. Conway began with two images of the same town, depicted in 1750 and 1900, and asked the students firstly to identify the range of changes that they could see, before inviting them to reflect on their significance, using a card-sorting exercise to rank them. His discussions with students alerted him to a range of preconceptions that he assigned to three different categories – those relating to the specific topic, those relating to their understanding of the nature of history (in this case to their assumptions about significance) and those relating to their wider understanding of the world. Conway's discussion is particularly interesting because of the interplay it reveals between preconceptions of different kinds and the strength of conviction that sometimes underpins students' unhelpful ideas. The article offers valuable suggestions about the importance of eliciting students' existing ideas at the start of any new topic – a key feature of assessment for learning – and illustrates the importance of using such discoveries to shape subsequent planning, in Conway's case, by narrowing the focus to allow him to target specific ideas in more depth.

In the United States, Linda Levstik and Keith Barton (2008) designed a flexible and very productive research instrument to explore adolescents' views of historical significance. They offered participants a collection of 20 captioned pictures relating to US history carefully chosen to represent a range of different periods and types of history, from which they were asked to select the eight that they regarded as the most significant. The historical timeline that the participants thus created then forms the basis of a semi-structured interview, usually conducted in small groups. Levstik and Barton have used this approach in a variety of ways, both to compare the views of students with those of teachers, and also to explore the perspectives of young people from several different countries, including Northern Ireland, New Zealand and Ghana.

The judgements about significance that the young people make effectively illuminate the narrative that they perceive as underpinning their nation's past, shaping a sense of collective identity in the present. What is most striking from the discussions is the contrast between the 'legitimating' history that the students tend to represent in their choices – a focus on the origin and development of the political and social structure of the United States, characterised by steadily expanding rights and opportunities – and the 'vernacular' history of struggle and unresolved tensions, of which many were aware. The latter tended to be transmitted through families and local communities, challenging the official visions of progress. The choices that the students made and the problems that they articulated when discussing events such as the Vietnam War, or the continued experience of racism (developments that do not fit a narrative of progress) – reveal the very real tension between the two versions of the past. As Peter Seixas (1997) had previously found in Canada, students from diverse backgrounds had difficulty coordinating their own perspectives on historical significance with those presented in the school curriculum. Most worrying, however, was the fact that the teachers and prospective teachers who took part in the research rarely focused on any form of vernacular history – choosing instead to share entirely positive images of nation building. As Levstik warns, history educators need to build a framework for making critical sense out of legitimating stories as well as alternative vernacular histories. Lacking such a framework, she fears that students 'may simply replace nationalist self-satisfaction with cynicism', which will leave them no better equipped to understand national history. The framework is needed to make critical sense of both, since each on their own, Levstik suggests, will leave students 'uninterested in history ... and lead [them] away from active civic participation' (Levstik and Barton 2008: 286).

References

Conway, R. (2006) What they think they know: The impact of pupils' preconceptions on their understanding of historical significance. *Teaching History*, 125, 10–15.

Hunt, M. (2000) Teaching historical significance. In J. Arthur and R. Phillips (eds) *Issues in History Teaching*. London: Routledge, 39–53.

Hunt, M. (2003) Historical significance. In M. Riley and R. Harris (eds) *Past Forward: A vision for school history 2002–2012*. London: Historical Association, 33–6.

Kitson, A. and Husbands C. with Steward, C. (2011) *Teaching and Learning History 11–18: Understanding the past*. Maidenhead: Open University Press.

Levstik, L. and Barton, K. (2008) *Researching History Education*. New York: Routledge. See particularly Chapter 11 'What makes the past worth knowing?'; Chapter 12 '"It wasn't a good part of history": National identity and students' explanations of historical significance'; and Chapter 13 'Articulating the silences: Teachers and adolescents' conceptions of historical significance'.

Lomas, T. (1990) *Teaching and Assessing Historical Understanding*. London: Historical Association.

Phillips, R. (2002) Historical significance – the forgotten 'Key Element'? *Teaching History*, 106, 14–19.

Seixas, P. (1997) Mapping the terrain of historical significance. *Social Education*, 61, 220–8.

Historical interpretations

Teaching young people about historical interpretations is a crucial element of history education and in England has been a formal part of the National Curriculum since it was first introduced. Indeed, in some senses its inclusion was a necessary guarantee that a national curriculum would not mean the imposition of a single view of the past. However, it has since caused considerable difficulties for teachers both in terms of understanding precisely what is required and how to teach it effectively. Essentially teaching about historical interpretations requires young people to see that our knowledge of the past is a construction rather than a direct copy of that past. Although constructing their *own* interpretations will help students to understand the nature of this process, the emphasis here is on understanding *how* and *why* the past has been interpreted in different ways, which of course requires knowledge of the context in which the different interpretations were constructed. The importance of teaching interpretations is explored in the first extract, whereas the other extracts focus on the challenges of teaching historical interpretations.

Extract 1

Source

Chapman, A. (2011) Historical interpretations. In I. Davies (ed.) *Debates in History Teaching*. London: Routledge, 96–105.

Introduction

This extract comes from a chapter on historical interpretations that focuses attention on historical, theoretical and logical dimensions of interpretation. Arthur Chapman draws on the work of a range of historians and history educationalists to provide an explanation of historical interpretation and a justification of its explicit place in the history classroom. Beyond this extract, the chapter goes on to consider a range of tools and criteria for comparing and evaluating interpretations.

Key words & phrases

Historical interpretations; discipline; validity of claims; claims about the past; historical culture; historian; fluidity of the past

---

Extract

Understanding historical interpretations involves thinking critically about the diverse ways in which human groups and societies make sense of time and change. Subject disciplines exist to enable us 'to approach questions of importance in a systematic and reliable way' (Gardner, 2000, p. 144) and the study of historical interpretations should aim to provide pupils with tools that they can use to systematically compare and evaluate claims about the past if not in order to establish total and definitive 'truth' then certainly to move beyond the view that 'anything goes' and towards an understanding of how the validity of claims about the past can be assessed.

Many good arguments have been advanced for the study of historical interpretations – citizenship arguments, political arguments and so on – and it is plausible to suggest that the study of plural historical interpretations is important to the health of democratic culture in a diverse and complex world. The most compelling arguments for the student of historical interpretation are, however, historical: there is no alternative to studying historical interpretation, if we want to help students think reflectively and critically about a key dimension of their humanity and about the ubiquitous and often competing history stories and memory practices that clamour for attention in the present.

Historical interpretation in the history curriculum

Historical interpretations are a key component of the history curriculum in England and Wales, from Key Stage 1 [ages 4–7] to AS and A2 [ages 16–18]. Simplifying the various curricular statements, we can say that it is intended that the study of 'interpretations' will enable students to:

1. *Understand that* the past has been interpreted in different ways;
2. *Understand how* the past has been interpreted in different ways;
3. *Explain why* the past has been interpreted in different ways; and
4. *Evaluate* different interpretations of the past.

The curriculum also requires that students engage with a broad range of historical culture and study the work of 'historians and others' (QCA, 2007, p. 113) …

The fluidity of the past and the plural nature of historical interpretation

In so far as it exists at all, the historical past only exists in the present and in the form of:

- traces of the past (relics and reports)
- interpretations of the past constructed subsequent to its passing.

What we can say about the past results from an ongoing *dialogue* between traces and present questions and purposes ...

Disciplined historical thinking is characterized, however, by an effort to make practices of interpretation explicit and available for scrutiny and an important purpose of history education is to make it clear to pupils that interpretation is open to rational discussion and evaluation. Engagement with the past is also a dynamic process: we are not stuck where we started and interpreting the traces of the past frequently involves the revision of questions and preconceptions (Megill, 2007).

In addition, all histories are in history: the ways in which we become conscious of the past, the ways in which we aim to interpret the past and the tools available for this task are as much reflections of who we are and of our particular place in time as they are of the traces of the past itself. Engagements with the past are always authored, driven by particular purposes or questions and undertaken by particular people or groups of people with particular beliefs and assumptions and even where 'facts' can be clearly and non-controversially established their meaning is inherently debateable (Koselleck, 2004, p. 149; Samuel, 1994).

The past is, therefore, inherently fluid and historical interpretations are inherently plural and variable; they are in history, have historicity and continually change as the present changes.

Summary

Chapman emphasises the importance of teaching historical interpretations to help pupils move towards an understanding of how the validity of claims about the past can be assessed. He points out that the past only exists in the present in traces of the past or interpretations of the past and argues that a purpose of history education is to show pupils that interpretation is open to rational discussion and evaluation. This has crucial implications for the history classroom where interpretations work has been seen to be weak or confused (see 'Think deeper' section below). Chapman is demanding in his expectations of teachers and students. He sets the challenge of disciplined historical thinking, which is vital in the teacher before it can be shared with students.

Questions to consider

1. Define historical interpretation. What strategies might you use to enable your students to engage with this definition or to create their own definition?

2. How explicit is the teaching of historical interpretations in your classroom? To what extent are your students able to fulfil the criteria of the National Curriculum set out in this extract?

3. At what age do you introduce your students to the concept of the historian? When do they become aware that they are working with the views of historians? When do you invite them to analyse the interpretations of specific named historians? What are the challenges inherent in this aspect of historical study? How might they be overcome?

Extract 2

Source

Card, J. (2004) Seeing double: How one period visualises another. *Teaching History*, 117, 6–11.

Introduction

Jane Card, a history teacher with a strong interest in art history, investigated the way in which pictures are used in history textbooks. She found that, due to the lack of appropriate images, some textbook authors use artists' constructions of what a person or event would have looked like. When these reconstructions date from a period prior to our own we get what Card calls 'double vision' – one historical period's visualisation of another. This extract details one way to put such pictures to good use in the teaching of interpretations.

Key words & phrases

Victorian paintings; Lady Jane Grey; interpretation; 'seeing double'

Extract

[M]any nineteenth and early twentieth-century paintings are so richly detailed, dramatic and 'realistic' that pupils are tempted to over-rate their value as evidence. These apparent drawbacks, however, can be turned to advantage by using these pictures as resources for how one period of history interprets another. In the days when we were heady with the excitement of helping pupils to realise that not everything written or painted in the past was trustworthy, I produced a simple exercise on Lady

Jane Grey's execution. It invited pupils to compare a written eye-witness account of the event with the dramatic, brightly coloured and evocative painting by Paul Delaroche (1834) … In time, this developed into an exploration of why the artist had chosen to put his painting together in this way … pupils came to see that, even if the painting was not an accurate depiction of the event, it still told us a great deal about the tastes and interests of the early nineteenth century. In its latest incarnation, the investigation is becoming, 'Why did the Victorians choose to show Lady Jane Grey like this?'; the activity has thus become one of analysing an *interpretation* … The focus has evolved into an exploration of how subsequent representations or accounts of the past are constructed.

I start by showing Delaroche's picture to the whole class … The first step is to focus on three key questions:

- Name something you can see.
- How does this picture make you feel?
- What tricks has the artist used to make you feel like that?

The last question often produces surprisingly sophisticated pupil responses. The teacher needs to draw out the gloomy darkness of the background; the attention drawn to Jane Grey by her central position and by the bright light shining on her white dress; the fact that she is small, childlike and pretty; the anguish of her ladies-in-waiting; the concern of the Lieutenant of the Tower, and the threatening presence of the block …

The essential point is that the picture is a piece of manipulation. It is now that I introduce the fact that we are dealing with a Victorian portrayal of an event from Tudor history, and explain that Victorians liked dramatic and sentimental pictures, especially if they showed vulnerable woman and children.

The next step is to focus on, 'Why did the Victorians admire Lady Jane Grey?' The first part of the worksheet conveys some basic information about Victorian attitudes to women in general and to Jane Grey in particular. Pupils go on to pick out parts of her story which would have had an appeal. They can also identify a key feature which was glossed over – her formidable academic intellect …

[After an investigation of Tudor accounts of Lady Jane Grey] [i]t should now be possible to embark on a comparison of the execution as shown by Tudor evidence, and the execution as shown by Delaroche. Points which can be highlighted in the feedback are:

- Jane Grey has been made blonde
- Her hair is loose (sexier). It would have been tied up in order not to impede the axe.
- Her dress is white, not black, and not Tudor in style.
- The costume of her ladies-in-waiting is from a period 20 to 30 years earlier.
- The execution is taking place inside, not on Tower Green.

■ Eye-witnesses do not mention a cushion.
■ The artist has selected the one moment in the ceremony of her execution when Lady Jane displayed any vulnerability.

Pupils can be invited to speculate on the reasons for some of the differences. Thus they are reflecting on how and why Delaroche chose to construct the painting as he did. For example, did Delaroche show her kneeling on a cushion in order to emphasise her small stature? Is the execution inside because that allows for more dramatic lighting? By the end of the session, students were indeed 'seeing double' – gaining an ability to date images by their style.

Summary

Card uses pictures and period style to approach one of the more challenging aspects of teaching historical interpretations – introducing pupils to two time periods simultaneously. Her metaphor of 'seeing double' and simple dichotomy of 'Tudor' and 'Victorian' periods are crucial in providing access for pupils to this concept. Her carefully crafted enquiry moves away from a limited focus on 'accuracy' to a richer exploration of purpose and the values of the time in which the interpretation was constructed.

Questions to consider

1.   Are pictures explored as interpretations in your classroom? Were they constructed recently or in another period subsequent to that being studied? Does the time period affect the way you introduce the picture?
2.   What range of interpretations do you include over a course of study? Do pupils find films, for example, easier to access than historian's accounts? Does the nature of the interpretation affect the way you introduce it to pupils?
3.   Card is quite clear that this enquiry is not about assessing accuracy, but rather about exploring the values of the period when the interpretation was constructed. Do you think she goes too far in simplifying the 'Victorian' period in this extract? What other dangers might history teachers face in trying to help pupils access the past as a construct?

Extract 3

Source

Moore, R. (2000) Using the Internet to teach about interpretations in Years 9 and 12. *Teaching History*, 101, 35–9.

Introduction

Reuben Moore wrote this piece as a practising history teacher reflecting on his practice with students in Year 9 (aged 13–14) and Year 12 (aged 16–17). It describes one of a wide range of pedagogic approaches to instigate students' thinking about historical interpretations. Moore is keen that the critical skills students can already apply to written accounts should not be left behind when opinions appear on a computer screen in the form of a website.

Key words & phrases

Interpretation; valid decision; enquiry; Irish history; Internet; website as interpretation

Extract

Whose idea was it that we should teach history through ICT? The answer is that it should have been ours. The skills, approaches and attitudes that we teach in history are the vital ones for teaching pupils to use the Internet. No one else teaches them as directly, as systematically, and with such attention to progression across Years 7 to 13, as we do ... The Internet has increased opportunity through its scope and its resources, but its proper use demands a certain kind of rigour that is already evident in the professional practices, language and debates of history teachers ...

The Internet is not a passing trend. Our young people will use it in their daily lives, no matter what they choose to do with them. And, on the Internet, they will continue to confront interpretations and representations of history. All adults, no matter what they do with their lives, need to be able to see how and why the historical interpretations that bombard them were constructed. Otherwise they are prey to propaganda and manipulation, not to mention cynicism or a lack of regard for truth ...

Whilst the Internet poses many of the same challenges as television, greater skill is required to deal with the Internet resource than with the television screen. Pupils need support in climbing in to this over time. Your current progression policy might help here. The simpler work that I have done on teaching pupils to infer ideas from sources at Key Stage 3 has shown that this process must begin with a visual image. Students find the concept of inference much more straightforward when applying it to pictures. Deconstructing interpretations also involves inference – inference about audience, intention and historical viewpoint (as opposed to points of view held in the past).

It is exactly this skill of inference that we should be asking the students to use every time a site is opened. Whether we are using the contents of a website as sources or whether the website itself and contributions to it are being analysed as interpretations, pupils need to start inferring matters such as audience and purpose and the impact that these are likely to have upon the tone or content of the site (or elements of the site) ...

Examining interpretations of Gladstone in Year 12

One particular session with an AS group began as quite a straightforward lesson on William Gladstone. A key aim was research, but the application of understanding about interpretations was soon to enrich it greatly. I wanted the students to fill in a data capture sheet on his main activities and roles, his successes and failures and a little of his personality. This data capture would inform the beginnings of discussion in class, getting them interested in Gladstone the man (Taylor and Temple, 1997). Owen Dudley Edwards from Edinburgh University's Department of History once said in a lecture that he found it much easier to discuss American Presidents as old friends and colleagues than mere facts in a book. This was our approach. I had bookmarked a number of sites, which the students used to build up their data capture. Answers to the first questions we had set were found with ease but, after a bit, one student piped up and said that it seemed a bit strange that Gladstone had no negative points at all – not one. Now, I do not wish to get into a debate on the career of the famous Liberal but one would surely have to say, even for the sake of balance, that Gladstone had made at least one error in his long political career. This led us into a discussion of the provenance of one site and the purpose of it. It turned out that the site was not for the use of historians but created for the general reader. We discovered that this had had an interesting effect on information choice and tone. The line of thinking had led us into high-level 'interpretations' skills.

Summary

Moore argues that history teachers have many strategies for helping pupils reach their own historically valid conclusions about the past, but that such strategies need to be applied when pupils are using the Internet. Interpretations work with websites could set up opportunities to move beyond simplistic views of 'hero' against 'villain' that have tended to be used in the past and to look instead at some of the more complex issues around the creation of interpretations. The wide range of websites available on most significant historical topics provides the opportunity to explore the creation of interpretations and look beyond how they are different to why they might be different. This is a key article as, a decade on, websites have proliferated, but the critical approach to them in history lessons has not necessarily developed at the same speed.

Questions to consider

1. How are websites used in your history classroom/schemes of work? Do you expect pupils to extract information from websites or to move beyond this to looking at how and why the interpretation has been constructed in this way? Which topics that you teach would benefit from an exploration of websites as interpretations?

2. If interpretations are potentially controversial, are there dangers to using the Internet in this way in the history classroom? How might such dangers be overcome?

3. How trusting are your students of what they find on the Internet? Is it the role of the history teacher to help students judge the validity of claims on websites?

Investigations

Audit your schemes of work: What interpretations are included for student evaluation across the age range you teach? Are students exposed to a variety of types of interpretation? What are pupils expected to do with the interpretations? Is there a sense of progression in understanding interpretations built in across the school experience? How do examination specifications affect your model of progression?

Talk to your department: Is there a consensus across your department over the definition of historical interpretations? How do your colleagues go about helping pupils understand the past as a construct? Is there a shared sense of what progression in understanding interpretations might mean across the department?

Analyse pupil responses: Create some focus groups with five or six pupils. Give them a popular historical interpretation to discuss. At the end of the year repeat the exercise with a similar interpretation. Repeat the exercise with older pupils. Do they show progression in understanding? If so, what does it look like? If not, what needs to be done?

Think deeper

Tony McAleavy (2000) sets out a background to the teaching of historical interpretations since the inception of the National Curriculum for England. He quotes from the History Working Group at the time advising two reasons for the inclusion of interpretations within the curriculum – the first being the perceived dangers of 'ideologically slanted school history' and the second being that the belief that school history made insufficient use of secondary sources, particularly the work of academic historians.

Some practitioners have introduced younger pupils to the work of historians as a way of establishing the purpose of the subject and the idea of history as a construct. Gary Howells (2005) has pointed out that school history, like all history, is a simplification, but suggests it is worth spending some time considering what it is we are simplifying. Howells points to the complexity of backgrounds and political persuasions that inform the 'baggage' of the individual historian and suggests that there is no one interpretation that dominates any one era. Howells suggests introducing the concept of cliometrics when studying slavery so that students are able to access a genuine historical controversy by assessing the methodology of historians. It places the process of historical research and evaluation at the heart of the investigation. Kate Hammond (2007), building on the work of Howells, describes and evaluates a learning sequence that introduced pupils aged 12–13 to two contrasting types of historian: the cliometrician and the micro-historian. Her learning activities enabled pupils to understand and develop their own increasingly informed views on these historians' theories and methods.

Peter Lee and Denis Shemilt (2004) have explored what a progression model might look like for pupils' understanding of historical accounts and suggest a series of 'break points' in pupils' thinking. An early break point is when students 'begin to recognise that the ideas of "being there" (the idea that if we weren't there to see we can't know) is problematic' (2004: 29). A later break point is when students 'begin to see that historical accounts cannot be copies of the past'. The authors suggest that 'Grappling with ways in which accounts may differ legitimately without being merely matters of "opinion", helps students to recognise that although the past is not fixed, this does not mean that "any story is as good as any other"' (2004: 31). Chapman (2005: 7) relates this back to classroom practice:

> There are a number of approaches that should be avoided – approaches that set up polarised judgements and that ask pupils to adjudicate between them, for example, often reinforce preconceptions that we should be seeking to challenge, including the idea that differences in interpretation are simply a matter of political bias and partisan 'distortion' and the idea that there might be some uninterpreted and transparent mirror of the past 'out there' somewhere (if we could only find it).

Think wider

Although McAleavy (2000) explains that interpretations work was originally included in the National Curriculum for England partly to address the relative neglect of historians' accounts (in comparison with original sources), he also argues that interpretations work should include far more than simply the work of historians, pointing to popular forms of history including historical fiction, films, songs and documentaries as well as pictures and historic sites.

It has become common practice to use popular representations of the past such as pictures or films in the classroom as they are arguably more accessible for younger pupils than the work of historians. Stephan Klein (2008), for example, has used the Oliver Stone film *Nixon,* analysing a particular scene as a work of art, a historical document and an interpretation. Dale Banham and Russell Hall (2003) have used the 2001 Oliver Stone film *JFK* in a similar way to explore the gulf between 'JFK the myth' and the politician who actually existed. They focus on the factors behind Kennedy's heroic reputation, 'allowing pupils to focus on the subsequent period – the period of film-making as well as on JFK himself' (2003: 6). This allows for one of the potential challenges of teaching historical interpretations, building knowledge at the same time as deconstructing a representation.

Andrew Wrenn (1998) has taken a creative approach in looking at sites as historical interpretations. He suggests that such sites change constantly because the guardians of the sites respond to new national or popular priorities. He took pupils aged 14–16 to visit cemeteries of the First World War. Here he found a 'clash of interpretations' as pupils' initial perceptions of the monument, in particular the placing of specific flags, acted on their existing preconceptions of what was appropriate. Wrenn suggests that 'well-structured learning activities can help pupils to discern and to reflect upon the cultural and political values of the period that created and altered the memorial site' (1998: 25).

In the past, concerns have been raised over whether sufficient time is given in history lessons to understanding interpretations of history and the potential for rigorous interpretations work to be confused with the rather different thinking involved in interpreting a source of evidence (Ofsted 2004). This report, focused on the teaching of historical interpretations, goes on to suggest the difference between having a 'light/non-existent interpretations focus' or having a 'strong interpretations focus'. In the first category pupils construct their own interpretations or use contemporary sources. In the latter, stronger category, pupils 'compare, contrast, discuss how/why their own interpretations differ' or 'consider how the availability of sources has shaped an interpretation'. However, the report concludes that '[i]nterpretations are a vital part of National Curriculum history'.

References

Banham, D. and Hall, R. (2003) JFK: The medium, the message and the myth. *Teaching History*, 113, 6–12.

Chapman, A. (2005) *Supporting High Achievement in History: Conclusions of the NAGTY History Think Tank 28/29 November 2005*. Available at http://www.uk.sagepub.com/secondary/Phillips/nagty_history_thinktank.doc (accessed 20 May 2013).

Gardner, H. (2000) *The Disciplined Mind*. New York: Penguin Group.

Hammond, K. (2007) Teaching Year 9 about historical theories and methods. *Teaching History*, 128, 4–9.

Howells, G. (2005) Interpretations and history teaching: Why Ronald Hutton's *Debates in Stuart History* matters. *Teaching History*, 121, 29–35.

Klein, S. (2008) History, citizenship and Oliver Stone: Classroom analysis of a key scene in Nixon. *Teaching History*, 132, 32–9.

Koselleck, R. (2004) *Futures Past: On the semantics of historical time*. New York: Columbia University Press.

Lee, P. and Shemilt, D. (2004) 'I just wish we could go back in the past and find out what really happened': Progression in understanding about historical accounts. *Teaching History*, 117, 25–31.

McAleavy, T. (2000) Teaching about interpretations. In J. Arthur and R. Philips (eds) *Issues in History Teaching*. London: RoutledgeFalmer, 72–82.

Megill, A. (2007) *Historical Knowledge/Historical Error: A contemporary guide to practice*. Chicago: University of Chicago Press.

Ofsted (2004) *Ofsted Subject Conference Report: History*. London: Ofsted.

QCA (2007) *History: Programme of study for Key Stage 3*. Coventry: QCA.

Samuel, R. (1994) *Theatres of Memory: Past and present in contemporary culture*. London and New York: Verso.

Taylor, C. and Temple, G. (1997) *Combating Copying*. Exeter: Devon Learning Resources.

Wrenn, A. (1998) Emotional response or objective enquiry? Using shared stories and a set of place in the study of interpretations for GCSE. *Teaching History*, 91, 25–30.

Chronological understanding and historical frameworks

All those with a stake in history education – teachers, researchers and policy makers – are united in the conviction that concepts of time and chronology are fundamental to the development of a child's historical understanding. It is the temporal dimension that sets history apart from other disciplines based on the interpretation of evidence and that provides its basic structure, without which no grasp of change or continuity, of progression or regression, is possible. There is agreement too that children need not merely a timeline of events (and knowledge of the dating systems by which it has been constructed so that they can relate one event to another), but also a 'sense of period' enabling them to recognise the distinctive features of particular periods, and a 'framework' or mental map that allows them to orient themselves in time – relating the past to the present and thus to the future (see Chapter 11 on historical consciousness with which this discussion has strong connections). There is also a strong consensus that so far history educators have not been very successful in equipping young people with such a framework. Agreement thereafter tends to break down, with arguments arising about the value of memorising dates; the necessity of studying different periods in chronological order; the value of themes rather than periods as an organising device; the most appropriate terminology for discussing the structures around which 'big pictures' or 'mental maps' could be built; the scale on which they should be constructed and the best time to focus on them within any given teaching sequence.

Extract 1

Source

Stow, W. and Haydn, T. (2000) Issues in the teaching of chronology. In J. Arthur and R. Phillips (eds) *Issues in History Teaching*. London: Routledge, 83–97.

Introduction

William Stow and Terry Haydn provide an illuminating summary of a range of research conducted into children's understanding of chronology over the course of the twentieth century. Their review is structured around two questions: 'What does research indicate about children's understanding of historical time?' and 'How can children's understanding of time be developed?' Their overview shows how earlier theories that had tended to rely on age-related models of development, such as that of Piaget, were increasingly challenged by empirical research that demonstrated both the wide variation in children's knowledge and understanding and strong 'school effects' that pointed to the influence of the particular ways in which the history teacher (and the curriculum that they followed) approached the teaching of chronology. They outline the key implications of these findings, encouraging teachers to debate them.

Key words & phrases

Chronology; time; dating systems; sequence; duration; frameworks; relationships; associative networks; misconceptions

Extract

A summary list of points can be drawn up from the[se] questions … which could form the basis of a discussion with colleagues or a check-list for the teaching of chronology across a primary or secondary school:

- a rigid, age-related scale of the development of children's understanding of time in history is inappropriate: children progress along this scale at different ages and pace;
- some children at Key Stage 1 may possess quite sophisticated knowledge of chronology; some in secondary schools may not yet have grasped very basic time concepts such as which century they are living in, or what AD means. We should not make assumptions about what children can achieve in this area: careful monitoring is necessary;
- systematic teaching about chronology does influence the rate of development of children's understanding;
- to understand chronological systems children need to be familiar with a range of terms, and to develop confidence in using these through modelling, instruction and discussion;
- misconceptions and stereotypical ideas about time need to be specifically addressed and challenged, but can form the basis for useful starting points in discussion;

- dates and period labels can be learned mechanically, alongside developing understanding of sequence, intervals of time and duration;
- the order in which periods of history are taught is not as important as the need to relate periods to a wider time-frame;
- early-years children may find it easier to distinguish the distant past than the recent past when comparing it to the present;
- visual representations of time should be used consistently throughout the primary years, but with increasing complexity;
- visual evidence (including artefacts and buildings) is a powerful way of developing children's associative networks in relation to period or age;
- all children have some familiarity with images of the past, which can be built on and widened through teaching. It can be helpful to draw on and try to engage with the ideas about time that they bring with them to the classroom;
- children's understanding of chronology can be most effectively developed through a range of methods, but methods that show some consistency through a child's school career;
- given the variety of experience of history that children encounter in the primary school, it can be helpful to do an audit of where the children are in their understanding of chronology when they start secondary school;
- sequencing work needs to be complemented by discussion of the relationship between the events, people or artefacts sequenced if we are to develop historical understanding effectively;
- teachers need to keep in mind the various strands of pupils' progress in time: the building up of a framework or mental map of the unfolding of the past, the development of an understanding of time-related vocabulary, and an understanding of dating systems so that children can make consistent progress in all these areas;
- teaching children about time needs to be sustained as well as systematic – there is a need to go back to aspects of time to check that understanding has been retained.

Summary

Chronological understanding involves much more than mastery of dating conventions or period labels, but constructing an overarching framework or mental map of the past cannot be achieved without these elements. The diverse strands and complexity of what is involved call for sustained attention and explicit teaching throughout a student's school career, using a variety of methods. At their heart should be a strong focus on developing appropriate vocabulary and a commitment to checking rather than making assumptions about students' existing understandings.

Questions to consider

1. What strategies can be used to explore students' existing knowledge and understanding about historical time, especially with a new class?
2. Although age-related theories about the development of children's chronological understanding have been challenged, students' personal experience of time is obviously limited to that of their own life-span. What effect do you think this may have on their understanding of historical time and the duration of particular periods?
3. While calling for 'some consistency in the methods' used to develop children's understanding of chronology over the course of child's school career, these principles also endorse the value of using a range of methods. How can these two approaches be combined to ensure the kind of 'systematic teaching of chronology' that has been shown to accelerate children's learning?

Extract 2

Source

Lee, P. (1991) Historical knowledge and the National Curriculum. In R. Aldrich (ed.) *History in the National Curriculum*. London: Kogan Page, 39–65.

Introduction

The history education researcher Peter Lee and his colleagues have been reflecting for many years on the challenges of developing appropriate kinds of 'framework' for helping students to construct 'big pictures' of the past. In this particular article, written in 1991 while the History Working Group was deliberating about the structure and content of the original National Curriculum for history in England, Lee accepts the claim that '*part* of the historical knowledge required by pupils should be a framework of British history set in the wider context of European and world history' (p. 58) and outlines the criteria that he thinks any such framework must meet.

Key words & phrases

Frameworks; overview; thematic; developmental; open and progressive structures

---

Extract

First, any framework must be an *overview*. In other words it must offer a coherent pattern, not a mere collection of facts and dates. Outlines which shed arbitrary pools of light in a sea of darkness have failed.

Second, a frame must be capable of *rapid* presentation: it should be a course that can be taught in two or three weeks, so that it does not degenerate into discrete factual outlines. If history teachers have learned anything in the last four decades it is that laying down facts gradually over the years in a slow chronological aggregation does not work. Unless pupils have some overall scheme into which to fit new knowledge, it cannot form part of a framework because there is no structure into which it can be fitted. Children simply forget most of what they learn in one year before they are half way through the next. A sedimentary model must give way to a metamorphic one.

Third, a framework must be *thematic*. Initially it should be developmental, not one all-encompassing official *story*, because a developmental overview allows legitimate simplification, without handing on an interpretation as though it were on a par with discrete statements of fact. In their simplest form developmental frameworks are concerned with change and continuity, with simplified long-term patterns that are not, in the first instance, causal, and do not offer a narrative in which actions are connected by reasons for doing things. They fall some way short of full historical accounts, which are organized in narrative form and are far more or less explicitly explanatory … We cannot produce a simplified single version of this kind of story to serve as a framework of British history which is not either Party history or absurdly too complicated for young children. A thematic and developmental framework avoids this dilemma.

Fourth, a framework must be a *progressive structure* which can gradually be elaborated and differentiated, gaining in thematic coherence through internal links, both causal and intentional. It must link an increasing range of themes and allow gradual geographical expansion.

Fifth, a framework must be an *open structure* offering perspectives which enable pupils to cope with new encounters with the past, and to handle the present and the future. History is only valuable when it is not inert: when it changes the way we see things.

The kind of framework suggested here depends on the notion of a developmental and thematic overview which is slowly elaborated and 'thickened' into full historical accounts as pupils move through school. Such a framework allows simplification in a legitimate way: themes can be articulated into a small number of parts, and from early on several strands are possible, not 'the' single version.

Summary

Lee advances five criteria for the design of a framework that could be used to teach British history within the wider context of European and world history. While the spatial scale is thus deliberately somewhat limited, his other criteria are much more ambitious. Lee expects the framework to be taught very quickly at the beginning of a course of study, providing a thematic or multi-stranded overview that is sufficiently open and flexible that it can both accommodate new material learned through the course of study and allow itself to be progressively challenged, modified and developed in light of that material.

Questions to consider

1. How feasible do you think it is to offer students a framework intended to structure their subsequent historical learning and yet expect them to question and perhaps even overturn that original framework?
2. Why does Lee suggest that any framework must be a thematic one, encompassing a number of different strands?
3. In subsequent reflections on 'frameworks', Lee (2004: 80) concluded that 'the subject of a framework should be human history, not some sub-set of it', apparently rejecting his endorsement here of the value of a framework focused on British history. How far do you agree with his later view that in a globalized and increasingly interdependent world young people would be better served by an over-arching framework focused on human rather than national history?

Extract 3

Source

Howson, J. and Shemilt, D. (2011) Frameworks of knowledge: Dilemmas and debates. In I. Davies (ed.) *Debates in History Teaching*. London: Routledge, 73–83.

Introduction

While the first version of the National Curriculum for England sought to establish a secure chronological structure to children's learning by including a series of core British history modules to be taught strictly in order, the 2008 version offered a radically different approach, outlining the prescribed 'range and content' of the curriculum in terms of themes rather than defined periods of history. Professional debate about the appropriateness of this strategy and published advice about how to construct thematic stories within such a curriculum generated a range of new models and terms for describing both the 'scaffolds' that teachers might use to structure their schemes of work and the pictures of the past that students might construct in response (see the references to Dawson in the 'Think deeper' section below). In this extract Jonathan Howson and Denis Shemilt seek to bring greater clarity and precision to the terminology used in these discussions and to locate the source of much of the disagreement in deeper differences about the fundamental aims and purposes of history education.

Extract

Definitions and distinctions

A framework of knowledge

1. Serves to assist teaching and/or to facilitate learning about the past without representing the ultimate shape or substance of the learning involved.
2. Enables the contextualization, organization and evaluation of historical data with reference to high-level and chronologically ordered generalizations about 'what life was like' and/or how things were done' at different points in time.

This definition distinguishes 'frameworks' from 'summaries', 'outlines' and 'pictures of the past'. The latter are *objects* of learning, intended or actual, whereas 'frameworks' are *instruments* used by teachers and students to accelerate learning. In short, 'frameworks' are provisional factual scaffolds as adaptive to student constructions of the past as to teacher intentions for the demolition, reconstruction or extension thereof.

Semantic boundaries between 'frameworks,' grids and timelines are more permeable. While all three instruments are used to facilitate learning, 'grids' serve to juxtapose and 'timelines' to sequence information; only 'frameworks' enable teachers and students to contextualize, organize and evaluate data against broad generalizations about human activity and experience.

Framework diversity [can] be analysed against five dimensions of difference (see Figure 11.1) … [which] shift in framework uses and purposes from the traditional in the left-hand column, the adventurous and experimental in the centre column through to the speculative in the right-hand column.

Debates about frameworks

… '[F]rameworks' have been offered as partial solutions to a range of problems and anxieties with respect to gaps and distortions in students' knowledge of our island story; to the seeming inability of most students to turn disconnected facts and stories into joined up narratives of national glory, human rights or anything else; and to the questionable relevance of parochial history education agendas to future citizens of a world dependent on globalized economic and financial systems, threatened by common problems of climate change, resource depletion, population growth and mass migration and looking for solutions to international treaties accords and agencies. It follows that 'framework' instruments and processes are diverse because they are optimized to address one or other of these issues. And because most issues relate to the aims and purposes of history education, debates about frameworks quickly

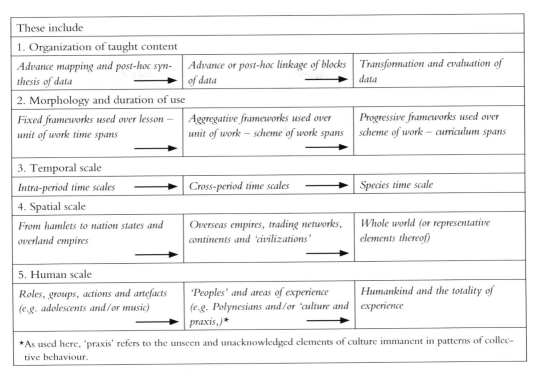

These include		
1. Organization of taught content		
Advance mapping and post-hoc synthesis of data ➔	*Advance or post-hoc linkage of blocks of data* ➔	*Transformation and evaluation of data*
2. Morphology and duration of use		
Fixed frameworks used over lesson – unit of work time spans ➔	*Aggregative frameworks used over unit of work – scheme of work spans* ➔	*Progressive frameworks used over scheme of work – curriculum spans*
3. Temporal scale		
Intra-period time scales ➔	*Cross-period time scales* ➔	*Species time scale*
4. Spatial scale		
From hamlets to nation states and overland empires ➔	*Overseas empires, trading networks, continents and 'civilizations'* ➔	*Whole world (or representative elements thereof)*
5. Human scale		
Roles, groups, actions and artefacts (e.g. adolescents and/or music) ➔	*'Peoples' and areas of experience (e.g. Polynesians and/or 'culture and praxis,)*★* ➔	*Humankind and the totality of experience*
★As used here, 'praxis' refers to the unseen and unacknowledged elements of culture immanent in patterns of collective behaviour.		

Figure 11.1 Five dimensions of difference

reduce to matters philosophical or political. For instance, variations in the temporal, spatial and human scales of frameworks follow from debates not just about the balance of content coverage – recent versus distant, social versus economic, national versus world – but also about the desirability of teaching *lessons from history* versus the *lessons of history*, of teaching identity-shaping yarns and cautionary tales potentially applicable to possible futures versus teaching where humankind has been, by what means it has arrived at its present position and where, by choice of compulsion is might from here.

Summary

Howson and Shemilt draw a distinction between 'frameworks' as the instruments or scaffolds that teachers use to shape and drive students' learning and the 'pictures' or 'outlines' that students construct or challenge or modify on the basis of that framework as they are learning. Frameworks allow them not merely to compare or sequence new data, but to organise and evaluate it in relation to broader generalisations about human experience over time – and so embellish or redesign the picture they have been working with so far. Frameworks can be used at different stages of the learning process, and may be more or less flexible. They can also be applied on very different scales. Arguments about the most appropriate frameworks to use tend to reflect different assumptions about the purpose of teaching history.

Questions to consider

1. What 'frameworks' do you use, implicitly or explicitly, in planning your schemes of work? How explicitly do you share these with students and at what stage in the process of learning new historical content?
2. On what scales do the frameworks that you use tend to operate? What would be the challenges involved in widening either the temporal or the spatial or the human scale?
3. How far do you agree with Howson and Shemilt that arguments about the most productive frameworks to use are essentially arguments about the purpose of teaching history, rather than reflections of different assumptions about how students learn best?

Investigations

Explore the kinds of ideas that your students hold about time and chronology: Design a series of tasks to help you to evaluate students' understanding of time and chronology. What ideas seem easier to grasp than others? What misconceptions do they seem to hold and how could they be addressed?

Review the different types of frameworks that you use to structure students' picture of the past: The five dimensions of difference that Howson and Shemilt identify in the extract above provide a useful way of categorising and comparing different sorts of frameworks. Review your schemes of work (within and/or across year groups) examining the range and types of framework that you offer to students (or encourage them to create). On what scales do they operate and when are they used? How effective do you think they are in allowing students to construct pictures of the past?

Experiment with different kinds of framework: Try out a different kind of framework from those that you tend to use and evaluate its effects in terms of students' capacity to make connections and to relate the past to the present.

Think deeper

In a fascinating and detailed account that draws on empirical data from learners ranging from Year 2 (6–7 year olds) to Year 7 (11–12 year olds) and even to history graduates applying for initial teacher education, Frances Blow, Peter Lee and Denis Shemilt (2012) explore students' ideas of *time* and *chronology*, challenging a common assumption that the two concepts are effectively indistinguishable. While chronology is a matter of convention that deals with the practicalities of time measurement, time itself, they point out, is 'deep, mysterious and inescapable'. Some temporal concepts – such as ideas related to sequencing and duration – can be understood at some level in relation to everyday life; others – such as period – are peculiar to the discipline of history and reliance on everyday assumptions in seeking to make sense of them may cause significant difficulties. The amusing and perplexing examples of students' responses that the authors analyse provide a vivid illustration of the need to pay careful attention to the ways in which students are thinking and reasoning, in order to support the development of more historical thinking. Their discussion of the particular temporal concepts that seem to be associated with developing a connected view of the relationship between the present is also extremely important in considering the kind of frameworks that are needed if students are to develop more usable big pictures.

In response to revisions to the National Curriculum is England in 2008 that presented the 'range and content' in terms of themes rather than distinct units, textbook author and former director of the Schools History Project, Ian Dawson contributed an influential pair of articles to *Teaching History* suggesting how teachers might begin to adapt their curriculum to exploit the potential for developing a new kind of coherence through 'thematic stories' and how such stories might also contribute to the development of a sense of period. In the first of these articles, Dawson (2008) shows how a variety of ways in which common topics from previous versions of the curriculum might be re-assembled as thematic stories of 'power and democracy' or 'empires'. In the second (Dawson 2009), she explored how the different components of a history curriculum – the process of historical enquiry and a series of depth studies each feeding into the different thematic stories work could work together, shaped by the historian's conceptual tools – to turn 'individual notes' into 'historical tunes'. While there are fundamental differences between their approaches, Dawson's conception of 'thematic stories' has the same emphasis as Lee's view of frameworks does on the *provisional* nature and importance of testing and revising the particular narratives to which the underlying structures give rise. While Dawson had originally suggested that such stories could simply be constructed at the end of a particular phase of study, as a way of pulling together what had been learnt, his conception of the enquiry process as fundamental to historical learning (see Chapter 16 on historical enquiry) means that he came to treat thematic stories as initial hypotheses to be tested as the students encounter successive events and developments over time.

Rick Rogers (2008), a history teacher working in a comprehensive school in the north of England outlines and evaluates the impact of a 'topic-based framework' that he taught to 11–12-year-old students over the course of seven lessons, in response to the kind of concerns revealed by the Usable Historical Pasts project (discussed in Chapter 7 on historical consciousness). The focus of his framework was Magna Carta and the framework grid that he used to structure and broaden students' learning beyond events directly associated with the charter itself was broken into five sub-periods: two that pre-dated

Magna Carta (before 1066; 1066–1215) and three afterwards (1215–1500; 1500–1837; 1837–present day). For each sub-period three key questions were addressed:

■ What's the story? What happened before and after Magna Carta?
■ Crime and punishment. What did Magna Carta have to do with getting a fair trial?
■ Who's the boss? What did the Magna Carta have to do with running the country?

Students were encouraged to produce their own interpretation of the answers to these key questions and any misconceptions emerging from their responses were addressed before moving on. Some of the teaching was also focused on projecting pupil thinking about the topic into the future.

The students' responses to a formal assessment task demonstrated significant progress in relation to their earlier achievements on a comparable 'baseline test' focused on the legacy of the Romans. While most of the students had clearly conceived of the Roman past as an entirely separate entity from the present, all the students' answers on the Magna Carta assessment suggested that they were thinking of the past of a continuum. While some consisted of 'strings of small stories, interconnected like the episodes of a soap-opera' (2008: 30), others included quite sophisticated comments more suggestive of a cohesive big picture within which students could even define some of the patterns that might be projected into the future.

In a lengthy and speculative, but very carefully argued, article, Shemilt (2009) reviews the strengths and weaknesses of what he regards as the three most carefully focused approaches attempted so far in the UK to support young people's construction of 'big pictures' of the past. The first are *thematic* approaches, and the most extensive and sustained examples can be found in the studies in development (such as 'Medicine through Time') taught within the Schools History Project. Evaluation of these courses suggests that when recursive strategies are used, beginning with an uncluttered and rapid overview, and close attention is paid to the second-order concepts of change, development and progress, students can indeed gain some sense of the shape of the past, but obviously only in relation to a narrow sliver of it, from which it would be impossible to generalise.

The second approach, *temporally contextualised topics* (of which Rogers' case study is one example) involves locating core topics within historical contexts that extend forwards and backwards in time, inviting comparisons and contrasts. The examples that Shemilt discusses suggest that this approach has met with mixed success, depending on whether the contextual focus is merely 'bolted-on' to existing schemes of work (in which case students tend to regard it as an extraneous preamble and coda) or whether the topics are taught in new ways that genuinely connect with and exploit the comparisons across time. Shemilt, however, doubts that the approach could be used to construct a coherent big picture because most topics taught in this way tend to be quite parochial in geographical terms, restricted in the time spans that they cover and still relatively narrow in their focus.

The third approach involves leaving time at the end of the school year for *summative reviews and tasks*, looping thematic threads (about such issues as the sharing of political power, individual freedom and rights) through and around otherwise discrete topics to construct a big story about the past. Although Shemilt offers some persuasive examples of the success of this approach in one selective secondary school, he questions whether the particular departmental teaching strategies adopted to achieve it could be replicated in comprehensive school contexts.

In light of these experiences Shemilt then outlines his own speculative proposal for designing secondary school history curricula around a maximum of four continuously updated chronological *frameworks of knowledge* focused on 'Modes of Production', Political and Social Organisation', 'Growth and Movement of Peoples' and 'Culture and Praxis'. He suggests that each framework should be taught first within a single lesson (50–70 minutes), and serve as a preview or advance organiser for subsequent topics, prompting key questions to ask of them, and subject to later review, elaboration and amendment. To illustrate his ideas, Shemilt outlines a number of specimen 'starter' frameworks, such as that for Modes of Production, entitled 'From Snails to Snacks', structured around three questions for five time periods ranging from 60,000 years ago to the present: 'How do you spend your time?' 'What do you eat?' and 'How long do you live?' He also draws on a wide range of research to offer a tentative model of the kind of progression that might become evident in students' thinking about the 'event space' of the past, as they began to use and connect these frameworks. Although the value of his suggestions cannot yet be assessed, he urges teachers to experiment on the basis of these conjectures, and so contribute to the production of the body of evidence that will be needed to evaluate whether such an approach does indeed facilitate the development of worthwhile and genuinely useful 'big pictures'.

Think wider

History teacher Matt Stanford (2008) was inspired by the emphasis in the 2008 National Curriculum for England on 'developing a sense of period' to focus on how he could develop his students' feeling for the characteristic features of the Renaissance in ways that would allow them to contextualise subsequent historical knowledge. While he felt reasonably confident about the basic scheme of work for year 7 students aged 11–12 that he devised, focused on the concept of significance and addressing the question 'What was so remarkable about Renaissance?', he was much less certain how to assess the 'sense' of period that students had developed. His article offers a rationale for the eventual decision to ask students to draw a picture, and draws on Roland Barthes' study of the layers of meaning communicated by images to justify the use of a non-verbal means of assessment, as a way of evaluating the sense that the students had made of this particular period.

World History for Us All is a project of San Diego State University in cooperation with the National Center for History in the Schools at the University of California (Burke et al. 2012). It offers a curriculum model and web-based resources for teaching world history structured around seven key themes and three over-arching or 'essential' questions related to 'humans and the environment', 'humans and other humans' and 'humans and ideas':

- How has the changing relationship between human beings and the physical and natural environment affected human life from early times to the present?
- Why have relations among humans become so complex since early times?
- How have human views of the world, nature and the cosmos changed?

The teaching and learning framework is described as fundamentally chronological, and is based on an assumption – challenged by the research on which Stow and Haydn (2000) drew in Extract 1 – that 'historical learning works best when students begin their studies with remote eras, and move forward, connecting patterns of cause and effect over time' (http://worldhistoryforusall.sdsu.edu/shared/themes.php). The seven themes are thus intended to be revisited within each of nine 'big eras' that deal with chronological periods on global scale. Each of the first eight eras covers a shorter time span than the previous one, while the final era – 'Reflecting on the past, thinking about the future' – is devoted to examining the connections between past, present and future. Teaching units, which are still being developed, are offered at different levels of resolution, ranging from 'panorama' units (intended to be taught in one or two weeks) through 'landscape' to 'close-up'. The outline programme and rationale, along with the teaching units, thus represent one of the most of the clearly articulated large-scale frameworks in use.

History teachers and curriculum planners are not the only professionals who wrestle with the challenge of devising appropriate frameworks to structure 'big pictures' of the past. Museum curators, especially those of large national or international collections, face similar sorts of questions about the frames that they use in selecting, interpreting and making connections between the artefacts that they display. The Ashmolean Museum in Oxford, for example, recently re-designed the layout of all its collections, using glass galleries and interconnecting bridges to end the distinction between 'eastern' and 'western' galleries and instead emphasise the links between cultures and regions. The British Museum undertook the challenge of selecting just 100 objects from its vast collection to tell a history of the whole world. While the structure of the framework chosen by Neil MacGregor (2009), the museum's director, was undoubtedly dictated in part by the requirements of a radio schedule (one object per 15-minute programme, and a single theme linking the five programmes presented each week), the decisions that he made about how to divide the 2,000,000 year time-span into coherent segments, and which themes to assign to each, provide a stimulating example that might be used with students or teachers to reflect on the scale and range and structure of their own pictures of the past. It is also worth considering whether and how a framework constructed in relation to material artefacts might differ from one that was more reliant on written sources.

References

Blow, F., Lee, P. and Shemilt, D. (2012) Time and chronology: Conjoined twins or distant cousins *Teaching History*, 147, 26–36.

Burke, E., Christian, D. and Dunn, R. (2012) *World History – The Big Eras: A compact history of humankind for teachers and students.* Los Angeles, CA.: National Center for History in the Schools, UCLA.

Dawson, I. (2008) Thinking across time: Planning and teaching the story of power and democracy at Key Stage 3. *Teaching History*, 130, 14–23.

Dawson, I. (2009) 'What time does the tune start?': From thinking about 'sense of period' to modelling history at Key Stage 3. *Teaching History*, 135, 50–7.

Lee, P. (2004) Walking backwards into tomorrow: Historical consciousness and understanding history. *International Journal of Historical Learning, Teaching and Research*, 4 (1), 69–114.

MacGregor, N. (2010) *A History of the World in 100 Objects.* London: Allen Lane.

Rogers, R. (2008) Raising the bar: Developing meaningful historical consciousness at Key Stage 2. *Teaching History*, 133, 24–31.

San Diego State University/National Center for History in the Schools (n.d.) worldhistoryforusall.sdsu.edu/bigeras.php

Shemilt, D. (2009) Drinking an ocean and pissing a cupful: How adolescents make sense of history. In L. Simcox and A. Wilshut (eds) *National History Standards: The problem of the canon and the future of teaching.* Charlotte, NC: Information Age Publishing, 141–209.

Stanford, M. (2008) Re-drawing the Renaissance: Non-verbal assessment in Year 7. *Teaching History*, 130, 4–12.

Change and continuity

Change and continuity is one of the fundamental organising concepts in history (often referred to as second-order concepts), used to shape the way in which we look at the past and thus how we understand it. It is essentially dependent on other ideas such as chronological understanding and is intimately connected with the process of developing 'frameworks' of the past (see Chapter 11) – the discernment of trends, patterns and turning points that give shape to the past. Yet there are a number of dimensions to the concept that make it complex to understand and therefore to teach – not least the interplay *between* change and continuity. The extracts in this chapter flesh out these dimensions and challenge us to clarify the ways in which we want young people to use ideas of change and continuity to think about the past.

Extract 1

Source

Foster, R. (2009) Speed cameras, dead ends, drivers and diversions: Year 9 use a 'road map' to problematise change and continuity. *Teaching History*, 131, 4–8.

Introduction

Rachel Foster is a practising history teacher working, in this example, with 13–14-year-old pupils. She wanted not only to introduce her pupils to the concept of change and continuity, but also to 'problematise' the concept and fascinate her pupils at the same time. This article describes the design of an activity in which pupils create road maps as metaphors, first for the American civil rights movement, and then for the history of medicine and the New Deal. The extract sets out the issues facing Foster and her justification for the activity.

Extract

How can change and continuity be made fascinating to pupils? *I* know that change and continuity is deeply and intrinsically interesting – the false starts, the twists and turns of the story, the unexpected breakthroughs – all these make the study of change a challenging yet ultimately satisfying undertaking. But how can pupils be convinced that this complexity is actually valuable, interesting and a challenge worth persisting with? How can I stop them sliding into defeatism as they collapse under the weight of detailed knowledge that a complex understanding of change and continuity demands? As Lee (2005) has argued, the key to understanding the complexity of change and continuity is the recognition that change is a *process*, and a frequently gradual and unintended one at that. If, as Lee suggests, pupils instead understand change as being intentional, episodic events, change becomes simple to explain, deterministic and even worse, dull. Therefore, if pupils are to be fascinated by change and moved to explain it, they need to be taught to understand change as a process. But how can I help my pupils to *see* this?

This was the challenge I set myself as I planned a six-lesson enquiry on the American civil rights movement. The sequence came at the end of a Year 9 course on the black peoples of the Americas. Pupils had already studied the slave trade, plantation life, the American Civil War, Reconstruction and the beginnings of Jim Crow. The existing scheme of work began the enquiry in 1955, with the Montgomery bus boycott. I was concerned that by jumping directly from Jim Crow to the civil rights movement, pupils could end up with a distorted view of the movement and of the role African Americans played in shaping their own history. More recent historiography emphasises the long history of resistance to segregation out of which the civil rights movement was born. By not setting the civil rights movement in its longer term historical context, I was concerned that pupils would come away with the mistaken belief that African Americans were simply victims in history, who passively waited for a Great Leader to deliver them from the tyranny of Jim Crow. I was also concerned that pupils' view of historical change as an event, rather than a process, would be reinforced. I therefore decided to begin the enquiry much earlier, with the early attacks on Jim Crow by the NAACP and trade union and women's movements from the 1920s onwards. By locating the civil rights movement within a broader pattern of long-term change and continuity, pupils would be better placed to explain it.

My second concern related to the teaching of the movement itself. How would pupils be able to understand the reasons for the movement's eventual success if they did not have a clear idea of how it evolved over time? Reducing the movement to a set of causal factors – media attention, mass action, presidential intervention – would be to ignore its complexity as an evolving, changing *movement*. By placing an explicit focus on change and continuity I hoped to deepen pupils' understanding of the movement's evolution through time and strengthen their causal reasoning. With this in mind I wanted to create an activity that would enable pupils to:

- handle the complexity of change;
- see change as a process, rather than as an event;
- consider the rate, pace and extent of change over time;
- analyse how factors acted to affect the process of change.

Summary

Foster's pupils drew a road map as a metaphor for a particular example of historical change and continuity. Pupils considered factors that would slow down or speed up a car journey and linked these to examples of the speed, rate, nature and direction of historical change. Road maps were created to support this metaphor and added to in subsequent lessons as pupils built up their knowledge. From a relatively simple idea Foster's pupils were then able to enjoy the complexity inherent in historical change and continuity.

Questions to consider

1. What are the challenges Foster faced in planning to teach an enquiry focused on change? How might you plan to overcome these challenges in your own teaching?
2. Foster uses the broader, long-term historical context to help students see change as a process rather than an event. What does it mean to consider change as a process?
3. Foster chooses a road-map as a metaphor for historical change. Could other metaphors work in a similar way in the classroom to develop students' understanding?

Extract 2

Source

Corfield, P. (2009) Teaching history's big pictures: Including continuity as well as change. *Teaching History*, 136, 53–9.

Introduction

Penelope Corfield writes as an established academic historian. She argues for a return to 'big history' or long-term frameworks in the history classroom, explaining how 'grand narratives' were out of fashion in the 1990s due to the brutal wars and genocides of the twentieth century and the collapse of Marxism. The destruction of the

Twin Towers in New York in September 2001 brought back a need to understand events in their full historical context. However, 'there is a justified concern that history must not be reduced to simple pieties, however rousing – whether those be ideological, religious, imperialist, nationalist, sexist, racist, hierarchic or classist' (p. 55). Here she presents an approach that teachers may find useful in presenting 'the big picture'.

Key words & phrases

Big picture; time; change; continuity; temporal; space; micro-change; macro-change; thinking long; grand narrative

Extract

So how can teachers present the big picture? There is not one big historical message which is universally agreed. That absence in itself makes an important point. It is not just a question of finding and teaching one new 'grand narrative', or of resurrecting and refurbishing one old one.

Nor is it helpful or plausible to divide the world into different cultural groups and propose a separate 'grand narrative' for each different group. That denies our common humanity and ignores the extent to which historic and current cultures overlap – people from all cultures intermarry, for example – and the diversities *within* as well as between cultures.

Perhaps instead a generic global platitude might be advanced, such as 'History incorporates elements of continuity and change.' But such a proposition, which often recurs in course outlines, does not add much to the sum of human understanding. We need to probe continuity more closely and, equally, to disentangle the many sorts of 'change'.

The study of history relishes its complexity and variety, because human diversity is an integral part of the story. Indeed, historians often find simplified 'universal' concepts from other disciplines, which they then test and criticise against the experience of history, invariably finding that one single formula will not explain everything … Thus plurality and diversity do not negate a single human story – instead, these elements add to its plausibility.

History, as the study of the past, is not so chaotic and tangled that it defies all systematic probing. We can see instead that there are recurrent ways of looking at the past – and we can weigh these and assess how their messages can be combined. Some of the various models that have been proposed at different times are outlined in Figure 12.1. But none integrate all history's features together: there are models of change that wrongly exclude continuity; or models of continuity that underplay change.

My own study, entitled *Time and the Shape of History* [Corfield, 2007], integrates not only different forms of change but also deep continuities (as identified by Zeldin, 1994). Having rejected the old and unproven assumption that there were different sorts of cosmic and historical time, I start from the view that everything is

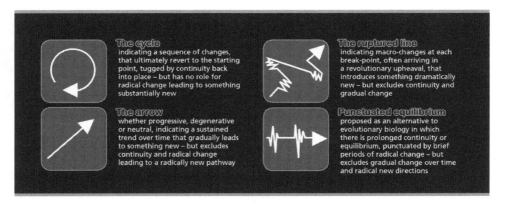

Figure 12.1 Partial models of change through time.

within time – or more properly, within time-space. Within that capacious framework, there are perennial dimensions, linked integrally together. Just as space has its three dimensions of longitude, latitude and altitude, so time – and so history which is integrally within time – has three interlocking dimensions of continuity (persistence), micro-change (momentum) and macro-change (turbulence) … These features interact in ever-varying permutations.

Continuity (or through-time persistence) provides ballast to the system and a benchmark against which change is assessed. This dimension has been under-studied and under-theorised. Zeldin salutes the importance of this theme, but also reveals how much it is entangled with change. The second dimension is micro-change, which refers to gradual, incremental adaptation. It adds a gentle, often almost imperceptible momentum to history and prevents the system from clogging. Meanwhile, the third dimension is that of radical transformation or revolutionary upheaval. This state contributes massive impetus and intense turmoil within the system. But even the greatest transformations are subtly assimilated over time by the forces of micro-change and continuity. History is not completely sundered. Hence each revolution can eventually settle into a new system and spawn a renewed continuity.

All these features of history can be identified and debated with reference to all periods and themes. My analysis in *Time and the Shape of History* is non-prescriptive. No one element or outcome is elevated above all others. Instead, it is the dynamic through-time interaction and interlocking of the core processes of continuity (persistence), micro-change (momentum) and macro-change (turbulent upheaval) which frame an ever-changing history.

Summary

Corfield promotes a model for big-picture history. She points out that while there are patterns in the past, current models tend to ignore continuity or underplay the role of change. Corfield argues that time, and so history within time, has three interlocking dimensions – continuity, micro-change and macro-change. These features interact in an infinite variety of ways. This model can be applied to all different periods and themes across history, and so provides a potential framework for approaching longer-term study in the history classroom.

Questions to consider

1. Corfield argues that human beings 'think long'. Could your pupils benefit from thinking about time, especially longer spans of time, within their history lessons?

2. Apply Corfield's three-point model to the period 1640 to 1660. Then use the same model to consider the seventeenth century as a whole, then the period 1450 to 1750. How do the longer time periods change perspective on periods of turbulence?

3. Is continuity ever explicitly considered in your schemes of work? What would be the best time to introduce your pupils to Corfield's three-dimensional model of continuity, micro-change and radical transformation?

Extract 3

Source

Counsell, C. (2011) What do we want students to *do* with historical change and continuity? In I. Davies (ed.) *Debates in History Teaching*. London: Routledge, 109–23.

Introduction

Historical change and continuity became more explicit in the 2008 version of the National Curriculum for England. While it had been discussed and included since Shemilt's (1980) evaluation of the Schools Council History Project 13–16, there was a focus on 'changes' that rather lacked historical rigour. Christine Counsell points to the lack of professional discourse around this second-order concept when compared, perhaps, with causation. She suggests the need to problematise change in the classroom/for pupils and provides examples of how this might be done. This extract deals with a possible solution to the issue of engaging pupils with big-picture history.

Key words & phrases

Change; continuity; making meaning; experience; time orientation

Extract

Attempts to characterize change and continuity through dispassionate analysis of its extent, type, speed or interplay still leave students at one remove from deep engagement with the *experience* of historical change and/or continuity. The study of change cannot, surely, be left at the abstract, distanced level of states of affairs – those large, discernible patterns in institutions and governments, in ideologies and beliefs, that history textbooks concern themselves with. It is the notion of 'experience' that interests me, not in the 1970s/1980s pedagogic sense of 'empathy' (although that is part of it), but rather in the sense of meaning-making – the structures of meaning held and continuously transformed by the people who were active and responsive agents living at the time. How did the citizens of Cordoba in the eleventh century actually experience change and what did it mean for them? A few paragraphs in a work of scholarship on the eleventh century or in a standard textbook might give the impression (for example) of mounting despair and terror at the encroachments of the Christians to the north, of the terrifying sacking of the city of the Berbers in 1013, of the desperate pleas to the Almoravids and then to the Almohads for help later in the century followed by the mixed benefits of the latter's rule. We hear from scholars that the population of Cordoba collapsed in that year, as did the size and the wealth of the city. But these are the necessary generalizations of the historian. How is an 11- to 12-year-old in the twenty-first century to make meaning out of these generalizations about change and continuity at the level of human experience *at the time?* If all school students are to be intrigued and compelled by enquiry into such broad historical developments, they will need a deeper engagement with and a curiosity about the way people at the time experienced these developments.

My contention is that judgements about degree or nature of 'change' or 'continuity' must be at least partly constructed out of the time orientation in which people lived. Humans can only ever make meaning temporally. We remember the past and anticipate the future. Memory and anticipation frame all our action and the meaning of our acts. It is possible to incorporate this emphasis on the temporal quality of human experience into students' enquiries. We would need to reflect on how (say) eleventh-century Cordobans positioned themselves temporally and historically. What did change and continuity mean to them? How did it *appear* to them in their consciousness? Their knowledge (or lack of knowledge) of their own past will be intricately involved here. Pain at seeing trade collapse, population fall or art destroyed must have emerged from the collective memory, from the collective historical consciousness of what Cordoba had once been. If this was constructed out of past experiences, was this mainly from their own living memory or from the collective memory of custom and oral stories? What forms did fears, hope and longings take? How did they envision the future? Were they resigned to eventual Christian conquest?

Summary

It is not enough to study the rate and extent of change. Pupils need to make meaning out of generalisations about high-level changes. This could be achieved through considering the changing experience of people at the time. What were their hopes and fears? How was their memory constructed? If pupils are to be intrigued by such broad developments over long periods of time they will need to consider the temporal quality of human experience.

Questions to consider

1. What, for Counsell, can often be missing from studies of change and continuity? What is the disadvantage of focusing at the level of governments and ideology when teaching change enquiries?
2. Do your pupils struggle to stay engaged with broad-brush studies about longer periods of historical change? How might you introduce the nature of change and/ or continuity as it was experienced by people at the time to make the past more meaningful to your pupils?
3. Counsell uses Cordoba as an exciting location for studying change across several centuries. Can you identify other places in the world that witnessed similar changes of culture over long periods? What would you need to do to use these as examples in your history classroom?

Investigations

Analysing current practice: Identify where change and continuity are taught in your current schemes of work. Is the concept or change simplified or problematised in the way Foster and Counsell suggest? Is continuity explicitly considered both within and across historical periods?

Pupil voice: Talk to a small group of pupils about their understanding of change and continuity. Do they seem to understand change as a process or change as an event? Do they simply see the past as different from the present or do they have a more nuanced view of change and continuity?

Action research: Find an opportunity to introduce pupils to Foster's road map or Corfield's three-dimensional model. Talk to a small group of pupils again after they have completed the exercise. Has their understanding of change or continuity developed?

Think deeper

Research into pupils' understanding of change supports this sense of confusion between event and process. Denis Shemilt (2000: 89) suggests that some pupils equate change in history with 'headline actions and events' rather than with 'the consequences thereof for people in general'. He states that the historical narrative comes to be seen as a 'series of changes (actions and events, inventions and discoveries) separated by periods of quiescence in which nothing happens' (2000: 90). He goes on to give a variety of examples to support this point from interview data with students who have completed the Schools History Project 'Medicine through Time' development study.

There are several examples of recent practice experimenting with ways of problematising change and continuity in the history classroom. The simplest, and perhaps one of the most effective, is Yosanne Vella's use of colour and timeline (2011). Vella wanted to teach pupils about change and continuity in medieval Maltese religious history within the confines of one 45-minute lesson. She didn't want to fall into the trap of giving an overview 'lecture', but wanted pupils to be able to discuss the views of two historians on whether Christianity had been an enduring phenomenon in Malta throughout the Medieval period or whether it had effectively died out for some time, effectively supplanted by Islam. Pupils were given a timeline with key dates of different invaders and some source material. They were asked to colour the timeline according to religion – orange for Christian and green for Muslim. The pupils were also to use a heavier or lighter shade according to how certain they felt or how reliable they thought the sources were. As Vella says, 'the beauty of colour is that, like historical periods, colour can fade in and fade out' (2011: 19). The author found that although some of the pupils struggled and could have done with more time and reinforcement, several were able show an appreciation of historical change as the gradual transformation of a situation.

Ben Jarman and Hywel Jones both attended a professional development course that focused on developing students' understanding of change through action research. Jarman (2009) chose a suitably rigorous enquiry question to get his Year 8 class thinking carefully about change: 'When were medieval Jews in most danger?' Students used cards to plot events on a graph that set time against 'level of danger'. Jarman decided to use a question and answer session with his class to draw out the explicit difference between an event and a change. The class preferred football metaphors, but were then able to transfer their models to the graph of events. When it came to writing up the task Jarman gave his pupils specific language relating to change to help them to express their ideas more precisely. Building on the work of Woodcock with causation, Jarman concludes that 'any attempt to get children to think and write about second-order concepts has to give them the language to do so first' (2009: 12). Jones (2009) was inspired by reading Malcolm Gaskill's (2005) *Witchfinders*. He decided to challenge students to trace and analyse the changing nature of several people's lives between 1641 and 1647. With the enquiry question 'Were the Witchfinder Trails in East Anglia a tragedy for everyone?' Jones found his students inspired, particularly when the life stories of those involved were covered in depth. He discovered that all pupils were able 'to select specific events and changes from the personal stories to illustrate how individuals were caught up in the witchcraft trials, using them to develop hypotheses as to why the trials were or were not a tragedy for different people' (2009: 15). This is one way to answer Counsell's concern, raised in Extract 3, of the difficulty engaging students with broader sweeps of change over time. Jones then wanted his students to move from a micro-analysis of personal stories 'to construct a narrative analysis of macro-changes in East Anglia at the time' (2009: 13). He used living graphs to plot the experience of change of three witchfinders, then asked students to audio-record their arguments in response to the enquiry question. This move from the micro- to the macro- that both Jones and Jarman encourage in students is ambitious, but does lead to engagement with macro-analysis.

Think wider

Shemilt has raised important concerns about students' understanding of longer time-frames, which are considered in more depth in Chapter 11 on chronological understanding and frameworks. However, it is obviously important to acknowledge them here since the teaching of longer themes and bigger pictures is inextricably linked to an understanding of change and continuity. His original evaluation of the Schools History Project (Shemilt 1980) had suggested that that while some students were able to debate the reasons and causes of actions and events in short time-frames, they seemed to have a more fixed, mechanical view of larger-scale spans of time. Shemilt (2000: 98) therefore offers several suggestions to develop students' understanding of 'polythetic narrative frameworks', which are 'ordered and coherent, complex and multidimensional' and admit the existence of alternative narratives. These include teaching and re-teaching the whole of human history, revisiting and elaborating the story frequently, inclusion of thematic studies over long spans of time and, in planning lessons, the identification of data that 'we wish pupils to retain for incorporation within emergent narrative frameworks' (2000: 99).

Thematic studies provide many opportunities for approaching change as a process; however, Sarah Gadd (2009: 36) found that this was not enough for her pupils who 'struggled to retain and transfer knowledge across topics and themes'. In a piece of action research that formed part of a Master's qualification, Gadd explored whether intensive use of story in 'depth' studies could help pupils cope with the challenges of creating an overview narrative. She found that the emphasis on narrative gave students something of what was missing in the initial thematic study: 'enduring, remembered meaning and a more natural fascination about broader trends and processes' (2009: 41). Gadd emphasises content to enable critical conceptual work, which would suggest that a selection of appropriate content and engaging methods of working with that content may be crucial precursors of effective work on longer term change.

References

Corfield, P.J. (2007) *Time and the Shape of History*. London: Yale University Press.

Gadd, S. (2009) Building memory and meaning: Supporting Year 8 in shaping their own big narratives. *Teaching History*, 136, 34–41.

Gaskill, M. (2005) *Witchfinders: A seventeenth-century English tragedy*. London: John Murray.

Jarman. B. (2009) When were Jews in medieval England most in danger? Exploring change and continuity with Year 7. *Teaching History*, 136, 4–12.

Jones, H. (2009) Shaping macro-analysis from micro-history: Developing a reflexive narrative of change in school history. *Teaching History*, 136, 13–21.

Lee, P. (2005) Putting principles into practice: Understanding history. In J. Bransford and M. Donovan (eds) *How Students Learn History in the Classroom*. Washington, DC: National Academy of Sciences, 31–78.

Shemilt, D. (1980) *History 13–16: Evaluation study*. Edinburgh: Holmes McDougall.

Shemilt, D. (2000) The caliph's coin. In P. Stearns, P. Seixas and S. Wineburg (eds) *Knowing, Teaching and Learning History: National and international perspectives*. New York: New York University Press, 83–101.

Vella, Y. (2011) The gradual transformation of historical situations: Understanding 'change and continuity' through colours and timelines. *Teaching History*, 144, 16–23.

Zeldin, T. (1994) *An Intimate History of Humanity*. London: Sinclair Stevenson.

13

Causal reasoning

E.H. Carr (1961), in his classic book *What Is History?*, argues that the primary role of the historian is to ask 'why?' In this sense causal reasoning lies at the heart of studying history. As a concept, causal reasoning can appear deceptively simple. It is not enough, however, simply to list a series of events that led to another event; students need to understand that causal reasoning involves explanation and argument about the relationships between events, and between individual actors and more impersonal structures. The fact that it involves consideration of motives and intentions, as well as of unintended consequences, means that it requires a very sophisticated level of reasoning – some of which may appear counter-intuitive. This chapter explores what we know about the assumptions young people make about causation, the way in which their understanding develops, and the kind of teaching strategies and analogies that can support this development.

Extract 1

Source

Lee, P. (2005) Putting principles into practice: Understanding history. In S. Donovan and J. Bransford (eds) *How Students Learn: History in the classroom*. Washington, DC: The National Academies Press; see pp. 49–54.

Introduction

This research stems from two sources – an American report on how people learn and British research on how children understand the past called 'Concepts of History and Teaching Approaches' (CHATA). This book sets the British research in the context of the American report, exploring children's preconceptions about history and pointing out some key concepts involved in making sense of the discipline.

Extract

Not all explanations in history are concerned with understanding peoples' reasons for acting or thinking as they did. We often want to explain why something happened that no one intended. Actions have unintended consequences, or simply fail to achieve their purposes. Historians also explain why large-scale events or processes occurred (for example the Renaissance, the Industrial Revolution, or American westward expansion). In such cases, understanding what people were trying to do – their reasons for action – can be only part of an explanation of how events turned out, and we are likely to have to start talking in terms of *causes* ...

Students often treat causes as special events that make new events happen in much the same way as individual people do things: causes act the way human agents act. When one fails to do something, nothing happens; similarly, if no causes act, nothing happens. It is as if the alternative to something happening is not something different occurring, but a hole being left in history (Shemilt, 1980). Students thinking like this misconceive the explanatory task, seeing it as explaining, for example, why the [American] Civil War happened as opposed to 'nothing' happening. But the task for historians is to explain why the Civil War occurred rather than other possibilities (such as a compromise solution or the gradual demise of slavery).

Another idea connected with seeing causes as special kinds of events is that causes are discrete entities, acting independently from each other. Construed this way, they can be thought of as piling up so that eventually there are enough causes to make something happen. Hence students make lists, and the more causes are on the list, the more likely the event is to happen. (The bigger the event, the longer the list needs to be.) Some students, while seeing causes as discrete events, go beyond the idea of a list and link the causes together as a linear chain .... This is a more powerful idea than simply piling causes up, but still makes it difficult for students to cope with the complex interactions that lie at the heart of historical explanations ...

In historical explanations, the relationship among the elements matter as much as the elements themselves – it is how they came together that determined whether the event we want to explain happened, rather than something else. Within this network of interacting elements, a key idea is that there are some elements without which the event we are explaining would not have occurred. This idea provides a basis for understanding that historians tend to select necessary conditions of events from the wider (sufficient) set. If these necessary conditions had not been present, the event we are explaining would not have happened; it is often these that are picked out as the 'causes' ...

If students think of causes as discrete events that act to produce results, they have difficulty recognizing that is the questions we choose to ask about the past that push some factors into the background and pull others to the foreground to be treated as causes. We select as a cause something absent in other, comparison cases. The question of why the Roman Empire in the west fell is a classic case. The question may be answered in at least two different ways: first, 'when it had successfully resisted attack for hundreds of years', and second, 'when it didn't end in the east'. In the first case we look for events or processes that were present in the fifth century but not (to the same degree) earlier. In the second we look for actors present in the west in the fifth century but not at that time in the east. What counts as a cause here, rather than a background condition, is determined in part by what question we ask (Martin, 1989).

Summary

Children can have misconceptions concerning the past. Their understanding of why something happened is often based around people's intentions rather than considering unintended consequences or larger-scale events. They can tend to list causes or lean towards linear patterns rather than see the complex relationships between causes. There are some (necessary) causes without which the event would not have occurred. Asking different questions leads to alternate patterns of causation emerging.

Questions to consider

1. According to the author, what misconceptions about causation do students often have? How might students be encouraged to form a web of causation rather than a series of linear causes?
2. What is the difference between a necessary cause and a sufficient cause? What examples might you use in the history classroom to help students to understand the difference?
3. Lee states that what counts as a cause, rather than a background condition, is determined in part by what question we ask. How could a variety of questions on the same topic be used in the history classroom to develop students' understanding of causation?

Extract 2

Source

Chapman, A. (2003) Camels, diamonds and counter-factuals: A model for teaching causal reasoning. *Teaching History*, 112, 6–13.

Introduction

Chapman wrote this piece when working intensively with 16–18-year-old A-level students at the introduction of a new set of examination specifications. Wanting his students to understand what robust causal analysis might look like he turned to the historian, Richard J. Evans with the intention of revising his own typology of causation.

Key words & phrases

Model; cause; causal reasoning; concepts; historian; typology

---

Extract

The model for teaching for progression in causal reasoning that emerged out of my experience ... can be summarised in the following principles:

(a) Start by clarifying concepts and by identifying a vocabulary that will enable analysis – a terminological sieve that students can use to sort materials.

(b) Work up exercises that will allow students to learn to use the vocabulary – wildly unhistorical exercises are as good (if not better) as historical ones.

(c) Once there is clarity about concepts, use them to drive investigation and research – students should not be let anywhere near the historical material without their conceptual lenses polished and their questions sharpened.

(d) Design open-ended tasks that allow students to model conceptual relationships in concrete ways (see Phillips, 2002).

(e) Focus on consequences as much as on classification and design tasks that require consequences to be explicitly specified – understanding causality is about reflecting on effects as much as about categorising causes.

(f) Use counterfactual questions (Phillips, 2002) to build student understanding of consequences – this is the royal road to evaluating and ranking or to the elusive 'hierarchy' that is the ultimate aim of causal analysis.

Conceptual clarity: rigour and *rigor mortis*

Because an understanding of causation underpins not only our analysis of so much in history but also our ability to understand and analyse different and often competing accounts of the past, it is worth exploring what causation actually *means* with students. What exactly characterises the sophisticated and complex pieces of causal reasoning that historians present us with? How do they attempt to classify causes and ascribe different values to them? What makes one explanation of, say, the abolition of slavery in the British Empire different – and perhaps even 'better' – than another? ...

... It seemed obvious that causes could be differentiated according to the kind of stuff they were made of; clearly there is mileage in contrasts between such things as economic causes, on the one hand, and ideological or cultural causes on the other. Noting differences such as these, I decided, could be called analysing causes by 'Content'. Causes could also be differentiated by 'Time' – we are all familiar with terms such as 'long term' and 'short term' (terms that usually have the same effect on the enjoyment of marking as phrases such as 'this is biased' or 'Source 2, on the other hand, is a secondary source'). So far – in 'Content' and 'Time' categories – I had a descriptive analysis of causes. Things were starting to fall into shape. 'Catalysts' or 'triggers' were great favourites amongst my abler students who, nevertheless, tended to treat them as interchangeable with 'Time' categories. They were conflating description with something else. A whole new family of distinctions began to become clearer – there were triggers, there were catalysts (or were they the same as triggers?) and there were 'preconditions' and what they all had in common was that they focused on the roles played by causes. A 'Role' category seemed like a contender and role terms seemed to be doing much more interesting work than those in the descriptive categories because they were explanatory in intent.

Finally, I had to confront Evans' [1997] glib talk of necessary and sufficient causes. Whatever else they were, they certainly seemed to be about importance or – to use that favourite of examiners – 'weight'. I had a four-term classification model or typology then. Causes could be distinguished in terms of content, time, role and importance. It seemed promising, in the sense that most things could be analysed using it. In the end, as Evans says, everything is probably 'over-determined', but this typology seemed to enable the drawing of distinctions (or, in other words, analysis) and it seemed to me that it would 'do'.

Summary

Having identified the need to develop his students' understanding of causation, Chapman starts by examining a key historian's work in this area. He aims to establish a relationship between the historical thinking taking place in his classroom and thinking and argument of academic historians. Chapman suggests the need to clarify concepts and identify a vocabulary for analysis so that students can explore what causation actually means, for example, through the use of games. One typology to distinguish causes is suggested: content, time, role and importance.

Questions to consider

1. What justification does Chapman offer for the need to understand causation? Would there be any value in sharing such a justification with your students?
2. How far does Chapman's model for teaching for progression in causation suit your students? What would a scheme of work designed around this model look like?

3. How do both Chapman and his students benefit from the thinking of a historian? What other key history texts might be worth revisiting to develop your thinking, or that of your students?

Extract 3

Source

Howells, G. (1998) Being ambitious with the causes of the First World War: Interrogating inevitability. *Teaching History*, 92, 16–19.

Introduction

Howells is a practising history teacher developing practical strategies to develop students' understanding of causation. He wants to go beyond the comprehension of simple terms such as 'trigger' or 'long-term' to challenge students' thinking with something more 'meaningful'. In this article he describes a sequence of lessons that led 13–14-year-old students to be able to question the inevitability, first of the assassination of Archduke Franz Ferdinand, and then of the First World War. He introduces a small part of the Fischer thesis to his students, the idea that German politicians and generals were intent on war well before 1914. This extract focuses on the final part of the sequence of lessons.

Key words & phrases

Causation; inevitability; First World War; attitudes; meaningful context; Fischer thesis; big questions; concepts

---

Extract

Once familiarity and confidence is assured we can then move to considering the steps to the war in relation to the broader (and ultimately key) question of inevitability. Hopefully the students have some appreciation of whether the assassination made the war inevitable and have viewed the reactions of the great powers as the key. But there remains a deeper question. Why did great powers react as they did? In effect, studying the causes of World War I offers the opportunity of studying more than one question of inevitability. One question is, 'Was the assassination inevitable?' Then, once the assassination has taken place, 'Was war inevitable?' Finally there is the deeper question of whether war was inevitable regardless of the above events. The circumstances surrounding the outbreak of World War I offer the opportunity to interrogate the notion of inevitability. By constantly returning to that one question, students are encouraged to explore an identical question in different contexts which provides the opportunity for rigorous thought and, ideally, a sophisticated notion of causation which extends far beyond classifying events or factors as short term, long term or trigger.

If we leave the study with the steps to war we have the long term causes and the trigger, but we do not have a dynamic notion of people's attitudes and preoccupations at the beginning of World War I. We have no meaningful context as to how the idea of war fitted into the general historical framework. Why did people gaily step onto the World War I roller coaster? An answer which involves the death of the archduke, some awareness of the Balkans, the arms race and scramble for Africa would be adequate. Yet somehow the ideas of the participants are lost. Can we place the assassination within a more meaningful context and encourage the students (in Year Nine) to take on board a bit of the Fischer thesis?

Try presenting students with three paraphrased attitude boxes of the German generals, German politicians and all generals ... Having equipped the students to think whether war was inevitable as a direct consequence of the assassination, we can now present sources which argue the opposite. Again, we are encouraging them to think and to think about big questions. Causation is shown as complex and shifting ...

The broad point is to ensure that pupils achieve meaningful understanding. As history teachers, we need to aim for meaningful outcomes. These outcomes need to be conceived as something broader than the immediate confines of the lesson. Concepts are difficult to teach. Inevitability might not seem an immediate concept at the top of the list. However, by determining to address one key term and by tenaciously holding on to that term a direction and purpose can be found to planning and students can be encouraged to think and express their views. As with all historical skills most students do not learn by osmosis. They need explicit direction and the opportunity to develop their thinking through concrete examples and over time. Furthermore, in teaching new concepts or developing thinking on concepts we should not expect total success, amenable to easy measurement, in terms of conceptual understanding. Yet that is no reason for not attempting to encourage an appreciation of those ideas. We persist, and return to those same concepts at a later date.

Summary

Howells' students understand the long-term causes and the trigger of the First World War, but he wants them to go beyond the labelling stage and construct something more meaningful. In choosing to contemplate inevitability he is doing two things. First, this precise question provides access and motivation to lower-attainers in the class by giving a focus to quite a complex series of events. Second, considering the inevitability of the war provides an opportunity for higher-attainers in that students are encouraged to move away from any misconception about causation being static and decided. Introducing the Fischer thesis shows causation as complex and shifting and challenges students to construct their own causal argument from the available evidence.

Questions to consider

1. How does the author justify a focus on inevitability? What other elements of causation might be used in a similar way to focus and challenge students?
2. When experimenting with the type of strategy that Howells advocates, should we expect total success? How does the author suggest progression in conceptual understanding might best be achieved?
3. Howells and Chapman both suggest using the ideas of historians in their classrooms. What might be the advantages of this approach? What challenges might need to be overcome?

Investigations

Building in opportunities for progression: The author suggests revisiting the concept of inevitability regularly over the course of the year so that students are given the opportunity to build up an understanding of the concept. What other topics might lend themselves to exploring questions of inevitability. Work out what 'big questions' might shape the enquiries.

Pupil assessment: What do your students understand about causation and what are their misconceptions? Set up a series of interviews with a group of students. Give them a written causation problem to consider and ask them to talk you through why the event happened. Record the interviews and analyse the data to explore current misconceptions among your own classes.

Drawing causation maps: After teaching a causation enquiry ask a class of students to draw or represent the causes and their relationship to one another in some other kind of visual format. They can then explain this pattern to the class teacher. Are they still thinking in a linear form or can they see the relationships between a range of causes?

Departmental consensus: As the 'Think deeper' section below shows, causal reasoning has been an area of contention between historians. Summarise the views of a number of historians and share them with departmental colleagues. Find out if different views of causal reasoning exist. Then use the reading and the discussion to sketch out a possible model of progression in causation that students might be expected to follow.

Think deeper

Historians have debated models of causation. Carr (1961: 87) devoted a chapter to the concept declaring that 'the study of history is the study of causes'. He wished to re-establish the place of determinism, that everything has a cause, against the idea that history was governed by chance and the free will of individuals. He went on to argue that causality is a matter of interpretation and that history must serve the present. In his *Defence of History*, R.J. Evans (1997) sets out a variety of responses from different historians to Carr's approach. More recently, David Cannadine (2002) has pointed to the collapse of grand narratives and large teleological theories in history and the re-emergence of individual beings, 'the losers and bystanders' in the process of historical change.

The ideas of historians might well inform the way teachers approach causation enquiries and the choice of strategies they use to problematise causation. James Woodcock (2011) has explored the work of C. Behan McCullagh, as an example of how the ideas of one historian might be deconstructed and employed in the classroom. This involves categorising the causes of human actions, whether mental, social or cultural. In contrast, Woodcock goes on to consider the role of macro, geographical factors in explaining causal processes.

For his evaluation of the Schools Council History Project (13–16) Shemilt (1980) looked at students' understanding of causation. Among many key findings he points to the conception of causal redundancy; that for some children having 'more than one cause is to have causal overkill; a surfeit of causes is like striking matches once the fire is lit' (1980: 31). He points out that students think 'quite reasonably and sensibly' when it comes to causal narrative, but that they struggle to think historically. This move from mono-causal to multi-causal thinking forms part of the tentative progression model for children's understanding of causation produced by the Teaching History Research Group (Scott 1990). Stage 1 describes a simple level of understanding where 'Stories and events just happen. They happen without relation to each other. No links are detected or sought.' Stage 5 refers to the historiography of causation, how relationships between causes can change over time, the ability to discuss chance, inevitability and the extent of freedom/determinism among several other markers. Counsell (2004: 37) has suggested that this stage is useful not only for ideas about what the most able students might be doing, but also for giving 'a sense of the deeper, more enduring or underlying purpose of the easy, basic activities that we devise for younger or weaker pupils'.

Think wider

Jesús Domínguez and Juan Pozo (1998) carried out empirical research in Spain into effective teaching strategies for promoting the learning of causal explanations in history. Through an experiment where 112 students wrote a series of answers and were taught in a variety of ways, they came to the conclusion that the explicit teaching of procedures of causal explanation has a clear effect on the explanatory level of students. Christine Counsell (2004) supports this in stating that when teachers suggest students struggle with the writing process, it is actually 'the history' they are having difficulty with. 'The history' is the practice of causal reasoning, the choices about how to cluster causes and how to name them, the making of judgements about which causal model has the most explanatory power, the judgement about the status of the causes. She links this explicitly with literacy (2004: 36), stating that

> this is at the same time the work of choosing themes for paragraphs, deciding how to order those paragraphs into a thematic analysis, exploring the best supporting evidence within those paragraphs, and above all, understanding the power of a paragraph when it becomes cohesive..

In *Analytic and Discursive Writing at Key Stage 3* (1997) and then in further depth in *History and Literacy in Year 7* (2004) Counsell sets out the detail of a wide variety of card-sorts and other strategies intended to develop the thinking and reasoning involved in students' causal explanation.

In the article 'Does the linguistic release the conceptual?' James Woodcock (2005) builds on the work of Arthur Chapman referred to above in Extract 3. He focuses in particular on the vocabulary students need to have an informed debate about causation and explicitly teaches words such as 'latent', 'excite' and 'nurture' in other contexts before students attempt to apply it to debates around the causes of the First World War. The article also includes a developed version of *Alphonse the Camel*, an analogous story about the straw that broke the camel's back, which was initially designed by Chapman to help students with causal reasoning.

References

Cannadine, D. (2002) *What Is History Now?* London: Palgrave Macmillan.

Carr, E.H. (1961) *What Is History?* Harmondsworth: Penguin.

Counsell, C. (1997) *Analytical and Discursive Writing at Key Stage 3.* London: Historical Association.

Counsell, C. (2004) *History and Literacy in Year 7.* London: Hodder Murray.

Domínguez, J. and Pozo, J. (1998) Promoting the learning of causal explanations in history through different teaching strategies. In J. Voss and M. Carretero (eds) *Learning and Reasoning in History: International review of history education, volume 2.* London: Woburn Press, 344–59.

Evans, R.J. (1997) *In Defence of History.* London: Granta.

Martin, R. (1989) *The Past Within Us.* Princeton, NJ: Princeton University Press.

McCullagh, C.B. (2004) *Putting Postmodernism in Perspective.* London: Routledge.

Phillips, R. (2002) *Reflective Teaching of History 11–18.* London: Continuum.

Scott, J. (ed.) (1990) *Teaching History Research Group, Understanding Cause and Effect: Learning and teaching about causation and consequence in history.* Harlow: Longman.

Shemilt, D. (1980) *History 13–16: Evaluation study.* Edinburgh: Holmes McDougall.

Woodcock, J. (2005) Does the linguistic release the conceptual? Helping Year 10 to improve their causal reasoning. *Teaching History,* 119, 5–14.

Woodcock, J. (2011) Causal explanation. In I. Davies (ed.) *Debates in History Teaching.* London: Routledge, 124–36.

Empathy

One of the most derided developments in history education, at least in the UK during the 1980s, was the teaching of empathy as an historical concept. As ideas originally developed within the Schools History Project were extended to all history teachers with the introduction of new public examinations at 16+ (GCSE), many in the history education community found themselves grappling with questions about the essential nature of the subject and what precisely they were trying to achieve when teaching about the past. The idea of empathy, seeking to understand the ideas, attitudes and ways of thinking of people in the past was considered an important aspect of historical thinking. However, empathy, as a concept, became an issue that was used to attack the 'new history'. Empathy was seen as lacking a clear conceptual focus, often being associated with tasks that asked pupils to 'imagine' and thus the distinction between historical imagination and literary invention became obscured. The extracts in this chapter explore the issues relating to defining empathy, trying to identify what it means to get better at empathising with people in the past, and the ways in which classroom teachers think about empathy in their own context.

Extract 1

Source

Portal, C. (1987) Empathy as an objective for history teaching. In C. Portal (ed.) *The History Curriculum for Teachers*. London: The Falmer Press, 89–99.

Introduction

One of the major difficulties for those in the history education community was trying to define precisely what was meant by empathy, for example did empathy require a cognitive or affective way of thinking, or something entirely different? Without this clear understanding it was difficult to identify precisely what students were expected to do, and therefore difficult to create tasks that would allow the students to develop any sense of empathy with the past. In this extract, written at the height of the controversy that accompanied empathy, Christopher Portal offers his understanding of the concept.

Key words & phrases

Empathy; historical imagination; projective imagination

Extract

The term 'empathy' (*Einfühlung*) derives from idealism of the nineteenth century and was seen by Wilhelm Dilthey as an essential element in 'understanding' history or any of the human sciences. As in the natural sciences we need evidence and the use of rational processes to relate it to the questions we want answered, but social studies carry an extra dimension – broadly that of the meanings carried by language. Words still in use today, such as 'marriage', 'rebellion', 'heresy', may be found in sources from the past, but they will often have important differences of sense from how we would now define them. And this is not a minor matter, confined to the semi-technical vocabulary of social institutions; it applies to every aspect of life and thought. So the historian's first task is precisely 'interpretation' (as Dilthey insisted). It is necessary to establish what people thought was going on and how they saw their own range of options before any explanation of their motives has a chance of success. It must be stressed that 'interpretation' in this sense applies as much to actions as it does to words and to articulate concepts, as much to customary social behaviour as it does to the individual point of view.

A modern definition of empathy is to grasp imaginatively 'the thinking, feelings and actions of another and so structure the world as he does' [Natale 1972: 16], to which corresponds, in historical terms, Collingwood's [1946] belief that the historian should reconstruct and 'rethink' the opinions and purposes of people in the past. But such an historical achievement presumes a high level of expertise in a whole range of historical skills; although empathy may be a necessary element in such insights, it is confusing to regard as empathy everything concerned with understanding historical ideas. Collingwood did not use the term empathy (although 'rethinking' implies something very like it) and more familiar mental operations such as inference from evidence and background knowledge will play a part in every historical reconstruction.

The role of empathy in understanding the ideas of the past is to project ourselves imaginatively into the historical situation and to use 'our mind's eye' to bring into play the standards of intuitive observation and judgement which we have developed in everyday life. It is possible to recognize in this way what 'makes sense' in an alien world by implicit analogy with our own way of looking at things. At this stage we may be a long way from the authentic thoughts of the past, but the attempt to apply our own categories can show us what 'doesn't work' as well as those aspects that do. Given such stimulus we may, as we do so often in daily life, arrive at a new and more challenging hypothesis to account for the behaviour that is otherwise strange and inexplicable.

Summary

Portal argues that part of studying history is trying to understand the thoughts and feelings of people in the past in order to understand their motivation. The ability to look at the world through the eyes of people who lived in the past is extremely difficult and requires an extensive level of knowledge and understanding of history. However, Portal implies that it is possible to use our understanding of the present and the way in which we understand our world now as a means to start reflecting on people's actions in the past. However, such an approach would lead to a low level of empathetic reasoning (as will be discussed in Extract 2). Although this low-level reasoning may be a valid starting point for students, it is potentially problematic, and still leaves questions about how to develop stronger levels of empathetic reasoning. The extract also suggests that empathetic reasoning has different dimensions, e.g. there is a level of cognitive thinking in terms of inferring from evidence, but there is also an affective level of engagement by trying to understand people's feelings.

Questions to consider

1. How do you define empathy?
2. What makes empathy difficult? And how far do you think it is possible to empathise with people in the past?
3. What knowledge and understanding needs to be in place for someone to be able to empathise with someone in the past?

Extract 2

Source

Lee, P. and Shemilt, D. (2011) The concept that dares not speak its name: Should empathy come out of the closet? *Teaching History*, 143, 39–49.

Introduction

Because it has proved so difficult to define precisely what form of thinking empathy actually entails, it has proved equally problematic to establish what it means to get better at thinking empathetically about the past. Within the article Peter Lee and Denis

Shemilt outline their understanding of what this kind of thinking does and does not involve. In Extract 2, they draw upon their extensive research in the CHATA project to outline the different ways in which pupils think about the past empathetically. The research data, which included pupils' responses to particular tasks and conversations with them, were used to examine and identify the range of different ways in which young people understood the past. Although Lee and Shemilt divide these ways of thinking into levels, they stress very strongly that these levels are not some form of assessment ladder; instead the levels denote different ways of thinking.

Key words & phrases

Empathy; progression; CHATA (Concepts of History and Teaching Approaches) project; pupil understanding

---

Extract

Level 1: explanation by description

People just did what they did and thought what they thought. Requests for explanation are met by the reiteration or addition of information …

Level 2: explanation by assimilation to the known present or by identification of deficits in the past

As per Level 1, students tend to regard people in the past as modern men and women in fancy dress who did what they did and thought what they thought … Only when faced with practices perceived to be abnormal, puzzling or disturbing do students recognise something as being in need of explanation. In such cases, they either cite deficits in knowledge, intelligence, sensibility, technology or whatever to explain differences between past and present … or explain how what may, at first sight, appear alien and nonsensical about the past is, in reality, not so different from contemporary practice.

Level 3: explanation by stereotype

Students tend to explain what is recognisable with reference to 'what they know about the world', which knowledge is usually deployed in the form of stereotypes …

Level 4: explanation by means of everyday empathy

Students move from explanations in terms of the strangeness of people in the past to explanations in terms of the strangeness of past situations. The key assumption is that past circumstances differed from those obtaining in the present, and our predecessors behaved much as we would have done in similar situations. But instead of being content with stereotypical assertions about how different sorts of people are likely to behave, they analyse the particularities of past situations in order to explain why a social practice or institution made sense in the circumstances, why in comparable positions people today might behave in similar ways ...

Level 5: explanation by means of historical empathy

At this watershed in the development of their historical understanding, many students achieve something remarkable: the realisation that, although people in the past had the same capacities for thought and feeling as we do, they did not see the world as we see it today. There are some past ideas and practices for which trying to make sense of situation (and assuming beliefs in the past were the same as ours) can offer no satisfactory explanation ... Some students take the even harder step of grasping that people in the past are likely to have seen things differently from us even when they appear to think and act in the same ways ...

Level 6: explanation with reference to 'forms of life'

Once students assume that, even when past practices appear comprehensible from the perspectives of the present, predecessors may have evaluated and made sense of the world rather differently, they may begin to ask why this is so. At least, they may understand what is going on when teachers ask why. We can explain how subscription to certain religious ideas explains why victims of scrofula followed kings around the country being touched hundreds of times, but why were these ideas so powerful? Since people in the Middle Ages were no dumber than people today, why did dogmas of faith trump the lessons of experience? Among explanations offered are those that demonstrate awareness of connections between perspectives and material conditions of life, between material and symbolic cultures ...

Summary

In this article Lee and Shemilt outline what they see as distinct steps in the way that students empathise with people in the past. The levels described are not necessarily sequential and students do not have to move up through the levels, rather they represent quite distinct ways of thinking. What is not clear though is how the students have been taught and therefore what types of empathy exercises help promote lower/higher levels of empathetic reasoning.

Questions to consider

1. How convincing do you find these levels of empathetic reasoning?
2. What knowledge and understanding of history would be necessary to reach the higher levels outlined here?
3. What types of activity would enable students to reach these higher levels?

Extract 3

Source

Cunningham, D. (2004) Empathy without illusions. *Teaching History*, 114, 24–9.

Introduction

In this article, which is based upon a PhD study, Deborah Cunningham looks at the dilemmas teachers faced when trying to get students to think in an empathetic way. The study focuses on how teachers understood empathy and therefore how they tried to negotiate the dilemmas that teaching in an empathetic way created. The dilemmas focus on the use of imagination in history, whether or not to allow present assumptions and attitudes to shape how students look at the past, whether students should be encouraged to actively identify with characters in the past and whether empathy should be used to help students make moral judgements about people in the past.

Key words & phrases

Empathy; historical imagination; everyday empathy; engagement; moral engagement

---

Extract

How to harness imagination while keeping it tied to evidence

Imagination in history has a number of meanings ... So what did the teachers in my study mean when they told students to 'imagine'? They were clear about the fact that the imagination sought was not, as historian Bernard Bailyn has put it, 'transcendental flights into the unknown,' but 'imagination in a straitjacket.' Ms. Joslin used the term infrequently, and in interviews she connected it firmly to making sense of evidence, to 'developing through the imagination a picture of how things were,' not 'just grasping at anything that comes to your mind and that leads you to everyday empathy and writing wildly off the topic and out of focus.'

Whether to frame empathy in personal or historical terms

Another dilemma for teachers involved clarity about whether to encourage reconstruction of 'your' feelings or 'another person's.' All of the teachers at times used both the 'you' and 'they' pronouns, asking students questions like 'What would you think (or feel) if you were in this situation?' and 'How did they view this?' Because of the usage of 'you' to mean 'one' (third person) in many cases, semantics often made it difficult to interpret precisely what the teachers wanted. During much interactive discussion, teachers did not seem to be choosing the pronouns consciously.

... Ms. Joslin had mostly banished the 'you' phrasing of the question from her in-class speech. She did not want to encourage students to put themselves into the past, but rather to stretch to understand authentic historical reactions. In fact, in a lesson on attitudes toward vagabonds, she gave dozens of reminders to 'put your sixteenth-century hat on' and to consider views 'at the time'; she also gave five warnings not to let the students' modern views and opinions interfere. The results in the presentations that followed were, she said, something to celebrate: 'they were totally immersed in the sixteenth-century way of thinking and none of the attitudes that they expressed seemed anachronistic.'

Whether to encourage identification and emotional connection with historical figures

To point out that 'you' questions more frequently led to presentist responses is not to suggest that such tactics have no positive role to play in the history classroom. It appears that students' ultimate understandings depend partly on the way that they are used. Ms. Hayes' decision about the rules for Jews aptly represented the value she placed on students' engagement, their relating to some of the emotional impact of the topic at hand. She used a broad variety of strategies to make students care about the issues.

Balancing empathy and moral judgment

... [Mr Dow] emphasized the historical type of judgments – understanding what led to certain actions – but after they were explored he saw a role for value judgments on past actions. These sorts of judgments incorporated empathy, because to judge people you needed to know the context in which they acted, but values were part of it.

Summary

The article summarises key issues facing teachers who attempted to get their students to empathise with the past. The views of the teachers varied, which illustrates the contested nature of this area. Many of the issues focus on the pupils and the extent to which they could/should be allowed to bring their present-day assumptions to understand the past, and how much distance the pupils should place between themselves and the characters they are studying.

Questions to consider

1. How far do you identify with these dilemmas when trying to get pupils to empathise with people in the past?
2. Empathy is a tricky concept, both in terms of defining it and finding ways for students to empathise. Is it therefore too difficult to teach?
3. What is the value of getting students to empathise with people in the past?

Investigations

Examine teachers' perspectives on empathy: Gather views from a group of history teachers, either as a survey or through a meeting. How do they define empathy? Do they deliberately set out to develop empathetic reasoning (if so, how and why; if not, why not)? What does a good empathetic response look like? What do they think it means to get better at empathy?

Explore pupil perceptions: Give them a dilemma facing someone in the past, without any contextual knowledge and see how they attempt to explain the person's action. Carry out a similar activity but with contextual knowledge and compare the quality of responses. What are the main differences in how pupils reason and what misconceptions/preconceptions and/or issues does this highlight?

Other curriculum areas: Talk to teachers in other subject areas. Which ones expect pupils to engage in empathetic reasoning? How do they attempt to do this and what lessons might you draw from these areas for your own practice.

Think deeper

Much material relating to empathy was written in the 1980s and 1990s, in part because the concept was emerging as part of classroom practice but also because it became the centre of very heated debate about what empathy actually was, whether it was possible to empathise with people in the past and, if it was possible, how could you assess empathetic responses. It is therefore possible to focus on different aspects of this debate.

Keith Jenkins and Peter Brickley (1989) and Jenkins (1991) state strong objections to the mere possibility of empathising with characters in the past. Arguing from a post-modernist perspective on the nature of history they raise a number of important issues that deserve consideration, but whether these points are valid very much depends on your position regarding the nature of history itself.

The nature of historical empathy itself and the types of reasoning required to engage in empathy have also been debated. A lack of clarity in this respect is problematic for as Peter Knight (1989: 45) rightly points out: 'effective teaching goes with a clear grasp of the central ideas of the subject matter. A term such as empathy seems unhelpful to clear thinking.' For Shemilt (1984) empathising is essentially a cognitive skill, for Ros Ashby and Peter Lee (1987) it is a disposition and an achievement, while Ann Low-Beer (1989) sees it as part of the affective domain.

Problems of assessment are also raised, for example by Low-Beer (1989), who suggests that they essentially stem from the lack of clarity about what empathy is, and therefore what is being assessed. Is it the ability to structure a plausible account based on evidential reconstruction (and therefore a largely cognitive activity) or is it more associated with examining the feelings and beliefs of people in the past (and therefore a more emotive response would be suitable)?

Much has also been written about the practical problems of getting pupils to engage in empathetic reasoning. This can be clearly seen in a chapter by Chris Husbands and

Anna Pendry (2000) who analyse a number of pupils' responses to an activity and highlight the difficulties they encounter. Although they do not use the word empathy, probably because it had become such a hotly contested term, they clearly explore the challenges of seeing events from the perspectives of people in the past, who are distant in time, often adults and often having to make major policy, political or personal decisions, all of which are outside of the life experiences of the average teenager.

It is only recently that attention has turned once again to the concept of empathy. Ian Luff (2000) has been successfully advocating the use of 'role play' or, as he prefers, 'practical demonstration' as a means of helping pupils engage with the mindset and dilemmas of people in the past. Counsell (2011), in her discussion of change and continuity (see Chapter 12 in this book) writes about enabling pupils to understand the lived experiences of people in the past and argues that this allows pupils to engage productively with empathetic reasoning.

Think wider

O.L. Davis, Elizabeth Yeager and Stuart Foster (2001) present research from different contexts in their book *Historical Empathy and Perspective Taking in the Social Studies*, but that are predominantly drawn from studies carried out in the United States. Many of the issues raised reflect the points already discussed above. The book presents a more positive view of the possibility of getting students to engage in historical empathy, and is very clear about what is required to enable this. In the concluding chapter the sub-headings used give an outline of how the authors understand empathy and what is required to allow students to think empathetically:

- Historical empathy primarily does not involve imagination, identification or sympathy.
- Historical empathy involves understanding people's actions in the past.
- Historical empathy involves a thorough appreciation of historical context.
- Historical empathy requires multiple forms of evidence and perspective.
- Historical empathy requires students to examine their own perspective.
- Historical empathy encourages well-grounded and tentative conclusions.

Historical empathy is seen as an attempt to explain actions in the past, so is a dimension of causal reasoning. It requires detailed knowledge of the period in question and it requires students to work with historical evidence. They also emphasise the need to be aware of a range of perspectives within any given period. Historical empathy, they argue, 'lies at the heart of historical inquiry' (Davis, Yeager and Foster 2001: 175). In this sense, it becomes difficult to do history without empathy, empathy is not simply *a* way of getting to understand the past, it is *the* way of understanding the past.

Stéphane Lévesque (2008) offers a more recent exploration of the nature of historical empathy. He argues that it is built on three aspects: historical imagination, historical contextualisation and moral judgement. Historical imagination is seen as a key disposition, where it is possible to entertain the beliefs, values and attitudes of people in the past, based on an evidential reconstruction of the past. On its own this is not enough to develop historical empathy and contextualisation is necessary. Lévesque argues that this requires personal contextualisation (i.e. what is known or can be deduced about particular individuals), sociocultural contextualisation (the broader social, cultural and economic context of the period) and contemporary contextualisation (understanding current ideas, attitudes and beliefs in order to avoid presentism). Moral judgements are based upon the idea that people in the past acted for rational reasons, thus to understand the alternatives available to people in the past and to examine their actual choices, makes it possible to understand their reasoning, but within a context that examines whether the choices made were fair, just, courageous and so forth. Lévesque's position is a highly nuanced one, as each aspect of contextualisation is made up of several elements.

It can therefore be seen that empathy is still an area of debate. It is becoming an area of renewed interest, following the problems that accompanied the development of historical empathy in the 1980s, but one that needs further exploration and development.

References

Ashby, R. and Lee, P. (1987) Children's concepts of empathy and understanding in history. In C. Portal (ed.) *The History Curriculum for Teachers*. London: The Falmer Press, 62–88.

Collingwood, R.G. (1946) *The Idea of History*. Oxford: Oxford University Press.

Counsell, C. (2011) What do we want students to *do* with historical change and continuity? In I. Davies (ed.) *Debates in History Teaching*. London: Routledge, 109–23.

Davis Jnr, O.L., Yeager, E. and Foster, S. (2001) *Historical Empathy and Perspective Taking in the Social Studies*. Lanham, MD: Rowman and Littlefield Publishers.

Husbands, C. and Pendry, A. (2000) Thinking and feeling: Pupils' preconceptions about the past and historical understanding. In J. Arthur and R. Phillips (eds) *Issues in History Teaching*. London: Routledge, 125–36.

Jenkins, K. (1991) *Re-thinking History*. London: Routledge.

Jenkins, K. and Brickley, P. (1989) Reflections on the empathy debate. *Teaching History*, 55, 18–23.

Knight, P. (1989) Empathy: Concept, confusion and consequence in a national curriculum. *Oxford Review of Education*, 15 (1), 41–53.

Lévesque, S. (2008) *Thinking Historically: Educating students for the twenty-first century*. Toronto: University of Toronto Press.

Low-Beer, A. (1989) Empathy and history. *Teaching History*, 55, 8–12.

Luff, I. (2000) 'I've been in the Reichstag': Re-thinking role-play. *Teaching History*, 100, 8–17.

Natale, S. (1972) *An Experiment in Empathy*. Slough: NfER.

Shemilt, D. (1984) Beauty and the philosopher: Empathy in history and classroom. In A. Dickinson, P. Lee and P. Rogers (eds) *Learning History*. London: Heinemann Educational Books, 39–84.

Diversity

Teaching a diverse past is seen as an important area for teachers to examine: the past, by its very nature, includes the history of an array of individuals, groups and societies, and is therefore inherently diverse in content. This raises questions about what should be taught and what balance there should be between what is taught. There are many different dimensions to consider: the topics to include (and, just as importantly, exclude); the proportion of national history (in relation to personal, local and global history); the different types of history (e.g. political, social, religious) to cover; and the perspectives from which to approach them. Yet including such a vast array of material may mean students lose sight of any coherent view of the past, and fail to see the patterns and structures that give history shape and meaning. This focus on content, however, represents a one-dimensional view of diversity. More recent discussions about diversity have explored the notion of diversity as a concept that provides teachers with a different sort of challenge, namely appreciating the dimensions of this concept and the nature of progression in students' understanding and ability to handle it.

Extract 1

Source

Bradshaw, M. (2009) Drilling down: How one history department is working towards progression in pupils' thinking about diversity across Years 7, 8 and 9. *Teaching History*, 135, 4–12.

Introduction

Although the importance of teaching about diversity in the past is widely acknowledged, its inclusion in the National Curriculum for England in 2008 as a concept explicitly labelled 'diversity' was a new step. For some, however, diversity is akin to the concept of 'similarity and difference', which was included in earlier versions of the curriculum. In this extract, Matthew Bradshaw reflects, as a head of department, on the challenges that this presents.

Key words & phrases

Diversity; historical content; National Curriculum; second-order concepts; pedagogy; progression

---

Extract

The 2008 National Curriculum for England refocused history teachers' attention on diversity. This was a wise move, as this curriculum also contains elements which could run counter to this. The 2008 curriculum could be said to encourage a more thematic approach to developing chronological understanding. While many departments, mine included, have moved away from the 'one damn thing after another' approach to history teaching, a thematic side-step could just as easily lead to new grand narratives being swallowed uncritically (whether this be the development of democracy, the role of imperialism or the development of war) and, with them, a renewed failure to appreciate or explore the intense diversity of the past.

When we turn to the National Curriculum (NC) itself for guidance, however, the detail of the statutory requirement is a slippery fish, difficult to introduce into a planning framework:

> 1.2 (a) Understanding the diverse experiences and ideas, beliefs and attitudes of men, women and children in past societies and how these have shaped the world.

Such a rubric leaves us with a requirement merely to include certain types of historical *content*. It is therefore important to turn to the NC Attainment Target where diversity is presented as an analytic lens on the past and here we get a sense of what pupils are expected to *do* with those 'diverse experiences, ideas, beliefs and attitudes'. In this context, it acquires the same status as other second-order concepts (such as historical change or causation) and it is clear that students are expected to *analyse and make judgements* about historical diversity. They are called upon to discern and establish the similarities and differences within past societies …

Enquiries where pupils actually have to investigate, think and draw conclusions about diversity are difficult to structure but incredibly rewarding. The challenge according to the NC Attainment Target is for students to assess both the *extent* and the *nature* of diversity. In one sense, judging the *extent* of diversity could be all too easy, as the past always contains infinite diversity even if we are limited by the sources in our powers to perceive it. But if our pupils are to attempt some sort of analysis beyond the obvious truism that people are infinitely diverse, we may find ourselves having to make it a little 'easier' for some of them. Even when planning the most complex diversity enquiry, we often have to compromise the amount of diversity to which students can be exposed. This is because throwing in *too* much diversity is likely to confuse those students who lack a sense of period or those students with whom we are still having to work very hard to secure essential chronological and narrative frameworks. A diversity enquiry might therefore be exciting for us as teachers, but a bridge too far for pupils …

So the challenge for history teachers is a complex pedagogic one as well as an historical one. We have to help students find some possible shapes, some tentative patterns which allow them to *see* the complexity and which, at the same time, begin to break that complexity down without losing it. We need to help them analyse in such a way that the complex colour and drama become more visible, more meaningful. This reveals the benefit of pupils trying to categorise or label the 'nature' or 'type' of diversity. Helping students engage in finding labels and working out how well (or badly) they fit various groups in various historical situations can involve students in building the story back up again and making it (temporarily) neat and tidy enough to hold in their heads. Having accepted that great diversity exists, they try to find or test categories that provide sense, meaning and clarity. This is not dissimilar to the work of a professional historian who works with many sources but reconstitutes them into descriptions and narratives which take account of diversity but which do not become lost in it. It is also an activity that can provide a rich sense of period, with the variety of the people and their diverse experiences paradoxically helping pupils to fix in their heads what is distinctive about that period (thoughtful work on 'diversity' can therefore help with perceiving historical change or continuity, too).

Clearly, therefore, simply presenting students with a huge amount of unstructured material to encourage them to consider diversity is likely to be counter-productive. We need to be explicit about the thinking we are after and the steps and stages which will help all pupils, gradually, to do that thinking for themselves.

Summary

Bradshaw identifies a number of issues relating to the teaching of diversity. While acknowledging that teaching a diverse range of content is important, diversity is more than this. He argues that diversity needs to be considered as a second-order concept involving processes of analysis and judgement. This, however, presents a number of challenges for both teachers and pupils. For example, there is the need to understand the conceptual nature of diversity more precisely – in this extract Bradshaw focuses on the idea of similarity and difference. There is also the need to understand what pupils will find difficult about diversity, such as finding the balance between over-simplifying and overcomplicating the past (see also Chapter 21 on issues of acceptable simplification). In the remainder of the article, Bradshaw goes on to explain how his history department builds in opportunities for pupils to develop a progressively more sophisticated awareness of diversity as a concept.

Questions to consider

1. Bradshaw makes the point that diversity is concerned with more than historical content. However, teaching diverse historical content is still important. What dimensions of diversity do you feel it is important to explore and why?
2. What do you feel are the challenges for teachers and pupils when it comes to understanding diversity as a concept?
3. What do you think it means to 'get better' at understanding diversity?

Extract 2

Source

Banks, J.A. (1989) Integrating the curriculum with ethnic content: Approaches and guidelines. In J. Banks and C. McGee Banks (eds) *Multicultural Education: Issues and perspectives.* Boston: Allyn and Bacon, 189–207.

Introduction

James Banks, an American educationalist, is one of the leading figures in the field of multicultural education. In this article he discusses the different ways in which multicultural content could be incorporated into the curriculum, and highlights the strengths and challenges of each approach, although it is clear that he regards some approaches as less beneficial overall. The following extract has been edited to include only the history-specific examples that Banks gives.

Key words & phrases

Diversity; multicultural; curriculum; curriculum model; purpose

---

Extract

Approaches	Examples	Strengths	Problems
Contributions	Famous Mexican-Americans are studied only during the week of Cinco de Mayo (May 5). Black Americans are studied during Black History Month in February but rarely during the rest of the year.	Provides a quick and relatively easy way to put ethnic content into the curriculum. Gives ethnic heroes visibility in the curriculum alongside mainstream heroes. Is popular among teachers and educators.	Results in a superficial understanding of ethnic cultures. Focuses on the life-styles and artifacts of ethnic groups and reinforces stereotypes and misconceptions. Mainstream criteria are used to select heroes and cultural elements for inclusion in the curriculum.
Additive	Adding a unit on the Japanese-American internment to a US history course without treating the Japanese in any other unit.	Makes it possible to add ethnic content to the curriculum without changing its structure, which requires substantial curriculum changes and staff development. Can be implemented within the existing curriculum structure.	Reinforces the idea that ethnic history and culture are not integral parts of US mainstream culture. Students view ethnic groups from Anglocentric and Eurocentric perspectives. Fails to help students understand how the dominant culture and ethnic cultures are interconnected and interrelated.
Transformation	A unit on the American Revolution describes the meaning of the revolution to Anglo revolutionaries, Anglo loyalists, Afro-Americans, Indians and the British.	Enables students to understand the complex ways in which diverse racial and cultural groups participated in the formation of US society and culture. Helps reduce racial and ethnic encapsulation. Enables diverse ethnic, racial, and religious groups to see their cultures, ethos, and perspectives in the school curriculum. Gives students a balanced view of the nature and development of US culture and society. Helps to empower victimized racial, ethnic, and cultural groups.	The implementation of this approach requires substantial curriculum revision, in-service training, and the identification and development of materials written from the perspectives of various racial and cultural groups. Staff development for the institutionalization of this approach must be continual and ongoing.

(Continued)

Approaches	Examples	Strengths	Problems
Decision Making and Social Action	A class studies prejudice and discrimination in their school and decides to take actions to improve race relations in the school. A class studies the treatment of ethnic groups in a local newspaper and writes a letter to the newspaper publisher suggesting ways that the treatment of ethnic minority groups in the newspaper should be improved.	Enables students to improve their thinking, value analysis, decision-making, and social-action skills. Enables students to improve their data-gathering skills. Helps students develop a sense of political efficacy. Helps students improve their skills to work in groups.	Requires a considerable amount of curriculum planning and materials identification. May be longer in duration than more traditional teaching units. May focus on problems and issues considered controversial by some members of the school staff and citizens of the community. Students may be able to take few meaningful actions that contribute to the resolution of the social issue of problem.

Summary

It is clear that Banks has a particular vision of education, in which the multicultural dimension is central to the curriculum and underpins all other aspects. History is seen as a crucial element in this system, and Banks has written at length elsewhere about the value of adopting a disciplinary approach to the study of historical topics. The intention is to ensure that students are well informed about the society in which they live and that they are able to appreciate the complexity of the past and to challenge the ways in which it is presented and interpreted. Within the decision-making curriculum model, there is an explicit citizenship element, as students are expected to use their knowledge and insights to bring about positive change and, in that sense, Banks is keen to use subjects such as history to empower young people. Banks does not see these curriculum models as being discrete and acknowledges that there may be a 'mixed economy'.

Questions to consider

1. Considering the models outlined above, which would you say most closely resembles the approach adopted in your context? Why has this particular approach been adopted? With which of these curriculum models would you be most comfortable and why?

2. What do you think are the aims of multicultural education and what would you want students to know, understand and do as a result of such education?

Extract 3

Source

Bracey, P., Gove-Humphries, A. and Jackson, D. (2011) Teaching diversity in the history classroom. In I. Davies (ed.) *Debates in History Teaching*. London: Routledge, 172–85.

Introduction

This chapter from the book *Debates in History Teaching* examines the development of diversity within the history curriculum in England, taking into account historical and contemporary issues, the relationship between diversity as a concept and as a principle of content selection, and the role of diversity in developing a 'big picture' of the past. Within this extract, the discussion is about taking diversity beyond a focus on ethnicity; too often diversity is equated to the history of minority ethnic groups, whereas in its fullest sense it embraces the full range of experiences of people in the past.

Key words & phrases

Diversity; historical content; second-order concepts; 'big picture' history

---

Extract

Diversity has also been related to the dynamics and nature of historical change. Byrom and Riley used multiple narratives to develop an understanding of the complexity of relationships between Islam and the West during both the period of the Crusades and the sixteenth and seventeenth centuries and used this as a model for planning a range of themes including 'Britain – the English Empire? (National Stories): Wales, Scotland and Ireland' and 'Moving Stories (Migration to and within): Prehistory', ' "The locals" – migration to the local area' and 'Multicultural Britain' (Byrom and Riley, 2007, p. 29)

Some writers have considered regional diversity within Britain's 'big story'. Corfield (2009) made reference to the diverse impact of the Norman invasion in 1066 and the arrival of William of Orange in 1688 made within England, Scotland, Wales and Ireland ....

There have been fewer publications and articles related to gender and class than ethnicity in recent years ... Nevertheless, Moorse and Claire (2007) provided useful guidelines which could be related to it. They recommend teaching young people through the use of sources and examples which reflected both men and women. As students progressed they argued that gender should be embedded into both what was taught, the full range of second order concepts and used to 'dig deep' into the social and gendered construction of the historical record.

Patel (1997) noted that social class had received little attention in recent years. Successive versions of the National Curriculum have required that different sections of society should be considered. Some history educators have focused on the implications of this for teaching about the working classes with respect to the selection of content. Claire (1996) argued that teaching ought to include opportunities to challenge the view that changes have always been made by rules and the powerful … Jackson (1998) argued that interpretations of nineteenth century working-class movements, such as the Chartists, as failures should be countered with those which related them to the struggle for political reform.

Summary

This extract shows diversity to be a complex idea. It has a conceptual element in that it relates to second-order concepts such as change and continuity. It has a role to play in building up a 'big picture' of the past and exploring the range of experiences within that broader view of the past. It also has a substantive element in terms of content to be taught, which should encompass the full range of human experience based not only on ethnicity but also gender and class.

Questions to consider

1. How does this view of diversity challenge, extend or reinforce your understanding of diversity?
2. To what extent do you feel within your own context that your curriculum reflects this broader view of diversity in terms of developing students' conceptual understanding and substantive knowledge?
3. What do you feel are the challenges of creating a curriculum that develops the view of diversity expressed above, and how might you overcome these challenges?

Investigations

Analysing textbooks and resources: Take a sample of classroom resources. Look at both the images/visuals used and the text/audio. To what extent do these present a diverse range of historical content (consider ethnicity, sexual orientation, gender, class, religion, geographic scale).

Exploring teachers' views on diversity: Working with a group of history teachers, ask them to write down their own definition of diversity, and also to explain what they see as progression in understanding diversity. What are the similarities and differences between their responses?

Exploring students' understanding of diversity: Ask a group of students to explain what they think is meant by diversity in history – do they see it simply as an issue of content? Get them to examine the extent to which they generalise about the past and then ask them to see if there are any examples that would challenge the general claims that they have made and so reflect a more diverse view of the past.

Think deeper

The past is inherently diverse, as it includes the history of different social groups, whether based on gender, ethnicity, sexual orientation, class or other characteristics. It follows that one way to address the question of diversity is to teach a more diverse range of content. This should not be done as a 'bolt on', which is often the criticism directed towards events such as Black history month or LGBT history month, but examples of diversity should be part of the 'background noise'. This requires teachers to have broad subject knowledge, so that they can draw on a range of examples as appropriate. Ian Grosvenor (2000) not only discusses some of the issues associated with adopting a multicultural perspective in the history curriculum, but also provides some useful ideas about how it can be done within commonly taught topics in the UK, such as the English Reformation and nineteenth-century political protest. Dan Lyndon (2006), a teacher in a London comprehensive school, has long advocated the 'mainstreaming' of black history, drip-feeding it into the curriculum at appropriate points, either through studying themes such as attitudes towards poverty (which would include Elizabethan views towards the Blackmoores); looking at key historic events such as the world wars and the role of black and Asian people in the war effort; or focusing on specific individuals such as William Cuffay. In Lyndon's experience this is a relatively straightforward way of diversifying the curriculum and has had the benefit of engaging students from minority ethnic backgrounds and helping to raise their attainment. Flora Wilson (2012) and Jo Pearson (2012) both offer suggestions about examining the role of women in history, which is an often neglected element of the curriculum. Wilson (2012) argues that it is imperative for teachers to develop their own historical subject knowledge, to build their confidence in what they teach, and to introduce intriguing stories into the classroom. For example, she uses the experiences of four women in the Spanish Civil War, two Spanish and two British, to examine the complex dimensions of people's experience in past conflicts. Pearson (2012) argues that teachers need to pay more attention to the criteria they use for selecting content. Drawing on work about historical significance she presents the case for paying far more attention to the actions, role and contribution of women in the past (see Chapter 9 on historical significance for debates about significance). Pearson's work does also suggest another way to integrate greater diversity into the curriculum by linking diversity to second-order concepts such as significance. The danger of simply introducing additional content is that a transmission model of teaching is adopted, which lacks challenge. Whereas an approach that combines different content with a rigorous conceptual challenge is likely to be engaging for students and provide a means for developing more sophisticated historical reasoning.

Teachers also need to be aware of the diversity of students in the classroom – in many ways, diversity overlaps with issues of inclusion. The need for engaging students from all backgrounds and providing intellectual challenge is crucial. There is plenty of data showing how students' background has a profound impact on their achievements in school. The reasons for this are complex, but one factor appears to be the content of the curriculum – if students are unable to see themselves reflected in the curriculum, it can seem less meaningful and irrelevant and so students feel excluded and become disengaged (see also Chapter 5 on history and identity for similar discussions).

Such concerns underpin a study by Veronica Boix-Mansilla (2001) who taught in an area of social deprivation in Harlem, New York, to students from a range of ethnic backgrounds. Teaching a unit on autobiography and history, she sought to 'help students place their personal life stories in the larger context of the social, political and cultural changes in America' (2001: 22). The course allowed students to revisit their personal lives through the discipline of history, which led to new personal insights and greater awareness of social, political and cultural issues.

Think wider

The challenge of addressing diversity seems to be deep-rooted. Discussions about diversifying the content of the curriculum have been taking place for decades, which suggests that only limited progress is being made. The examination results for many students from minority ethnic groups remain lower than those from the dominant social groups and, although results have improved, there is a gap in attainment between different ethnic and social groups that remains relatively consistent. This issue has been the focus of much research, and the following suggestions provide some uncomfortable but thought-provoking insights.

Explanations for the attainment gap are complex and often controversial. For example, David Gillborn (2008) uses Critical Race Theory (CRT) to examine the lower attainment of many black and Asian youngsters. CRT was developed in the US as a means of highlighting social injustice. It makes a number of assumptions that can challenge those of the dominant social group. It assumes that racism is endemic in society, not necessarily explicitly so, but the fact that the *de facto* way of viewing the world is from the perspective of the dominant social group implies that institutional racism exists. Gillborn's argument is that the lower attainment of certain ethnic groups is a sign of that institutional racism. Acknowledging that institutions are racist does not mean that individuals are racist, but it does require individuals to recognise the issues within an institution and then take action to remedy them. Using a CRT lens helps reveal how societal constructs such as school curricula are dominated by the majority perspective, yet this perspective is so pervasive that it becomes the norm and therefore invisible. Only by acknowledging that 'whiteness' generates a privileged position for particular groups within society, is it possible to understand the ways in which discrimination operates and thereby find ways to tackle it.

This is a particularly important issue for teachers, as the majority of them come from the dominant social group, and may be unaware of the ways in which many minority groups are disadvantaged by the 'system', and how their own background provides automatic privileges for them. These issues are explored by Sarah Pearce (2005) who draws upon her own experiences as a white teacher in a multicultural school environment; she explains her own feelings of inadequacy when teaching pupils from culturally different backgrounds and her own misconceptions about them. Pearce, who describes her background as mono-cultural, only really had to interact with people from other ethnic backgrounds when she started teaching in a primary school where 90 per cent of the pupils spoke English as an additional language, with a predominance of pupils from Pakistani and Bangladeshi backgrounds. She explores how her understanding of the needs of her pupils shifted as she came to realise how her own sense of 'whiteness' and her 'racial' identify influenced her conduct in the classroom.

Teachers need to be aware of their own preconceptions in relation to pupils from different ethnic backgrounds. Louise Archer (2008) argues that teachers' beliefs can have a powerfully detrimental effect on the achievement of young people from minority ethnic backgrounds. Drawing on four separate studies she analyses the discourse of 'success' amongst teachers, pupils and parents and the ways in which pupils are labelled by teachers. White middle-class pupils, who are seen as the 'ideal' pupil usually achieve good academic success, because they are expected and encouraged to aim high and work hard, while black and Muslim pupils who achieve average results are often seen as 'good enough' by the teachers who have lower expectations of them – a view that contrasts with that of the pupils themselves and that of their parents who recognise that they are failing to achieve their potential. Similarly teachers see the model female pupil as quiet and diligent, so black female students who see 'loudness' and speaking their minds as strength of character become 'demonised' in the eyes of teachers. Even pupils who are successful, such as Chinese students, are described by teachers as being too quiet, too passive and repressed, which Archer claims is seen as the 'wrong' sort of success.

References

Archer, L. (2008) The impossibility of minority ethnic educational 'success'? An examination of the discourses of teachers and pupils in British secondary school. *European Educational Research Journal*, 7 (1), 89–107.

Boix-Mansilla, V. (2001) Expecting high standards from inner-city students. In A. Dickinson, P. Gordon and P. Lee (eds) *Raising Standards in History Education: International review of history education, volume 3*. London: Woburn Press, 20–35.

Byrom, J. and Riley, M. (2007) Identity-shakers: Cultural encounters and the development of pupils' multiple identities. *Teaching History*, 127, 22–9.

Claire, H. (1996) *Reclaiming our Pasts: Equality and diversity in the primary school*. Stoke-on-Trent: Trentham Books.

Corfield, P. (2009) Teaching history's big pictures: Including continuity and change. *Teaching History*, 136, 53–9.

Gillborn, D. (2008) *Racism and Education: Coincidence or conspiracy?* London: Routledge.

Grosvenor, I. (2000) History for the nation: Multiculturalism and the teaching of history. In J. Arthur and R. Phillips (eds) *Issues in History Teaching*. London: Routledge, 148–58.

Jackson, T. (1998) History. In D. Hill and M. Cole (eds) *Promoting Equality in Secondary Schools*. London: Cassell, 135–6.

Lyndon, D. (2006) Integrating black British history into the National Curriculum. *Teaching History*, 122, 37–43.

Moorse, K. and Claire, H. (2007) History. In K. Myers, H. Taylor, H. Adler and D. Leonard (eds) *Gender Watch: Still watching* … Stoke-on-Trent: Trentham Books, 188–91.

Patel, L. (1997) History. In M. Cole, D. Hill and S. Sharanjeet (eds) *Promoting Equality in Primary Schools*. London: Cassell, 215–42.

Pearce, S. (2005) *You Wouldn't Understand: White teachers in multi-ethnic classrooms*. Stoke-on-Trent: Trentham Books.

Pearson, J. (2012) Where are we? The place of women in history curricula. *Teaching History*, 147, 47–52.

Wilson, F. (2012) Warrior queens, regal trade unionists and warring nurses: How my interest in what I don't teach has informed my teaching and enriched my students' learning. *Teaching History*, 146, 52–6.

Structuring learning in history

Historical enquiry

The notion of 'enquiry' is fundamental to the study of history. Indeed the title of the first work of history, written by Herodotus in the fifth century BCE was simply 'Enquiry' – the Greek word ' ἱστορία' or 'historia'. While his first motive was to ensure that 'the great deeds of men would not be forgotten' the *questions* he set out to answer were why the Greek city states came into conflict with the Persian Empire and why they were able to resist them. Although the idea of enquiry-based learning has deep roots in progressive and constructivist conceptions of learning, in history teaching the principle of structuring students' learning around a series of questions or enquiries that drives each unit of work was popularised in England by the series of Schools History Project textbooks published in response to the first National Curriculum. Many schools' schemes of work (and some public exam specifications) are now structured around a series of key questions.

Extract 1

Source

Riley, M. (2000) Into the Key Stage 3 history garden: Choosing and planting your enquiry questions. *Teaching History*, 99, 8–13.

Introduction

When the National Curriculum for England was revised (for the second time) in 2000, Michael Riley, who was then working as a local authority adviser helping schools to re-plan their schemes of work, wrote a highly influential article in an edition of the professional journal *Teaching History* dedicated to curriculum planning. Riley not only defined the key characteristics of an effective enquiry, but also illustrated how well-chosen and carefully crafted enquiry questions could be mapped out across the whole Key Stage 3 age range (11–14 years old) curriculum to achieve resonance and progression for students, as they revisited particular concepts and patterns of question type.

Key words & phrases

Enquiry questions; interest and imagination; historical thinking; historical concepts; substantial outcome activities; mystery; pith and puzzle; purpose; intellectual curiosity

---

Extract

Crafting the enquiry question

First, what makes an individual enquiry question a good one? Does each of your enquiry questions:

- capture the interest and imagination of your pupils?
- place an aspect of historical thinking, concept or process at the forefront of the pupils' minds?
- result in a tangible, lively, substantial, enjoyable 'outcome activity' (i.e. at the end of the lesson sequence) through which pupils can genuinely answer the enquiry question?

It is very easy for these criteria to conflict. For example, 'Why did medieval towns grow?' is certainly historically rigorous and would allow a strong learning focus to be placed upon change and/or causation as the organising idea for work on towns. But is it exciting? Will each teacher in your department be able to reiterate it with passion and mystery, lesson by lesson, as they lead pupils towards its resolution in a final concluding activity? Possibly not. It could, however, be converted into something more pithy, something with a more obvious puzzle element, that can be used to intrigue pupils and connect one set of facts with another. For example, the enquiry question might keep its historical scope, but gain more pith and puzzle by being worded in one of these ways:

EITHER

How much did towns matter in the Middle Ages?

It would be impossible to do this reasonably well, even with the least able of pupils, without placing some emphasis upon change during the medieval period. Admittedly, the change/cause focus is more implicit here, but the teacher will find it easier to build in learning devices that lead pupils to reflect on nuances and distinctions: towns clearly mattered to these people more than to these people; towns clearly did matter to these people, but they didn't realise it; towns clearly mattered more in this period than in this period, more in this region than in this region. The question carries within it the notion of to whom did towns 'matter'? and when? and why? There is much meat and potential detail here for the more able, and many entry points for the less able ...

OR

When were the turning points in the development of medieval towns?
This would shift teachers' content selection into examples of the impact of domestic and international trade, and many other factors. Pupils could be set all kinds of mini-problems, with given criteria, to wrestle with the idea of what constitutes a 'turning point' and what does not.

But town growth may still not be that thrilling. What other big historical ideas, concepts or themes might enliven a study of medieval towns? A question like 'Did the towns make people free?' pushes a study of the towns into a new area of historical learning. Teachers need a question that places all the grind through guilds and apprentices and masters and rules about the sale of mouldy fish into a very clear context – a specific and intriguing learning journey. Towns were supposed to make you 'free' weren't they? ... Start delving into town life and all kinds of rules and restrictions and customs start to abound – all kinds of rules, rules to make you safe, rules to make you free, rules to make some people privileged, rules to keep some people out, rules to encourage some people in ...? So just how 'free' were the townspeople? What did 'freedom' mean, then, anyway? ...

Whatever your focus, clearly a question like 'What was life like in the towns?' or 'How did people live in the towns?' is just not of the same order. Many PGCE students are now trained right from the outset to sniff out such weak questions. We need to be clear about what exactly is wrong with them. Such a question is merely descriptive. Quite apart from the fact that it is far from intriguing and will leave neither lower nor higher attainers buzzing with intellectual curiosity and excitement, it is just not historically rigorous. It does not take you into an understanding of the way history works. It says nothing about the status of the information that will render it history. It is in danger of drifting into mere antiquarianism.

Summary

All three features of Riley's checklist for identifying a good enquiry question need to be addressed simultaneously. It is no good capturing students' interest and imagination, tempting them with an intriguing mystery, if the question they are seeking to answer is not sufficiently rigorous, clearly rooted in the key historical concepts and processes. Nor is it enough to provide a tantalising hook, a real puzzle to solve, if students never actually develop a substantial and well-substantiated answer to the question. Good questions work effectively for students working at very different levels of attainment, allowing scope for more nuanced and developed argument.

Questions to consider

1. Why does Riley put so much emphasis on creating a sense of puzzle and intrigue? How might you begin to provoke students' curiosity about medieval towns?
2. What historical concepts would students address in tackling the question 'Did towns make you free'? Would this question allow you to address the issues that you think it is important for 11–12-year-old students to learn about medieval towns?
3. Why is Riley so critical of purely descriptive questions that ask, for example, 'What was life like in the towns?' Do you think his concern about them is justified?

Extract 2

Source

Dawson, I. (2009) *Developing Enquiry Skills.* Available at: www.thinkinghistory.co.uk/ EnquirySkill/Index.html (accessed 23 May 2013).

Introduction

Ian Dawson, who (like Riley) has served as Director of the Schools History Project and written numerous textbooks, endorses the same principle of using enquiries to plan systematically for students' progression within and across all stages of their history education, building not just their conceptual understanding as they revisit different types of question but also their capacity to draw comparisons and make links across time. In this article he explains what the enquiry process involves and why it is so valuable, before going on to demonstrate how good enquiry questions can be used to structure learning for public exams at 16+ and 18+ just as effectively as for lower secondary age students.

Key words & phrases

Historical enquiry; conceptual understanding; map of the past; process of enquiry; formulating and testing hypotheses; evidence; purpose; problem-solving; transferable skills

---

Extract

Why is historical enquiry important?

One major reason is that it provides continuity across history courses, from primary to university level. Students often find history difficult because they constantly feel they're starting again. They see the surface details and think each new topic is different because it features new or mostly new names, dates, places etc. This camouflage prevents students realising that they can use what they've learned before to help them with a new topic. Therefore we need to help students realise that what they learned in Year 7 is useful in Year 8 and even in Years 10 and 12.

Several elements contribute to how we do this:

a) developing conceptual understandings so that, for example, students use sources more effectively as evidence as they mature.

b) building knowledge and understanding of the map of the past so that, for example, students are better able to compare and contrast events, periods and individuals, making those elusive links across time and developing a sense of period.

c) and perhaps even more fundamentally, understanding how we go about the process of enquiry, being able to move from knowing nothing or next to nothing about a topic to having a satisfying grasp of the issues and being able to answer questions about it with confidence – be they informal oral questions or demanding written exam questions. Students can then use this explicit process as a template when faced with other enquiries on other topics.

So what is the process of enquiry? This has doubtless been the subject of much learned debate but I'm afraid that has passed me by. My pragmatic definition is along the lines of:

'question – hypothesis – use of evidence to test the hypothesis – reformulation of hypothesis'

and so on, repeating the last two stages for as long as time and patience allow.

This short description could be debated and occasionally teachers at courses have debated it, asserting that this pattern is 'wrong' in some way or begins with the 'wrong' item. However, over-prescriptive precision can get in the way of a broadly useful idea. I agree that sometimes we begin with a question, at others with evidence or contextual information that inspires a question – these are variations on the theme. What's far more important is that there's a readily comprehensible sequence of activity that students can explicitly describe, apply and continue to apply as their history studies continue – and which helps them tackle their history more effectively and more confidently.

Apart from its centrality to the study of history, enquiry is also important because it's at the heart of arguments about the value of studying history. Explicit focus on enquiry helps students, parents and school management see one of the important benefits of studying history – thinking and planning a way through a problem, asking questions, undertaking research, independent thinking, making judgments, and effective communication. This is all the more important given the findings in the research of Richard Harris and Terry Haydn (2008), which concludes that 'large numbers of [pupils] have a limited grasp of the intended purposes of a historical education' (p. 47) [For another extract from this research see Chapter 4 on pupil perspectives on history education] …

If we are to make significant in-roads on students' ideas about the purposes of studying history then it seems essential to make clear the process of enquiry and its transferability to the world outside the classroom. Enquiry encompasses how to go about problem-solving, independent and team-driven research, identifying relevant evidence and evaluating its reliability, moving from tentative to firmer conclusions on the basis of that evidence and finally reaching a judgement and knowing how certain that judgement is, balancing the arguments for and against. These are widely transferable skills, both in the contexts of individuals and teamwork – and developed in history in the most important context of all, the actions and motives of real, individual people.

Summary

One of the benefits that Dawson claims for an approach to planning built around enquiry questions is that it builds students' confidence. Because they understand the process of posing questions, formulating and testing hypotheses using evidence and successively refining their ideas, they can approach new topics with assurance, knowing exactly how they need to tackle them. While enquiry is central to history, engagement in thinking and planning their way through a problem, assessing the weight of competing claims and communicating their judgements effectively also gives students important skills that are prized far beyond the history classroom.

Questions to consider

1. Is the template that Dawson outlines one that you think could indeed be used with students of all ages?
2. What risks, if any, do you think might be associated with adopting this kind of approach to your planning and teaching?
3. How far do you agree with Dawson's claim that the enquiry model in history is one that can be readily transferred to problem-solving in the world beyond the classroom? If these skills are indeed transferable to other contexts, does that suggest that they could be developed equally well elsewhere?

Extract 3

Source

Barton, K. and Levstik, L. (2004) *Teaching History for the Common Good*. Mahwah, NJ: Lawrence Erlbuam Associates; see pp. 188–91.

Introduction

While most advocates of an enquiry-based approach to teaching history base their argument on an appeal to the practice of professional historians, the American researchers and history educators Keith Barton and Linda Levstik declare that they 'do not believe that history's contribution to participatory democracy depends on teaching students how historians as a professional community go about their investigations' (p. 187). Instead, their defence of 'inquiry' rests on its compatibility with constructivist understandings of the nature of learning, its capacity to reduce educational inequalities and the opportunities it creates for meaningful communication.

Key words & phrases

Inquiry; participatory democracy; constructivism; conceptual understanding; engagement; educational differences; deliberation; transparency

---

Extract

The process of inquiry can contribute to a humanistic study of history – and to participatory democracy in at least three important ways. The first seems somewhat obvious, but it bears stating explicitly: People learn through inquiry. The process of gathering evidence to reach conclusions about important questions matches contemporary theories of human learning in which people are seen as active constructors of meaning. Given the match between inquiry as an instructional process and constructivism as a theoretical model, we can expect students will know more if they have engaged in inquiry than if they have filled in worksheets in pursuit of grades, stickers or teachers' praise. Having said that, though, we must point out that there are no comprehensive investigations of the superiority of inquiry as a form of learning in history: that is, there are no large-scale experiments in which students in some classrooms are rewarded for correctly mastering information related to the Civil War, while those in other rooms take part in inquiry-based investigations into the same subject. Indeed such experiments probably are not possible, because what counts as knowledge in behaviourist and constructivist classrooms differs – retention of factual information in one case, judgments and conceptual understanding in the other ... When we say that people learn through inquiry, then, we mean that inquiry is an approach consistent with current theory and research on human learning. When understanding is needed, inquiry appears to be one of the best ways to get there ...

Moreover, by engaging students in the process of knowledge construction, inquiry has the potential to spread historical knowledge more equitably ... Children begin to learn about history from a very young age, but what they learn may be heavily influenced by the settings in which they grow up

– African–American students, for example, do not always learn the same information and perspectives as those from European backgrounds … [These] initial perspectives may influence children's engagement with the content of the curriculum: African American and White students do not always come away from their history lessons with the same ideas.

… [I]f inquiry can live up to its potential as a means of engaging students in the construction of knowledge, the impact of these initial differences may be lessened. By allowing students to pursue their own investigations and reach their own conclusions, inquiry should enable those whose experiences have not traditionally been represented in the official curriculum to deepen and expand their historical understanding rather than simply to remain distanced from school history. Meanwhile, because inquiry can engage students with a variety of sources of evidence, those whose understandings have traditionally been privileged may be more likely to encounter conflicting perspectives that force them to question their beliefs. Again, at this point there is little empirical evidence that this is so; we can only suggest that one possible advantage of enquiry is that through its use, all students will be positioned to develop a more complete and nuanced understanding of history and that this understanding may be more equitably distributed …

This brings us to the third principal advantage of inquiry. It gives us something to talk about … [T]he kind of pluralistic democracy we envision depends on deliberation among equals in pursuit of shared knowledge and understanding. Without inquiry, this kind of communication is unlikely to take place, because the sources of knowledge and belief are either hidden or unquestioned. If attempts at discussion simply pit the knowledge some people have gained from their authorities and tradition against the knowledge others have gained from their authorities and tradition, the encounter is unlikely to result in meaningful communication or shared knowledge – more likely the result will be frustration and hostility … However, inquiry makes the process of knowledge construction more transparent. By laying out questions, evidence and conclusions (and the links among them) in clear view, inquiry allows ideas to be challenged without attacking anyone's identity or belief system.

Summary

An approach to learning history that makes the process of knowledge construction explicit to students has three major advantages. The first is that it is consistent with constructivist theories of learning and thus is likely to promote conceptual understanding. The second is that it reduces the impact of different levels of prior knowledge and diverse perspectives, making history education more equitable. The third is that it promotes genuine communication and deliberation on the basis of shared evidence rather than sterile appeal to competing authorities.

Questions to consider

1. Barton and Levstik acknowledge that there have been no large-scale empirical studies demonstrating the superiority of enquiry-based approaches to history teaching. Is it right to endorse enquiry-based approaches without such evidence? Do you think there are ways in which the claims about enquiry-based approaches could be, or have been, tested in practice?
2. Do you agree with the suggestion that an enquiry-based approach offers a more equitable approach to learning history, or is it one that squanders the intellectual resources that certain students already possess?
3. Does the principle of making knowledge construction transparent mean that students *always* need to study the evidence for claims that are made about the past?

Investigations

Experiment with different ways of provoking students' own questions: Burnham (whose work is discussed in the 'Think deeper' section below) concluded that of the different strategies she had used, role-playing the part of an Islamic physician in the Middle Ages proved to be the most accessible, prompting all students to suggest questions. Hammond (also in 'Think deeper' section) began with a simple database of medieval kings, which provoked excellent questions about causation but far fewer about change. Try experimenting with different kinds of stimulus and with inviting students to pose or refine their questions at different stages within a scheme of work.

Find out what historical questions, if any, your students would most like answered: Most teachers who invite students to frame their own questions do so within the context of a predefined curriculum focus. What kinds of questions (if any) would your students be most interested to answer if they were given free rein, as Barton and Levstik think they sometimes should? What scope might you have to address them and how valuable do you think it would be to do so?

Explore the recurring patterns (if any) that your students perceive within the history curriculum: If your current curriculum is already mapped out in terms of key questions that drive sequences of learning, what evidence is there (or could you gather) to examine its impact on (1) students' understanding of the processes involved in formulating, testing and refining an answer to a question; (2) students' recognition of the second-order concepts addressed with the questions and the way in which they are gradually building their understanding of these; and (3) students' assumptions about the value of studying history?

Think deeper

Barton and Levstik's claims in Extract 3 about the potential of enquiry to create a more equitable distribution of knowledge depend not merely on students being given the opportunity to *answer* significant questions about the past. It is also of critical importance to their argument about the contribution of history education to a pluralist, participatory democracy that students should be given the chance to frame their own historical questions. This means allowing them to pursue the questions that matter to them in the present: questions, for example, about American involvement in Vietnam, an issue that continues to haunt foreign policy and public debate in the United States. But it does not mean restricting their enquiry to those historical questions that students already have when they enter the classroom. The task for teachers is to provide students with genuinely stimulating resources about significant past events, thereby arousing their interest and provoking worthwhile and meaningful questions from them.

This use of well-chosen sources to prompt questions from the students was also acknowledged by Dawson, but it has, for obvious reasons, been teachers rather than textbook writers who have actually begun to explore what it might mean to allow students to ask their own questions, and how such a process can possibly be managed. Independent investigations have, of course, long played a part in history teaching and assessment at A level (for students aged 16–18), and Sally Burnham's (2007) interest in asking her class of 11–12-year olds to ask their own questions was borne out of frustration at the inability of her 17-year-old students to frame good historical enquiries for their coursework. Recognising that if this was an important skill for historians she ought to be developing it throughout their history education, she decided to allow her Year 7 to join her in planning the enquiry questions that would structure their scheme of work on Islamic civilisations. Her first step was to help the students distinguish between 'big' and 'little' questions related to their previous study of medieval history, before offering several kinds of stimulus in turn – maps, a role play, visual sources and written descriptions – to generate questions for the new topic. The pupils then worked in groups, not only to plan and sequence the questions that they judged most interesting and worthwhile, but also to ensure that they addressed the key aspects of the topic that they would need to cover. The final scheme of work was developed by Burnham drawing on planning grids produced by the students working in groups, with each of them able to identify where their questions had been used. Burnham was sufficiently convinced of the value of the strategy to repeat it in Year 8, building on the process by inviting the students to evaluate and, if necessary, adjust the questions in light of the available resources.

Robin Conway (2011: 51), with similar ambitions for students to be able to 'devise outcomes themselves' and 'assess the effectiveness of those objectives as a means of deepening their learning', explains in detail how his department learned to manage the complex process of inviting 13–14-year-old students not merely to frame their own enquiry questions but also to plan the scheme of work (determining which aspects they could research themselves and where they would need explicit teacher input), and to determine the format of their final response to the question, including the success criteria by which it should be judged. His article, which shows how the department's approach evolved over a number of years, illustrates the importance of the ways in which the teachers and not merely the students learned to evaluate and refine what they were doing, drawing on the principles of assessment for learning.

Another teacher, Kate Hammond (2011), inspired by Burnham's work and the fact that the key process of 'historical enquiry' set out in the 2008 National Curriculum in England expected students to 'identify and investigate, individually and as part of a team, specific historical questions or issues', was working very deliberately with the intention of equipping her students to act as 'apprentice historians' and was very keen to learn about how to develop students' independence in working in this way. In order to plan for progression, she drew on the practice of profession historians alongside recent government guidance about the promotion of Personal Learning and Thinking Skills (PLTS) to generate a list of 11 attributes that might characterise the work of a student successfully undertaking professional enquiry. This list formed the basis of discussion and debate with her colleagues, allowing them to identify and address immediate priorities, one of which remained that of helping students to frame good enquiry questions. Hammond felt that judging the value of questions as Burnham had done simply by categorising them as 'big' or 'little' was insufficient, and she focused on helping them to identify the historical concepts that lay at their heart. While she too began by using initial stimulus material to generate questions, a very small-scale experiment undertaken with her students aged 15–16 suggested that giving students an opportunity to refine their questions as they gained more substantive knowledge tended to result in questions with a 'sharper focus and a fresh energy about them', as well as greater 'meatiness' – calling for 'more thought, more research and more analysis' (2011: 50). A second attribute explored in the article is that of determining 'when enough is enough' (2011: 46). Hammond explains the strategies that she used to help 12–13-year-old students to explore the issue and apply their ideas in relation to a study of nineteenth-century factory conditions, determining when they had sufficient evidence to accept a particular hypothesis.

Think wider

Barton and Levstik trace their view of 'inquiry' back to the work of the American educational philosopher John Dewey (1910: 5), who argued that, while beliefs about what is true might be based on whole variety of foundations (such as tradition, authority or the imitation of others), important beliefs ought to be grounded in evidence, resulting from 'conscious inquiry into the nature, conditions and bearings of the belief'. This requires engagement in what Dewey called reflective thought: 'active, persistent and careful consideration of any belief or supposed form of knowledge in light of the grounds that support it, and the further conclusions to which it tends' (1910: 6). Dewey's ideas not only offer a model of the enquiry process entirely consistent with the definition outlined by Dawson in Extract 2 – a process of identifying and defining the problem, hypothesising alternative solutions and testing them to see which best match the evidence – they also help to explain why the process of generating questions is so important to successful enquiries. According to Dewey, the process always begins with a problem – a 'felt difficulty' or 'some perplexity, confusion or doubt' (1910: 12). Trying to get someone to engage in reflective thinking without there being any genuine puzzle is, he suggests, as futile as telling them to lift themselves up by their own bootstraps. It is precisely their interest in resolving the problem that provides 'the steadying and guiding factor in the entire process of reflection' (1910: 11).

While Dewey thus focuses attention on the starting point of any enquiry, Mike Gorman (1998), who is generally credited (see Counsell 2011) with the first explicit statement of what was meant by an enquiry question within history curriculum planning, focused as much attention on the processes by which students might record their findings and communicate their judgements. Written in the language of the second version of the National Curriculum for England published in 1995, his article draws attention to the essential interplay between what were then 'Key Elements 4 and 5', which required pupils: (4) to 'investigate independently aspects of the periods studied' by using and evaluating a range of sources, recording relevant information and reaching conclusions; and (5) to 'recall, select and organise historical information' in order to be able to communicate their knowledge and understanding of history, 'using a range of techniques, including extended narratives and descriptions, and substantiated explanations' (DfEE 1995: 11). In addition to outlining a wide variety of ways in which students might capture data relevant to their questions, Gorman also identifies the value of the requirement to provide a final answer – a 'worthwhile resolution, albeit one albeit one that is full of tentative and provisional conclusions' (Gorman 1998: 25). Not only can the eventual goal – which might also take a wide variety of forms (including advertisements, instruction manuals, film storyboards, theme park designs, board games, debates, TV show formats, diagrams or role plays as well as various forms of extended writing) – serve to motivate students and guide their planning, the process of sharing what they have learned with others also plays a fundamental role in securing and reinforcing their knowledge and understanding.

Counsell (2011) draws on the work of Gorman and Riley and the teachers whom they inspired to illustrate the nature of teachers' own practical theorising as they have wrestled with the challenges of developing disciplinary rigour for all students within the context of successive National Curriculum specifications. As she points out, the development of historical enquiries, in which students actually set out to answer meaningful and worthwhile historical questions, represented a concerted response to the sterility and artificiality of the 'sourcework' widely practised in classrooms in the early 1990s. Counsell outlines a variety of causes for this problem and highlights the damage that it did, not merely boring pupils with 'mechanical tasks rehearsing formulaic responses to snippets from sources' (Hamer 1990: 24), but als creating conceptual confusing by conflating 'source' and evidence'. (See Ashby 2011 in Extract 2 of Chapter 8 on evidence.) While the history inspectorate drew attention to the problem, Counsell (2011: 204–5) argues that the work of reconstructing 'sourcework' fell to teachers, achieved in large part through the development of an enquiry-based approach, of the kind inspired and exemplified by Gorman (1998) and Riley (2000) (see Extract 1):

What occurred in the late 1990s and early 2000s was a gradual, collective reconstruction of classroom source use. Although by no means universal, what is noteworthy is the capacity of teachers to discern problems, to generate solutions for nurturing evidential thinking and to give these currency through public discussion.

Her argument is that the development and refinement of teachers' practice through such examples, whether presented as published articles or shared through websites and workshops, reflects the coherence and power of teachers' professional discourse that should not be overlooked by curriculum reformers.

Another seminal article in the development of the use of over-arching enquiry questions to drive a scheme of work was written by Dale Banham (2000) a head of department (and textbook author), who courted controversy by deciding to devote eight weeks of curriculum time to a study of King John, addressing the question 'Was John really a bad king?' to determine whether he really deserved his reputation as one of Britain's 'worst ever' monarchs. The rationale that he offered was based not merely on a defence of the place of depth study – a detailed focus allowing students to develop familiarity with the fundamental features of a particular period, and to engage effectively with the way in which interpretations are created – but also on the powerful impact of a careful blending of overview and depth. This blending took a variety of forms, both *within* the depth study itself with focus questions such as 'Did King John ever have a chance?' guiding students to examine what was expected of medieval monarchs, as well as the specific problems that he inherited from his father, and through the *subsequent*, much shorter comparative enquiries that it made possible. The detailed enquiry into the assumed failings of highly controversial medieval monarch, vulnerable to the demands of his barons and unable to defend the empire he inherited, served as powerful motivation for students to address the wide-ranging questions that his reign had made meaningful to them: Were kings still in charge at the end of the Middle Ages? Did any other king ever win back his lost empire? The hypotheses to be tested in this case could be presented by an irascible king on his death-bed, fearful that the greedy barons would claw more power away from subsequent monarchs and arrogant enough to assume that if even he had failed to re-capture the lost territories, no future monarch would be able to do so.

References

Banham, D. (2000) The return of King John: Using depth to strengthen overview in the teaching of political change. *Teaching History*, 99, 22–31.

Burnham, S. (2007) Getting Year 7 to set their own questions about the Islamic Empire, 600–1600. *Teaching History*, 128, 11–17.

Conway, R. (2011) Owning their learning: Using 'assessment for learning' to help students assume responsibility for planning, (some) teaching and evaluation. *Teaching History*, 144, 51–7.

Counsell, C. (2011): Disciplinary knowledge for all, the secondary history curriculum and history teachers' achievement. *Curriculum Journal*, 22 (2), 201–25.

Dewey, J. (1910) *How We Think*. New York: Heath.

DfEE (1995) *History in the National Curriculum: England*. London: HMSO.

Gorman, M. (1998) The structured enquiry is not a contradiction in terms: Focused teaching for independent learning. *Teaching History*, 92, 20–5.

Hamer, J. (1990) Ofsted and history in schools. *The Historian*, 53, 24–5.

Hammond, K. (2011) Pupil-led historical enquiry: What might this actually be? *Teaching History*, 144, 44–50.

Harris, R. and Haydn, T. (2008) Children's ideas about school history and why they matter. *Teaching History*, 132, 40–9.

Literacy and oracy

Language is fundamental to the study of history and therefore developing language, and an understanding of language is central to history teaching. Language is not only the medium by which an interpretation of the past is most often conveyed, but it is also the source of our understanding in written and spoken historical evidence. It is through choice of language that our understanding of the past can be nuanced and given strength. Focusing on historians' or contemporaries' careful choice of words can help us gain a new level of understanding. However, the changing nature and meaning of language can cause difficulties for students in the history classroom. The need for precise selection of appropriate language when communicating about the past can add another layer of challenge. These extracts focus on three aspects of language. The first sets out definitions of language within the discipline of history; the second gives examples of how pupils might be helped to engage with the complex language of a historian; the third focuses on the development of students' spoken language in the history classroom.

Extract 1

Source

Husbands, C. (1996) *What Is History Teaching? Language, ideas and meaning in learning about the past.* Buckingham: Open University Press; see pp. 30–42.

Introduction

This is an extract from a general but seminal text in history education. It is a book that brings language to the forefront of learning history. Chris Husbands points out that while some historians and history teachers suggest that history is 'riven with linguistic difficulty', others argue that history has 'no specialist language' (p. 30) since it is a subject linked so closely with human experience. Here he highlights some of the aspects of historical language that might prove challenging for students and suggests initial ways of approaching such challenges in the classroom.

Key words & phrases

Historical language; expression; historical process; organising principles; concept of time; historical interpretation; teacher talk; pupil talk

---

Extract

Historical language, of course, has several quite distinct components; it refers to the ways in which we make sense of how people in the past expressed their actions thoughts and beliefs, but it also refers to the ways in which historians have tried to describe the historical processes which those people experienced and shaped. This in turn involves considering both the way historians use difficult, abstract concepts and the way in which they use what I want to call the *organizing principles* of the subject. By this I mean the ideas of causation, similarity, difference, continuity and so on which we draw on to give shape, meaning and structure to our interpretations of the past ...

Historians frequently use language in ways which are far from literal or immediately straightforward, or in ways which create difficulties for learners. As Edwards [1978] has pointed out, these characteristics of history drag the subject always towards higher levels of abstraction in its use of language. Talk about the past is full of metaphor, generalization and concepts which we use in often shifting ways ...

A further aspect of historians' language is the language of the organizing principles of history. The language of time and of change and of historical description is an easily taken for granted element of historical knowledge. The language of time – year, century, millennium, era – is difficult for many pupils because of their own limited experience of time. Historians use the language and concept of time for more than to calibrate the sequencing of events. The idea of chronology and sequencing is meaningless in isolation; it becomes an element in the construction of knowledge about the past when it provides a framework for organizing ideas about historical change, historical causation and consequence ...

There is a language of historical interpretation and debate which shapes understanding in ways which may be unanticipated. The language we use to describe past events may validate some interpretations of them and, if only implicitly, rule out others. Indians, for example, do not describe the events of 1857 as an 'Indian Mutiny'. The difficulties we have with these words present real problems for language and its use in the classroom: shall we call the Indian Mutiny a 'mutiny'? Will we describe the events of 1640–1660 as a civil war or a revolution?

All of this suggests that the linguistic difficulty of history is also what we can call an interpretive and epistemological difficulty: the way we describe the past also expresses a series of interpretations of it and the way we understand the past is inseparable from the way we know the past. These sorts of linguistic difficulty pose real problems in the classroom, but they are compounded because the typical encounter with them is not single, but multiple. Concepts, ideas and historical language spill into each other at high speed. This is true of even relatively simple sentences. The statement 'In 1642 a Civil War broke out between King and Parliament' assumes grasp of a dating convention, familiarity with the concept of a Civil War ... and some understanding of the nature of kingship and role of Parliament in seventeenth-century England ...

Teachers need through their own talk to be aware of the interpretive nature of language, to understand that the language of history and the language of historical description are fuzzy and to use the opportunities they have for explaining and communicating to provide their pupils with opportunities to understand these aspects of language. Pupil talk is important, too, for the opportunities it gives pupils to explore language in the context of the history classroom: was this a 'civil war' or a 'revolution' is as important a question for pupils to discuss as 'what do you think were the causes of ...'

Summary

Husbands raises important points about the use of language in the history classroom, first concerning the changing meaning of some words over time and then the use of language by historians in the creation of historical interpretations. In the years since this book was written it has become more common to place such issues at the centre of historical enquiry, planning a lesson or series of lessons around what a word or concept might mean in this instance or exploring why particular words of interpretation might have been used at a specific point in time (see Counsell 2004 in Extract 2 for examples). The language associated with concepts of change and causation has also been used more explicitly in helping students develop their writing skills in the history classroom. Woodcock (2005) is a particularly useful example of such practice (see Chapter 13 on causal reasoning, 'Think wider' section).

Questions to consider

1. What are the challenges your history students face with regard to language? What strategies do you have in place to overcome such difficulties?

2. Husbands highlights the language of historical interpretation and gives the example of Indians not describing the events of 1857 as an 'Indian Mutiny'. What are other examples of controversial terms within the topics you teach? How should such terms be introduced to your students?

3. How aware are you of the language your students use to discuss the past? Is there a relationship between the precision of student talk and the language they use for writing? How could you develop the quality and precision of students' language in talking about the past?

Extract 2

Source

Counsell, C. (2004) *History and Literacy in Year 7: Building the lesson around the text.* London: Hodder Murray; see pp. 1 and 107–13.

Introduction

This extract comes from a book aimed at history teachers, that is full of innovative ideas and activities for developing literacy and history in tandem. Counsell aims to build the lesson around the text and supports the use of longer texts by 11–12-year-old pupils provided that they are supported to understand and use such texts. Counsell stresses the importance, in history, of doing more with a text than simply reading for information. In these activities, centred around *Medieval Women* by Eileen Power (1975), Counsell gets the students first to listen for tone and style and then to imitate some of Power's literary devices in their own use of evidence.

Key words & phrases

Style and tone; analytic vocabulary; collaborative writing; evidential information; argument

---

Extract

Why 'reading for information' just won't do

[A] genuinely *historical* question will launch the search for a historically significant conclusion, allowing pupils to see – if not actually to carry out – aspects of the knowledge-construction process. This may require attention to the status of the text as evidence or as interpretation, to the author's deliberate *choice* of detail from a myriad of accurate details, or to the qualifying, speculative language in which a narrative or a problem of historical causation clothes itself.

How does Eileen Power let us know what she thinks?

In Activity 22, pupils listen to a passage from Eileen Power's book read aloud without a copy of the text in front of them. They comment on the changes in style and tone that they can hear. They see the text only at the end of the activity, after oral work has made them both ready and curious to read it.

Activity 23 is closely linked. Having heard Eileen Power, and having acquired an analytic vocabulary for talking about her style, they attempt to borrow an aspect of her style in a collaborative writing exercise. To help them with their writing, they receive a mixture of source extracts and pieces of evidential information that Eileen Power herself uses in one section of her book. This is part of their 'Eileen Power kit'.

The two activities are closely linked, the first making the second possible. Moreover, each activity has a central feature in common – almost all of the activity is designed *to prepare* pupils to meet a demanding text by a real historian. In each case, pupils only actually read the text right at the end of the activity sequence, *when they are ready*.

Understanding the rationale for the activity

In deliberate contrast to the kind of activity that asks pupils to 'read for information', pupils are here explicitly asked to listen for style and tone, and so engage with something of the subtext. To begin with, they are simply helped to *feel* the force of the argument, rather than to do anything particularly analytical with it. This has the effect of making the tricky words less of a problem. If we read the passage well, the energy of the text can be used like a powerful wave that washes away the distraction of small confusions.

The reading aloud also forces pupils to listen and to tune into rhythms and cadences in the writing. Carefully structured exercises help to give pupils a listening agenda. The listening part of the activity comes in three stages so that pupils build confidence with the text, steadily. These stages, each with its own mini-plenary, give the teacher opportunity to monitor pupil response, to check that understanding really is being achieved and to re-teach as necessary ....

Writing in Eileen Power's style using the Eileen Power kit

Understanding the rationale for the activity

Having listened to Eileen Power's voice, pupils are now ready to develop their thinking about the characteristics of her style by experimenting with some imitation. This activity involves pupils in collaborative writing using the same sources and evidential information that Eileen Power used .... Once again, the bulk of the activity involves *preparation* for reading the text. But the additional challenge this time is to notice the wide range of conventions, many of them vivid, for integrating reference to the evidential record smoothly into the prose. Here, pupils are required to borrow not only some features of Power's style explored in Activity 22, but also to experiment with conventions for integrating sources ....

Summary

This short extract comes from a very detailed chapter that includes a much longer justification and explanation of such activities, as well as resources and precise notes on how to use them in the classroom – well worth reading in full if you intend using the work of historians in your own classroom. The message in this extract is clear, however. If students are to improve their own written work in the history classroom, they need to be exposed to the articulate and opinionated work of real historians, exploring how claims are constructed and testing how tentative claims are. Exposure should, however, be careful and structured. It would be simply too much to give an 11-year-old an extract from a historian and ask them to read and understand it. Various activities can be used to explore style and tone and then encourage some limited imitation of the historian as a way of preparing the students to understand the actual text and how it has been constructed.

Questions to consider

1. What challenges does extended writing present for your students across the ability range? Counsell helps students deconstruct longer, challenging texts as one way of helping them write independently and at length. What strategies do you have in place to help your students both engage with and make progress in their historical writing?

2. How do you use modelling as a teaching strategy in the history classroom? How might you use a historian's work as a model for your students? Which historian would you choose and why?

3. Reading the work of a historian is often a challenge for students aged 11–14. What strategies does Counsell suggest for supporting students *before* they actually get the chance to read the text? Would these strategies be suitable for your students? What other strategies could you use?

Extract 3

Source

Fullard, G. and Dacey, K. (2008) Holistic assessment through speaking and listening: An experiment with causal reasoning and evidential thinking in Year 8. *Teaching History*, 131, 25–9.

Introduction

Giles Fullard and Kate Dacey wanted to move away from purely written assessment with their 12–13-year-old students. At the same time they wanted to help them integrate their understanding of cause and evidence. They decided to plan a series of debates around the English Civil War that would focus on speaking, argument and listening. The results are intriguing as, although many students responded very well to the opportunity to use evidence and debate, Fullard and Dacey found that those who struggled with marshalling evidence in written form also struggled in this oral format.

Extract

For a long time our history department believed in the primacy of writing as the greatest test of a student's ability in history. Whilst other subjects moved towards ever-shorter responses we ploughed the furrow of the essay. Although we still see this as important, its limits became ever more obvious. We therefore tried to think of ways to access students' extended thinking on a different basis but with the same academic rigour as before. Speaking and listening seemed to provide part of the answer.

After many years of trying to teach argument through writing, another tactic was needed. According to Clark (2001), speaking and listening forces students 'to feel the need to build an argument'. In his rationale for speaking and listening activities, Luff argues, 'any student capable of absorbing and marshalling ideas quickly will always be at an advantage in a written assessment carried out under pressure of time' (2001, p.11). Luff suggests that, over time, speaking and listening tasks may well enable students to develop their ideas more fully in their writing. Such tasks put pressure on students to think carefully about the validity of other arguments in order to counter them effectively. Additionally, we felt that such a task might secure some of our wider educational goals – it would build an ethos of co-operation among our students, fostering an awareness of and respect for others' opinions whilst feeling free to take these apart.

What we wanted to avoid was mere lip service to the listening element. Sometimes, there is little difference between writing an essay and delivering a pre-planned speech. It was the process of listening to an argument and assessing its relative strengths and weaknesses that we were keen to develop. Even in ordinary group work, students can avoid deep listening. Cohen's (1994) systematic study of group work points out, 'there is a tendency for members to be so concerned about saying their piece that they don't listen to what someone has just said'. For this reason we decided, early on, that students would be assessed on all aspects of their performance from what they had written in preparation to notes that they took during others' contributions.

Having selected the seventeenth-century 'English' Civil War – a subject that naturally lent itself to debate – we developed a sequence of three, linked mini-enquiries, each culminating in a debate which would be accessible to a mixed–ability Year 8 class. Each mini-enquiry within the scheme led up to, and enabled students to engage with, its concluding debate. This debate, along with the preparatory work, provided the evidence of historical thinking on which students were assessed. The three enquiry questions were:

- Why was there a Civil War in 1642?
- How far do you agree with the view that the Civil War was, 'fought by a minority in a sea of apathy and neutrality'?
- Why did Parliament win the Civil War?

The debate itself forms only one part of the material to be assessed. A planning sheet and observation notes also form part of the evidence ....

To some extent we embarked on this project on the basis that some of our students were put off history by the amount of written work. We wanted to provide them with a way in which they could explore their ideas without the pressure of an essay. One limitation we found, however, is that those students who struggle with marshalling their ideas in a written assessment, struggled in exactly the same way with our speaking and listening assessment. The fact that students still struggled with the issues that they struggled with before gives us a greater insight into what those problems are. This process has therefore been diagnostically significant for our department. Perhaps we started this with a simplistic division between written assessment and speaking and listening. Speaking and listening is not 'the answer'; rather, it is part of the answer to the problem of assessment.

Summary

This example of small-scale practitioner research in the reality of a history department raises some interesting questions. The authors identified two problems facing their students – the challenge of constant written assignments and the difficulty of combining the ideas of cause and evidence. The results they share here are not final or conclusive. However, they have explored the possibility of oral debate as a form of assessment in the history classroom and are prepared to make further changes to help their students develop their skills in this area. The detailed planning of the debate is perhaps of particular importance as it seems to produce more structured, prepared responses than a similar ad hoc debate. Using a different form of assessment helped the authors to notice that students were struggling, not just with writing, but with marshalling their ideas. In order to get better at writing, or better at arguing, the students need help to get better at selecting, organising and deploying their ideas.

Questions to consider

1. What opportunities do your students have for oral assessment in the history classroom? Should such assessments carry the same weighting as written assessments? How might you overcome the challenge of getting lots of students involved while still being able to assess and moderate their work effectively?
2. To what extent do the same students struggle in organising structured oral work and structured written work in your history lessons? What historical thinking

needs to take place before students can form such structure? What strategies could be put in place to support your students with the necessary thought processes?

3. Fullard and Dacey emphasise the importance of listening in this research, asking pupils to listen carefully to the argument of their peers and to use this to inform their own position. How might you place more of an emphasis on listening in your own classroom to enable the construction of more sophisticated argument?

Investigations

Carry out an audit: How does your history department view the relationship between literacy and history? How do you go about supporting the development of literacy? Use schemes of work, conversations with department teachers, scrutinies of student work and existing observations to analyse the way literacy is currently approached. Could this approach be developed to enhance the study of history in the department? What strategies and resources would need to be put in place this term, this year, next year? How might the department benefit from this new approach?

Introduce modelling: Create opportunities for your students to read the work of opinionated historians. Help them to unpick both what the historian has written and the way that they have written it for effect. Create a toolkit for this historian, similar to the Eileen Power toolkit described above. Let your students use the toolkit to see if they can write in the style of this particular historian. Evaluate the impact that this process has on your students' subsequent writing.

Help students to listen: Ask someone to observe you teach and focus on the way talk is used in your classroom. Come up with strategies to move beyond initiation-response-evaluation formats. Explain to your students that you want them to listen to each other's points and include consideration of those points in their own answers. Praise those who manage to do so. Ask the same person (or the students) to complete a similar observation schedule. Has the pattern of talk changed in the class?

Think deeper

Caroline Coffin (2006) has undertaken research from a linguistic perspective to explore the way students of history use language to write, think about and conceptualise the past. This book focuses on the discourse that takes place in secondary schools, examining the kinds of texts that students are required to read and write across their time in school. Interviews and a study of comments in student books were used to explore what teachers expect and value in student reading and writing. Team-teaching approaches were used to trial a language-based model of teaching history. Coffin considers three purposes of writing about the past – recording, explaining and arguing about past events – and shows how these purposes require different text structures and different uses of vocabulary and grammar. She also explains how successful students develop a repertoire of linguistic resources for constructing different types of causal explanation as they move through secondary school. This research highlights some of the linguistic challenges involved in teaching history, but through such a close analysis offers constructive ways forward.

Grant Bage (2000) comments on the 'textual balance' that history offers, between building on the familiar and exploring the strange. He emphasises the need for teachers to use real historical sources and texts in order to promote textual variety. He points out that learning history is not just about decoding semantic texts, but that it involves the learner in decoding big ideas about cultures from small fragments of evidence. He argues that becoming literate through history therefore involves reading words, sentences and texts, but extends into reading artefacts, arts, cultures and self.

There has been a recent refocusing on the importance of narrative in writing history. Sean Lang (2003) points to the way it has tended to be devalued by examination markschemes that reward analysis and mark down description. He suggests that constructing narrative does involve 'knowledge transformation' and that a good narrative is incredibly challenging to write. Dave Martin and Beth Brooke (2002) give some suggestions towards helping students write historical fiction, which is one form of narrative that involves knowledge transformation. The range of strategies and ideas in the article and in a textbook emerging from the project, *Write Your Own Roman Story* (Martin et al. 2001), shows that rather than encouraging ahistorical, imagination-based pieces, it is possible to get students writing rigorous, evidence-based historical fiction that demonstrates a deep understanding of a particular period.

Think wider

Through recent research into secondary students' compositional writing processes Debra Myhill (2009) has found different students have different composing patterns. This article, which looks at the broader spectrum of writing in the secondary school, holds many interesting points for history teachers. It explains the three processes of planning, translating and reviewing that occur when writing takes place and suggests that these processes are not necessarily linear. The research used close observation of student actions – writing and pausing – during ten minutes of writing task, followed by interviews with the writing students and the piece of writing they composed. Myhill suggests that 'flow writers' who take few pauses when writing may be using a strategy that enables composition, but not the shaping of that composition for purpose and effect, which are crucial in the history classroom. She suggests that such writers might need greater support for later drafting and revision. Equally, the dominant pattern of stop-start writers, where writers paused to generate the next idea, might be a productive process, but these writers may need further support in advance planning or sophisticated revision – two strategies that are common in the history classroom, but not necessarily differentiated towards the students who might need them most. A final point of the article is the metacognitive awareness of writing for students – who tend to be encouraged to focus on the writing produced rather than the process they are going through when writing. Being aware of different styles of writer in the history classroom may enable a more individualised approach to support.

Linda Levstik and Keith Barton (2001) warn that much classroom talk follows an initiation-response-evaluation format that isn't particularly realistic. Instead they offer some suggestions on how to promote reasoned, evidence-based discussion in the history classroom. Choice of topic was crucial, as not all controversies were worth discussion or would lead to evidence-based historical discussion. Giving sufficient resources, both primary and secondary, to students led to higher quality discussion. Small group background work was more effective than initial individual work in promoting discussion as it gave students a richer array of background information to draw on and a beginning understanding of different perspectives on the topic.

The work of Neil Mercer (1995) provides interesting insights into the ways in which students talk to each other. Drawing upon extensive classroom recordings of pupils talking to each other in groups, Mercer has identified three main forms of classroom discussion that he calls cumulative, disputational and exploratory. In cumulative discussions students readily agree with each other and alternative ideas are not explored; although it may be productive in allowing students to get work done, it does little to extend potential insights. Disputational talk, on the other hand, is characterised by disagreement. In this situation, students hold entrenched positions and do not listen to the points being made by someone else. Exploratory talk, however, is seen as the most effective for promoting higher level thinking. In this situation students explore a range of possible ideas, the reasons behind each, before deciding on a course of action or a position on an issue. Exploratory talk is characterised by plenty of questions, such as 'why', 'what do you think', 'can you explain your view', with the expectation that everyone needs to be open to challenge. Mercer stresses the connection between talk and thinking, and essentially argues that students need to be taught to talk and interact in particular ways, in order to improve the quality of thinking. His research has shown that the promotion of exploratory talk can lead to much higher levels of attainment for a wide range of students. His work also offers practical ways of establishing exploratory talk in the classroom; essentially students have to take ownership of the process by identifying their own ground rules for classroom discourse.

References

Bage, G. (2000) *Thinking History 4–14: Teaching, learning, curricula and communities*. London: RoutledgeFalmer.

Clark, V. (2001) Illuminating the shadow: Making progress happen in causal thinking through speaking and listening. *Teaching History*, 105, 26–33.

Coffin, C. (2006) *Historical Discourse: The language of time, cause and evaluation*. London: Continuum.

Cohen, E. G. (1994) *Designing Groupwork: Strategies for the heterogenous classroom*. New York: Teachers College Press.

Edwards, A. (1978) The 'language of history' and the communication of historical knowledge. In A. Dickinson and P. Lee (eds) *History Teaching and Historical Understanding*. London: Heinemann, 54–71.

Lang, S. (2003) Narrative: The under-rated skill. *Teaching History*, 110, 8–17.

Levstik, L. and Barton, K. (2001) *Doing History: Investigating with children in elementary and middle schools*. Mahwah, NJ: Lawrence Erlbaum Associates.

Luff, I. (2001) Beyond 'I speak, you listen, boy!' Exploring diversity of attitudes and experiences through speaking and listening. *Teaching History*, 105, 10–18.

Martin, D. and Brooke, B. (2002) Getting personal: Making effective use of historical fiction in the history classroom. *Teaching History*, 108, 30–5.

Martin, D., Brooke, B. and Dawson, I. (2001) *Write Your Own Roman Story: Pupil's Book, This is History Series*, London: Hodder Education.

Mercer, N. (1995) *The Guided Construction of Knowledge: Talk amongst teachers and learners.* Clevedon: Multilingual Matters.

Myhill, D. (2009) Children's patterns of composition and their reflections on their composing processes. *British Educational Research Journal*, 35 (1), 47–64.

Power, E. (1975) *Medieval Women* (ed. Postam, E. E.). Cambridge: Cambridge University Press.

Progression

The notion of 'progression' as distinct from 'progress' has tended to be used by history education researchers and classroom practitioners seeking a more holistic view of development in students' historical thinking or understanding than the mere accumulation of specific items of factual knowledge. Indeed, the most extensive programme of research in the UK into the development of children's understanding of history, conducted by Denis Shemilt and Peter Lee in association with various colleagues, has its origins in the evaluation of the Schools Council History Project (Shemilt 1980), which sought to promote students' understanding of history as a particular form of knowledge. As the extracts in this chapter reveal, seeking to account for the development of conceptual understanding (of both of the structure of historical accounts and the processes by which they are constructed) without neglecting the substantive content that remains fundamental to any claim to knowledge, is necessarily a complex process. Research-based models of progression, which seek to account for development in relation to a range of different concepts, and which describe general patterns in students' responses rather than predicting individual learning trajectories, are extremely useful both in curriculum planning and diagnosis of particular misconceptions. However, they often conflict with national assessment systems that tend to demand simpler measures of students' learning and pay less attention to different forms of knowledge. (The issues explored in this chapter thus have strong links both with Chapter 19 on assessment, and with debates about the role and nature of knowledge in learning history explored in Chapter 2.)

Extract 1

Source

Lee, P. and Shemilt, D. (2003) A scaffold, not a cage: Progression and progression models in history. *Teaching History*, 113, 13–23.

Introduction

Project CHATA (Concepts of History and Teaching Approaches), which built on the insights into children's conceptual development in Shemilt's (1980) original Schools Council History Project evaluation, sought to map changes in students' ideas about history between the ages of seven and fourteen. Different aspects of the findings have been published in a range of collections, but the article from which this extract comes was the first in a series of articles specially commissioned by *Teaching History* to make them easily available to practising teachers. (Several of the others are cited in the chapters related to students' understanding of particular second-order concepts, such as change and empathy, and further details are given below.) While this particular article includes a focus on students' understanding of evidence – how we come to know about the past – it also explains the nature of research-based progression models and how they differ from the National Curriculum attainment target that was then in use in England as a measure of students' achievement. While the authors do not claim that any model is perfect, they explore ways in which models based on empirical research – rather than on educational expediency – can be genuinely useful in understanding how to move students forward in their historical understanding, particularly by identifying and clarifying the misconceptions that hold them back.

Key words & phrases

Progress; progression; aggregation; development; more powerful idea; preconceptions; misconceptions; counter-intuitive; progression models; inductive categories

---

Extract

What is progression?

Pupils can make progress in any area of history, whether it is in keeping better notes, writing better essays, or giving better presentations to the class. But what counts as 'better' is likely to differ considerably for different activities. Better notes will probably mean a higher degree of organization and quicker retrieval. Better essays will involve (among other things) clearer structure and greater sensitivity to the question. Better presentations will mean stronger engagement with audiences and more acute judgement of what must be explained ....

The relatively recent appearance of another word – 'progression' – hints that we sometimes want to talk about something rather different from a general notion of progress. 'Progression' was juxtaposed with 'aggregation' to emphasize that progress in history could be more than an increase in the amount of information pupils could recall: learning history was not just learning 'one damn thing after another'. Research suggested that children's ideas about history and about the past changed as they grew older and that it was possible to view these changes in terms of development ....

Progression as acquiring more powerful ideas

The common sense idea that we can only really know what we witness ourselves makes history a dubious proposition for many children. Once young children start to wonder how we know about the past (rather than taking it as given) they often assume that we can't know anything 'because no-one was there in them days'. For pupils who believe this history is a non-starter. Of course many students soon recognize that people who did witness events may have left reports of what they saw, and so history becomes possible once more. Unfortunately, testimony has its own problems: children know that we don't always tell the truth and adolescents are only too aware that we can slant our stories of what happened for ulterior motives. History is once again revealed as a highly suspect activity. But as they begin to grasp that we can ask questions of sources that they were not intended to answer, pupils come to see how 'bias' is not the disaster they thought it was and that historians can operate successfully without being dependent on reports. The later ideas in this series are more powerful than the earlier ones in that whereas the earlier ones bring history to a grinding halt, the later ideas allow it to go on. In this way progression is the acquisition of more powerful ideas.

What are progression models?

If key historical concepts are counter-intuitive, it is clearly important to understand students' preconceptions (Bransford et al. 1999). In mapping the 'ideas' students are likely to hold about history as a discipline, a progression model is, of course, uncovering students' prior conceptions. Understanding such prior conceptions is essential if our teaching is to correct misconceptions or to build on students' ideas.

... Models of progression ... derive from research employing inductive categories to pick out broad divisions of ideas in children's responses to tasks, but they also owe much to the early days of SHP [Schools Council History Project] analysis of examination responses, which added considerably to our knowledge of children's ideas.

Progression models grounded in research do not, like the National Curriculum attainment target, simply combine complex ideas into a single target, and then cut it into an arbitrary number of convenient slices. Nor can they fall back on the conceptual crudity of generic and imprecise language like 'simple', 'begin to' and 'show some independence' as a substitute for identification of important shifts in understanding. Moreover, because there is some research evidence that students' ideas are decoupled – so that, for example, a student's ideas about evidence may remain the same while his or her ideas about historical accounts are changing quite rapidly – it is a mistake to try to bundle progression in different concepts together (Lee and Ashby, 2000). We must therefore construct separate models for key concepts like 'change', 'evidence', 'accounts', 'cause' and 'empathy'.

... The 'levels' in a progression model are not a sequence of ladder-like rungs that every student must step on as he or she climbs. Indeed, a model of the development of students' ideas does not set out a learning path for individuals at all. Assuming it is well founded, it is valid for groups, not for individuals. That is, it sets out the ideas likely to be found in any reasonably large group of children, the likely distribution of those ideas among students of different ages, and the pattern of developing ideas we might expect.

A progression model can therefore help us to predict the range of ideas we are likely to encounter, and the kind of changes we are likely to see as students' ideas develop. But a model gives no warrant for the kind of 'stagism' that says that if a pupil is in year nine, he or she must be at level 'n', and even less to the assumption that the next move the pupil must make is to level 'n + 1'.

Summary

While students can make 'progress' in many different aspects of history, including the aggregation of more information, the idea of 'progression' is used to mean the development of more powerful ideas about history. The idea, for example, that particular sources can be used as unwitting testimony – by asking questions of them that they were not intended to answer – moves students beyond the problem that biased sources cannot be useful in finding out about the past. Models of progression, based on inductive analysis to discern patterns of ideas in large collections of students' responses, are particularly useful for identifying the kind of misconceptions about history that students are likely to hold. Since the understanding of one second-order concept (such as evidence) does not develop in parallel with others (such as change or causation) separate models need to be created for *each* of the different concepts regarded as important in historical understanding.

Questions to consider

1. How do you think your students understand the notion of progression in history? How do you help them to understand the range of different elements that are combined in developing more powerful historical thinking?
2. The idea of using progression models as a means of identifying likely misconceptions might be seen as a rather negative approach to learning. How could you use it productively to guide your planning, without restricting your expectations of students' achievements?
3. Lee and Shemilt are highly critical of models that combine students' abilities to use different ideas into a single target. What are the implications of the finding that students' ideas about different concepts in history are 'decoupled' – both when it comes both to curriculum planning and when assessing and reporting on students' progress?

Extract 2

Source

Vermeulen, E. (2000) What is progress in history? *Teaching History*, 98, 35–41.

Introduction

The article from which this extract is taken presents the reflections of a newly qualified teacher, examining a wide range of research and research literature in the light of her early classroom experiences. Recognising that historical understanding is necessarily complex because of its dependence on the interplay between propositional, procedural and conceptual knowledge, Evelyn Vermeulen seeks to build a workable definition of progression to inform her planning and her interpretation of students' thinking as revealed in what they say and do. Progression is certainly not something that happens naturally; it has to be initiated and secured through the deliberate, active interventions of the history teacher to move pupils on.

Key words & phrases

Judgement; possibility thinking; hypothesis testing; confidence; doubt; framing questions; propositional knowledge; procedural knowledge; conceptual knowledge; interplay; complexity

Extract

History is a derivative of the Greek *historia* or 'judgement'. If we reject the notion of history as the 'archaeology of truth' as unpalatable in the postmodern era, then we are left with seeing history as the exercise of judgement, in which our judgement is the best possible, rather than the truth. We judge why William won the battle of Hastings, or whether Cromwell was a tyrant or an idealist. Prior to that we make judgements about which evidence to use and how best to use it; post hoc we make judgements about how best to express our theories. Progress in history must mean to 'get better' at making those judgements.

Using a single word ('judgement') might imply that the discipline is simple. Nothing is further from the truth. A single judgement in itself requires at least three characteristics of Piaget's formal operational reasoning: possibility thinking, the ability to generate and test hypotheses and the ability to think in purely propositional terms (Shemilt, 1980). The answering of an historical question demands a whole series of such judgements, each building on and taking account of the preceding ones. In addition, flexibility of mind is required to acknowledge that a previous judgement may be wrong. The ability to balance confidence with doubt, in fact, to have the confidence to doubt, is therefore crucial. Equally vital is the ability to frame the questions that invite our doubt and judgement in.

The ability to make these judgements rests on the interplay between what Rogers (1978) has termed the 'forms of knowledge'. He argues that any form of knowledge has a three-fold character: the propositional (know-that), the procedural (know-how) and the conceptual (both of these together) ....

… Children need both propositional and procedural knowledge, but must ultimately rely on the interplay between them. The question is, therefore, how one characterises the progression journey. For a teacher to isolate supposed skills and to test these in isolation, as some choose to do using the National Curriculum [NC] Level Descriptions, may not secure progress at all. The more aware children are of integrated historical processes, the more rapid progress is likely to be ….

The complexity of history as a discipline means that any description of what constitutes progress is likely to be caught in a trap between the dangers of extremes: over-simplification or confusion. Moreover, it is never a discipline in a vacuum; rather, it is engaged in through a whole range of individual filters and experiences, which will affect how the knowledge and the skills are framed. Progress may be expressed as the increasing ability to utilise the grammar of history independently, something that calls for a consciousness of what history is on the part of both pupils and teachers. If teachers do not think for themselves about progression frameworks, analysing both the discipline and pupils' learning in relation to it, they will just accept stages and hierarchies hopelessly filtered and diluted by NC levels or GCSE mark schemes. This could cause pupils to miss out on the full excitement and challenge of properly assessed progress that will provide access to demanding work.

Summary

Although Vermeulen recognises that getting better at history depends on students' understanding of, and ability to integrate, three different kinds of knowledge (propositional, procedural and conceptual), she suggests that these can all be compassed in the idea of making judgements. This central idea gives clarity of focus to her planning, and clearly indicates that historical knowledge is the result of a process of interpretation. However, since the application of judgement occurs at several stages in the process, and requires the revisiting of earlier, provisional, conclusions it is also sufficiently flexible to accommodate the different kinds of thinking that history demands. The notion of judgement also holds the different components together, rather than breaking them into separate 'skills' that make little sense, particularly to students, in isolation. Vermeulen is adamant that all teachers need to engage in the same kind of theorising as she has done examining the discipline of history themselves, alongside research literature, rather than merely accepting what are often arbitrary distinctions within national assessment systems.

Questions to consider

1. How useful do you find the idea of getting better at 'making judgements' as a summary of progression in history? Are there any important aspects that you think may not be adequately represented by this idea?
2. What are the potential benefits and drawbacks of seeking to focus at different times on particular aspects of conceptual understanding, rather than consistently emphasising their interconnections?

3. Vermeulen thinks that it is extremely important for teachers to think critically about any models of progression presented to them – interrogating them in light of their understanding of the discipline of history, and their experience of students' learning. Why do you think she regards this as so important? How appropriate do you think it is for teachers (even those with relatively little experience) to adopt this kind of critical approach to established assessment schemes?

Extract 3

Source

Counsell, C. (2000) Historical knowledge and historical skills: A distracting dichotomy. In J. Arthur and R. Phillips (eds) *Issues in History Teaching*. London: Routledge, 54–71.

Introduction

One of the unintended, but highly damaging, effects of the 'new history' movement (discussed by Rogers in Extract 1, Chapter 2) was a tendency among some of its enthusiastic supporters to assume that propositional knowledge ('know that') was of far less importance than conceptual or procedural knowledge (often referred to as 'skills'). Although the essential interplay between different kinds of knowledge has been repeatedly re-affirmed by its original advocates, the complex nature of that interplay, and fears that specified content might be interpreted merely as given 'facts' to be learned by rote, mean that there has been relatively little discussion of the role of substantive knowledge in securing progression. In the article from which this extract is taken, the history educator Christine Counsell highlights the need to redress this balance.

Key words & phrases

Historical knowledge; progression; fingertip knowledge; residual knowledge; sense of period; overview; depth

---

Extract

One result of the uneasy status of historical knowledge in history-teaching discourse has been the lack of thorough, shared professional debate about the function of knowledge in progression. Most general guides on progression refer to such things as 'expanding knowledge and understanding of the past' (Grosvenor and Watts 1995: 25) but how one bit of knowledge might contribute to another is not an area about which teachers and authors have theorised in depth. Even having acknowledged that knowledge might be important in some way, most commentators fall back on hierarchies of skill with which to define progression.

… If teachers can shake off assumptions that historical knowledge consists of neutral, value-free atomised pieces of information to be learned and, instead, see knowledge as a cumulative process of active critical construction, it will be timely to theorise about the function of knowledge in securing learning across longer time-scales.

… One very helpful distinction is that between the temporary or 'working' knowledge that pupils build up during a detailed study, and the broader and lasting understandings such as broad chronological awareness, awareness of institutional structures or cultural values of a period. The first might be called 'fingertip' knowledge. It is the kind of detail that one needs in ready memory and that is acquired through familiarity after extensive enquiry. It does not matter if much of the detail then falls away. The second type can be likened to the residue in a sieve. It is not just the ability to remember that the Tudors came before the Stuarts and that they used Parliament a lot. It is also that loose, amorphous objective of 'a sense of period' – the retention of all manner of mental furniture, gleaned from a rich visual and active experience of period stories and scenes. Such a residue is bound to enrich current and future study by preventing anachronism and sharpening judgment, even after the particular stories and scenes have long receded.

… That is why it is essential to think of knowledge in the context of medium- and long-term planning. What professionals need is a language for describing such knowledge for the purposes of planning. It is rather meaningless to state (although we do it all the time), that the objective is 'By the end of this lesson pupils will have gained knowledge of Henry VIII's wives' or '… of the Act of Supremacy'. What matters is the teacher's awareness of the *role of that knowledge in future learning* – the types and layers of knowledge that will endure and the types that will function as temporary working knowledge, the details of which will quite naturally and properly fall through the sieve. This defines and delineates the amount or type of knowledge the teaching is trying to deal with. Lesson objectives are more helpful when they indicate the proposed function of the knowledge area within wider planning. Words like 'anticipate', 'revisit', 'prepare for' tell us much more about the layer of knowledge being worked on – the teacher's rationale for its specificity or generality.

… Coming to know is a valuable experience in its own right but it may be a different thing from the concomitant awareness that results and endures. A study in depth in Year 8 or Year 10 is valuable in its own right for the opportunities that in-depth knowledge gives, allowing the pupil, for example, to examine sources closely and critically. Yet 'overview' understandings probably lurk in every depth study. The paradox that needs to inform the planning of school history is that pupils do not necessarily acquire 'overview' knowledge by doing 'overviews'. This is why it is essential to distinguish between curriculum outcomes and teaching processes. Although it may seem logical to 'teach the pupil an overview' if one wants an 'overview' it is not that simple. 'Depth' knowledge, memorable and thrilling in its period detail, creates certain kinds of overview knowledge. In turn, overview understandings might support pupils' work in a depth study. It is likely to be the *interplay* of 'depth' and 'overview' components within a work-scheme that is critical to quality, not their mere incidence (Riley 1997; Counsell 1998).

Summary

Counsell draws an important distinction between temporary (working) knowledge and enduring (residual) knowledge, acknowledging that while certain details will, quite rightly, be lost from memory, the rich insights into particular periods that they make possible will be retained. She urges teachers to pay more systematic attention to the way in which topics are sequenced across the curriculum in order to build, revisit and gradually enhance students' understanding of substantive issues and recurring themes (and the ways in which they change over time). Her argument about the way in which vivid and thrilling insights, gained through detailed study of particular topics or individual stories, can contribute to enduring understandings presents an important challenge to Hirsch's call for much more extensive use of survey courses (see Extract 2, Chapter 2), although Hirsch too recognises the need for some 'intensive' depth studies.

Questions to consider

1. How feasible do you think it would be to develop models of progression in which substantive knowledge is effectively integrated with other kinds of conceptual and procedural understanding? Do you think this could be done in terms of general 'levels' of understanding, or only in the context of specified topics?
2. How would thinking about the future uses of knowledge that students are developing impact on the way in which you planned lessons and how your learning objectives were expressed?
3. What kinds of strategies can you use to ensure that knowledge you are seeking to develop as a foundation for future learning is preserved in students' memories and can be readily accessed?

Investigations

Compare the assumptions about progression made by different series of textbooks: Focus on a particular second-order concept (such as change or continuity). In what specific ways do successive textbooks in an age-related series seek to build on students' prior understandings and seek to develop more powerful ideas when these concepts are re-visited?

Develop your own departmental vision of the highest levels of achievement in school history: Work together with colleagues – as they did at the National

Academy for Gifted and Talented Youth (discussed in the 'Think deeper' section below) – to develop a description of the highest levels of achievement to which you think students could aspire. You might begin by debating the sources on which such a description should be based: what importance should be ascribed to National Curriculum statements, public exam criteria, the practices of academic historians? How does your description compare with students' conceptions of high-level achievement?

Explore the misconceptions that your students hold: Experiment with planning lessons at the beginning of new topics or enquiries explicitly designed to elicit students' prior understandings and possible misconceptions about particular (substantive or 'second-order') concepts. How does this awareness inform and sharpen your planning for students' progress in subsequent lessons?

Think deeper

As noted above, the original Schools Council History Project evaluation (Shemilt 1980) marks the beginning of a rich tradition of empirical research into the patterns of thinking demonstrated by students, and the ways in which they change in response to more or less explicit teaching about the second-order concepts that underpin the construction of historical narratives and explanations. Other early accounts of aspects of this work, explaining the research methods as well as the key findings can be found in collections edited by Dickinson, Lee and Rogers (1984) and by Portal (1987). A good introduction to the later investigations conducted as part of Project CHATA can found in Lee, Ashby and Dickinson (1996). The series commissioned by *Teaching History* that distils key findings of these projects for teachers includes other articles on progression in students' understanding of historical accounts (Lee and Shemilt 2004) causal explanation (Lee and Shemilt 2009), empathy (Lee and Shemilt 2011), change and continuity and chronology (Blow 2011; Blow, Lee and Shemilt 2012).

In an article based on regular in-service training sessions that she had run for teachers, Counsell (2000) draws a powerful contrast between a lively and engaging activity used essentially in isolation, and the *same* activity carefully located, not merely within a challenging enquiry, but as part of a well-planned developmental sequence focused on securing progression in students' evidential understanding. The deliberately partial and complex collection of sources that she has assembled about experiences during the Blitz (all written by women and taken either from letters and diary entries written at the time or from interviews given to a women's magazine in the 1990s), are intended not to generate superficial conclusions or sweeping generalisations by forcing students to make premature judgements, but to raise a lot of complex problems quickly, informed by an understanding of likely misconceptions. The enquiry question, 'Why is it difficult to tell if there was a "Blitz Spirit"?' sharpens the conceptual focus on evidential understanding, and helps to highlight the importance of drawing on specific substantive knowledge about the Second World War, such as government policies and the role of Winston Churchill in raising morale. Counsell concludes the article with more specific proposals about where this enquiry might fit in a longer term planning for progression, suggesting exactly what students in Year 7 (aged 11–12) might be taught about using evidence and what the same students should then be taught in Year 8 (aged 12–13).

One potentially fruitful way of thinking about progression is to explore the characteristics of the very highest levels of historical understanding and then analyse how the features of that kind of reasoning and the dispositions that reflect and underpin it can be actively nurtured. This approach is obviously very different from the kind of inductive reasoning that researchers have used to make sense of the different types or levels of understanding that groups of students actually demonstrate but – particularly if the ideas about high levels of thinking are rooted in the actual practice of experts (i.e. historians) – it offers a very useful starting point for curriculum planning and creative thinking about the kinds of ideas that students need to work with and the sorts of opportunities and challenges that they need to encounter. In 2005, the National Academy for Gifted and Talented Youth brought together 25 highly experienced history practitioners, including classroom teachers, heads of department, academic historians and history teacher educators, to describe what they thought were the characteristics of the highest achievement in school history, and to suggest how they could be nurtured (Chapman 2005). The length and variety of the list of characteristics that they generated not only exemplify the complex interplay of different kinds of knowledge in historical learning, but also highlight the need for sophisticated linguistic skills and the ability both to contextualise specific information and sources and to work at a level of abstraction, drawing comparisons and thinking analogically. Mastering and integrating so many different aspects of knowledge and understanding calls for learners who are excited and intrigued by historical puzzles; who are as capable of framing useful questions as they are of generating and testing hypotheses; and who recognise and embrace the tentative and provisional nature of the judgements that they make. This would suggest that students' affective dispositions towards the subject – their enjoyment of history and their attitudes in the face of challenge or uncertainty – are perhaps as important to cultivate as their cognitive abilities.

While planning for progression obviously needs to inform curriculum design, it also needs to be considered in relation to the needs of diverse students within a particular class. Kate Hammond (1999) offers a very thoughtful reflection on a short series of lessons that she taught to a class of 11–12 year olds, explaining and evaluating the strategies that she used to try to ensure that Joe, a very high-achieving student, was enabled to extend the range of his substantive knowledge and deepen his conceptual understanding without the need for entirely different learning experiences that would risk isolating him from his peers. She adopted a variety of approaches to differentiation at different stages in the sequence, informed by careful analysis of her objectives for all students and consideration of the ways in which any additional substantive knowledge that Joe might gain needed to be *used* in the construction of more powerful explanation or argument. Just as important as the examples that Hammond shares is her rigorous reflection on their strengths and limitations, which helps to refine her understanding of the precise challenges that each next step forward presents.

Think wider

The Dutch history education researchers Jannet van Drie and Carla van Boxtel (2008) have drawn on an extensive review of empirical literature, including their own research studies, to develop a framework for analysing 'historical reasoning', the term that they use to encompass the combination of 'knowing' and 'doing' history that is widely claimed to result in deep historical understanding. Various kinds of task call for historical reasoning – whether in evaluating or constructing a description of processes of change and continuity, or in explaining a particular historical phenomenon, or in comparing different historical phenomena or periods – and they point out that such thinking can be demonstrated by individuals in written tasks, or by small groups and even whole classes in discussion. The researchers' theoretical framework consists of six components: asking historical questions, using sources, contextualization, argumentation, using substantive concepts and using meta-concepts. They first discuss and illustrate each component, using examples from their own research, and then provide preliminary suggestions about how to use the framework both in future research and in designing teaching strategies to enhance students' historical reasoning.

One of the ideas explored in the 'think-tank' convened by the National Academy for Gifted and Talented Youth for nurturing the development of high achievement was that of bringing school students into closer contact with expert historians in order to refine the students' understanding of the nature of the process in which they were engaged. Strategies for doing this with which members of the group had begun to experiment included inviting PhD students into school on a regular basis to talk about their research and its ongoing development and to support the school pupils as they engaged in historical research. Such initiatives were seen as particularly valuable in drawing attention to the nature of history as an ongoing process of creative thinking and problem-solving, a dimension that is often lost when higher education professionals simply deliver lectures to school groups. Another, which is discussed in Chapter 3, involved the creation of 'virtual academies' in which sixth-form students engaged in online debate both with other students and with academic historians (Thompson and Cole 2003).

The notion of defining the characteristics of the highest levels of achievement as a first step in defining progression towards them has inspired a number of studies into the differences between the practices of 'novices' and experts. The American psychologist Sam Wineburg (2001), for example, invited eight historians and eight senior high school students to share their reasoning with him by 'thinking aloud' as they read documents about the Battle of Lexington. Wineburg attributes their vastly different approaches not to differences in the level of their substantive knowledge (in fact since the historians were not all experts in this particular topic, two of the students actually achieved more correct answers on questions of fact), but to the assumptions they made about what it means to read a historical text. For the students, reading history was 'not a process of puzzling about authors' intentions or situating texts in a social world but of simply gathering information, with texts serving as bearers of information' (2001: 76). Wineburg not only uses these findings to call for much greater attention to be given to students' beliefs about the nature of the subject, but also to look critically at the nature of school textbooks (which tend to obscure the process by which the knowledge they present has been constructed) and to highlight the danger of thinking in *generic* terms about teaching students to read for comprehension. In an another article (Wineburg and Schneider 2010), written with one of his doctoral students, further comparisons between the practices of historians and high school students (reading documents written in 1892 about the commemoration of Columbus) are used to highlight the dangers of applying a highly influential but generic model of progression to the discipline of history. Bloom's (1956) taxonomy of educational objectives is usually depicted as a pyramid with knowledge at the lowest level and evaluation at the top. While this certainly *seems* to make it clear that substantive knowledge is the 'foundation for all further acts of mind', the visual metaphor of the pyramid, and the way in which it is actually used, often tend both to imply that such knowledge is far less important than critical thinking, and to ignore the ways in which evaluation (of sources in context) is necessary *before* new knowledge can be learned:

> For students of history, the pyramid posters have it wrong – or at least upside down. Putting knowledge at the base implies that the world of ideas is fully known and that critical thinking involves gathering known facts to cast judgment. The pyramid treats knowledge with all the glamour of a dank concrete basement – necessary for a house's foundation but hardly the place to host honored guests. Such an approach inverts the process of historical thinking and distorts why we study history in the first place. New knowledge, the prize of intellectual activity, gets locked in the basement.
>
> (Wineburg and Schneider 2010: 61)

References

Bloom, B. (1956) *Taxonomy of Educational Objectives*. Boston: Allyn and Bacon.

Blow, F. (2011) 'Everything flows and nothing stays': How students make sense of the historical concepts of change, continuity and development. *Teaching History*, 145, 47–56.

Blow, F., Lee, P. and Shemilt, D. (2012) Time and chronology: Conjoined twins or distant cousins. *Teaching History*, 147, 26–36.

Bransford, J., Brown, A. and Cocking, R. (eds) (1999) *How People Learn: Brain, mind, experience and school*. Washington, DC: National Academy Press.

Chapman, A. (2005) *Supporting High Achievement in History: Conclusions of the NAGTY History Think Tank 28/29 November 2005*. Available at http://www.uk.sagepub.com/secondary/Phillips/nagty_history_thinktank.doc (accessed 24 May 2013).

Counsell, C. (1998) Big stories, little stories. *The Times Educational Supplement*, 8 September.

Counsell, C. (2000) 'Didn't we do that in Year 7?' Planning for progression in evidential understanding. *Teaching History*, 99, 36–41.

Dickinson, A., Lee, P. and Rogers, P. (1984) *Learning History*. London: Heinemann Educational.

Grosvenor, I. and Watts, R. (1995) *Crossing the Key Stages of History*. London: David Fulton.

Hammond, K. (1999) And Joe arrives … stretching the very able pupil in a mixed ability classroom. *Teaching History*, 94, 23–31.

Lee, P. and Ashby, R. (2000) Progression in historical understanding among students ages 7–14. In P. Stearns, P. Seixas and S. Wineburg (eds) *Knowing, Teaching and Learning History*. New York: New York University Press, 199–222.

Lee, P. Asbhy, R. and Dickinson, A. (1996) Progression in children's ideas about history. In M. Hughes (ed.) *Progression in Learning. BERA Dialogues 11*. Clevedon: Multilingual Matters.

Lee, P. and Shemilt, D. (2004) 'I just wish we could go back in the past and find out what really happened': Progression in understanding about historical accounts. *Teaching History*, 117, 25–31.

Lee. P. and Shemilt, D. (2009) Is any explanation better than none? Over-determined narratives, senseless agencies and one-way streets in students' learning about cause and consequence in history. *Teaching History*, 137, 42–9.

Lee, P. and Shemilt, D. (2011) The concept that dares not speak its name: Should empathy come out of the closet? *Teaching History*, 143, 39–49.

Portal, C. (1987) *The History Curriculum for Teachers*. London: The Falmer Press.

Riley, M. (1997) Big stories and big pictures: Making outlines and overviews interesting. *Teaching History*, 88, 20–2.

Rogers, P. (1978) *The New History: Theory into practice*. London: The Historical Association.

Shemilt, D. (1980) *History 13–16: Evaluation study*. Edinburgh: Holmes McDougall.

Thompson, D. and Cole, N. (2003) Keeping the kids on message: One school's attempt at helping sixth form students to engage in historical debate using ICT. *Teaching History*, 113, 38–43.

van Drie, J. and van Boxtel, C. (2008). Historical reasoning: Towards a framework for analyzing students' reasoning about the past. *Educational Psychology Review*, 20 (2), 87–110.

Wineburg, S. (2001) On the reading of historical texts: Notes on the breach between school and academy. In *Historical Thinking and Other Unnatural Acts: Charting the future of teaching the past*. Philadelphia: Temple University Press, 63–88.

Wineburg, S. and Schneider, J. (2010) Was Bloom's taxonomy pointed in the wrong direction? *Phi Delta Kappan*, 91 (4), 56–61.

Assessment

Assessment is an important area in education; it is needed to judge the success of any teaching and learning and thus to inform the design and adaptation of plans for future learning. In recent years, particularly following the publication of Paul Black and Dylan Wiliam's (1990) *Inside the Black Box*, a greater distinction has been made between summative and formative assessment, the former being a judgement about what has been learnt and the latter focusing on what still needs to be learnt. However, there is always a danger that assessment dominates teaching and learning, and encourages 'teaching to the test'. Consideration of assessment also raises serious questions about what should be, and what actually is being assessed; it seems that we often value what we assess, but do not always assess what we value. As Chapter 18 explores, debates about the nature of progression in history – particularly about the different kinds of knowledge that need to be combined in developing historical understanding, and the extent to which they can be developed independently of each other – make the process of assessment similarly complex and contested. Certain kinds of knowledge may seem easier to assess than others, prompting assessment systems to prioritise particular kinds of knowledge or to treat each of them in isolation. These challenges are explored in the extracts within this chapter, which address fundamental questions about how assessment should be conducted in order to inform students and teachers – as well as wider stakeholders – about the students' learning.

Extract 1

Source

Kitson, A. and Husbands, C. with Steward, S. (2011) *Teaching and Learning History 11–18: Understanding the past.* Maidenhead: Open University Press; see pp. 97–8.

Introduction

This extract comes from a chapter on communicating and assessing history. Alison Kitson, Chris Husbands and Susan Steward argue that assessment is an integral component of communicating in the history classroom. They detail the myriad ways in which the term 'assessment' can be understood in education today and stress the recent focus on formative assessment to inform the 'moment-to-moment' decisions teachers make. However, here they go on to raise questions about the particular challenges in providing authentic contexts to assess understanding in the history classroom.

Key words & phrases

Authentic assessment context; oral assessment; written assessment; challenge of authenticity

---

Extract

The best assessment practices are embedded in realistic contexts: the best way to assess whether someone can ride a bicycle is to ask them to ride one. In some subjects, authentic assessment contexts are easier to establish than in others. Authentic assessment contexts pose some obvious challenges for history teachers: pupils are asked to demonstrate their understanding of the past at one remove through oral or written assessment which is – by definition – inauthentic in context. The 'authentic' past is unrecoverable; understandings of the past are always partial. This challenge of authenticity is a profound one for history teaching: it is relatively easy to ask pupils to provide the date of the Battle of Waterloo, or to sequence later nineteenth-century American presidents, but these very simple questions in themselves generate little valid evidence of a pupil's historical understanding. Such knowledge may be *necessary* but it is far from sufficient. For this reason, assessment in history has sought to become more authentic through the posing of more challenging questions. Some of these may be relatively conventional in focus – for example, asking pupils to explain the causes or consequences of a particular event, or asking them to account for the significance of a specific action or piece of evidence. Others may be more challenging: for example asking pupils to consider what alternative courses of action were open to a particular historical figure or to explore competing interpretations of an event. These tasks derive their authenticity from the ways in which they require pupils to identify, select, organize and present relevant knowledge to shape interpretations of an historical event or episode. However, classrooms also impose inauthenticity on pupil responses because of pressure of time or an insistence that some communicative modes are more 'useful' for assessment purposes than others. This frequently means that assessment opportunities in history lessons are either trivialized to factual recall questions or formalized to written work produced under time pressures.

In history teaching, contextualized and authentic assessment is that which asks pupils to think about their work *in context*. This can be achieved in a number of ways. Pupils might be asked to jot down – perhaps on a small whiteboard – their initial thinking about a problem before sharing it, so that time to reflect on a causal relationship or a challenging moral choice facing a historical figure is built in; they might be asked to think through and propose a hypothesis or generate ideas on the basis of having read some source material or seen a video. As Barzun and Graff point out, 'a note is a first thought' (Barzun and Graff, 1970); in classrooms, this can be modelled. Most important of all, however, contextualized and authentic assessment needs to be located in the context of historical enquiries which span sequences of lessons, and the enquiry itself needs to sustain the assessment focus. The enquiry 'Why did the Romans come to Britain?' generates a series of investigations which are relevant to the explanation of an action, such as the Roman invasion of 43 CE, but equally rules out of authentic contextualization a series of different investigations, such as 'What was Roman Britain like?', which may divert the enquiry. Assessment of pupils' learning in this enquiry is likely to be developed over a number of tasks, a number of lessons as pupils develop ideas and present conclusions which help to conclude the enquiry.

Summary

There is something distinctive about the challenge of assessment in history – understandings of the past are always partial. This has led the history education community to ask more challenging questions in a search for authenticity, but pressures including time can lead to such questions being trivialised. Initial thoughts and notes should be given prominence; overarching enquiry questions (as discussed in Chapter 16) are vital for authentic assessment. It is important to question what we value in terms of assessment and plan accordingly.

Questions to consider

1. How do you assess? Why do you assess in this way? What is an authentic context for assessment in history? Is this provided in your lessons? If not, what are the challenges you need to overcome to provide such a context?
2. Do your historical enquiries span sequences of lessons? Do the enquiries sustain the assessment focus? How does the focus of the final assessment affect the moment-to-moment decisions you make during the enquiry?
3. How often do you ask pupils to 'jot down their initial thinking about a problem before sharing it'? Would this be worthwhile? Why? What are the advantages of this approach? How can small whiteboards be used to promote authentic assessment in the history classroom?

Extract 2

Source

Burnham, S. and Brown, G. (2004) Assessment without level descriptions. *Teaching History*, 115, 5–15.

Introduction

Since 1995 the National Curriculum for England and Wales has set out attainment targets, broken down into 'level descriptions', to guide the assessment of students' learning across all subjects from the ages of 5 to 14. While official guidance suggests that students should be graded against these levels at the end of each Key Stage in the UK, schools increasingly encourage teachers to use the descriptors more often. Sally Burnham and Geraint Brown argue strongly that this is totally inappropriate and can indeed stand in the way of teachers and their students understanding what 'getting better' at history really means. Instead they offer some precise opportunities for meaningful, formative assessment that will help pupils and inform future planning and teaching.

Key words & phrases

National Curriculum level descriptions; assessment for learning; progression; formative assessment

---

Extract

Has your department asked itself recently, why do we assess pupils? … Ever since becoming heads of history, we have had heated discussions with colleagues, managers and LEA [local education authority] advisors over this issue. As subject leaders, we have thought long and hard about what is progress in history and how we should measure and support that progress ….

We strongly support the notion that assessment is *for* learning. The Level Descriptions cannot get anywhere near achieving this. They do not define the changing ideas, patterns of reasoning and layers of knowledge that make up progression in historical learning, and they certainly do not offer guidance for designing the detailed learning paths that will secure such progression ….

[We provide written] feedback designed to secure progress, based on a close knowledge of [individual pupils'] thinking and learning, linked to a thoughtful appreciation of the nature of causation in history. Simply trying to get this pupil to move forwards to the next Level or a sublevel drawn from a scheme not designed for this purpose, as though this were the ideal learning path, would not be a pupil-centred or history-sensitive way forward ….

For teachers, a key purpose of assessment is to establish how they are changing pupils' understandings, across a lesson or a sequence of lessons. We need multiple ways of doing this if we are to work out whether our teaching is any good and in order to change tack, sometimes even within a lesson. Are we really shifting pupils' thinking? Are we really enabling them to transform their knowledge? For example, using pupil discussion when teaching the causes of the First World War, Sally was able to assess pupils' understanding of the concept of 'imperialism' by getting pupils to explain to each other why imperialism was one of the causes. Sally could hear immediately who was still unsure of the term, who was operating with a limited idea of the term, who was questioning the boundaries of the term, who was ready to have their existing conceptions of the term challenged and so on. She was then able to adapt the lesson to ensure that all pupils were sufficiently confident with the concept of imperialism to use it meaningfully within this lesson. She was also able to adapt future planning to make sure that residual misconceptions were remediated and that certain pupils were eventually pushed out of their comfortable confidence into more demanding reflection on the term. In this particular case, several pupils with English as an additional language were unable to use the concept confidently. This prompted her to return to where she had taught about imperialism much earlier in the Key Stage and to strengthen her long-term planning.

This is one of the vital parts of assessment – for teachers to be able constantly to evaluate and improve their teaching, on different scales of planning. Sally used this assessment to tweak the way she did things within the lesson itself. She could also record such an assessment, by placing a simple device in her markbook such as a sentence or qualitative comment or a simple coding system to highlight those pupils who she felt would need specific additional work on it. This is extremely valuable data. It can be used by the individual teacher and by the whole department in assessing their effectiveness and reviewing medium- and long-term plans ....

Historical learning is recursive

Our assessment therefore informs our subsequent planning very directly and it informs pupils' later work in similar spheres. Learning in history has to be recursive: whenever pupils return to a causation piece of work they are then encouraged to turn back to the piece of work they did and look at the targets that they were set and think about how they are going to get better .... After all, to get better here might involve the pupil simply using (or choosing to use) identical causal reasoning moves and techniques as last time. The learning will come from exploring how that works in different knowledge settings, or perhaps in another variable such as the use of new substantive concepts for classifying (religious, cultural, technological, ideological, social etc.). So 'getting better' often cannot be seen as finding the next increment. It is about revisiting, reshaping, reconnecting.

After the introduction to the causes of the English Civil War, for example, we revisit the work on the Battle of Hastings, putting a piece of work on the OHT [Overhead Transparency] to analyse as a class ....

This use of prior knowledge and prior learning ensures that pupils really think about what we are asking them to do so that they can build on what they have already achieved. This reinforces the concept of assessment being for learning and has a significant impact on pupil progression, enabling us really to drive progression, and make it happen, rather than just letting them coast.

Summary

Burnham and Brown argue against the use of level descriptors as a regular form of assessment. Instead they promote individual markschemes devised for each individual assignment as a result of reading and careful consideration over what it means to get better at that aspect of history. The markschemes are intended to open a personalised dialogue with individual pupils about the next steps they should take. To produce such markschemes teachers need an understanding of the discipline of history and careful consideration of the finer points of progression that the level descriptions simply do not accommodate. (For a fuller discussion of the limitations of the level descriptions see Chapter 18.) The full article includes several examples of how the methods suggested by Burnham and Brown work in practice so that assessment becomes useful for teachers, parents and pupils.

Questions to consider

1. Who is assessment for? How far does the assessment model in your department benefit pupils, teachers and parents? What are the tensions in trying to satisfy all three parties?
2. What opportunities exist on your schemes of work for recursive learning? How might such reminders help pupils develop in their understanding of the past?
3. What is the relationship between assessment and progression? What opportunities for close, formative assessment are built into your planning? How far does your recording of pupil progress influence your planning?

Extract 3

Source

Facey, J. (2011) 'A is for assessment'… Strategies for A-level marking to motivate and enable students of all abilities to progress. *Teaching History*, 144, 36–43.

Introduction

Jane Facey teaches history in a sixth-form college for students aged 16–19. She had become aware of 'assessment for learning' initiatives being used with younger pupils and wanted to see if these strategies could be used effectively to motivate older students.

Over a number of years she experimented with a variety of practical assessment strategies, tailoring them to meet the needs of her students. These included directed self- and peer-marking, 'conveyer belt' peer marking and small group assessment. She concludes that it is important to include students in the assessment process and aims now to foster an ethos of immediate rewriting and revising work in the light of feedback.

Key words & phrases

Assessment for learning; A-level; self-assessment; peer-assessment; formative assessment; group assessment; essay writing

---

Extract

What I found to be the most effective strategy in using assessment formatively was a form of small group assessment which got students not only discussing, drafting and peer-marking, but also then rewriting their paragraphs in the lesson, commenting on how they had improved their work. In an AS-Level lesson on Gandhi's non-violent civil disobedience against British rule in India, I set up mixed ability groups to evaluate this policy of 'satyagraha', with two students arguing for and two against its effectiveness. In the second half of the lesson, the groups were given an essay title and two sources and had to decide on the points they wished to make, allocating one to each student to write on behalf of the group. Clear success criteria were essential here so that students were aware of both the necessary content and the underlying learning intention. To reinforce earlier work on paragraph structuring and ensure that all students could participate in the task with confidence, a simple grid was provided. It was important to emphasise that this was a draft so that students accepted from the start that they could further improve their work. The group then assessed each other's paragraphs, adding comments under the grid headings, and discussed how their group essay could further be improved. Ellen, for instance, was asked to explain what she meant more clearly in both her point and her conclusion, and to refer to a specific event to support her point. Her writing generally tended to be undeveloped and the group's challenge proved to be a more effective way for her to see this than previous essay targets. Joe's written work did not reflect his good understanding of a topic as it tended to be rushed and minimal. This was picked up by the group, who asked him to be more explicit and to explain in more detail. In response to the group assessment, students revised and rewrote their paragraphs and were asked to comment upon how they had improved. Ellen was able to see that she was now writing more clearly and specifically, and was linking her answer to the question. Joe also realised that he had improved his answer with more explanation and a more developed point ....

As a department we now expect students to include with their submitted essay their own comments on 'what went well' (WWW) and 'even better if' (EBI). Sometimes we ask them to indicate which mark scheme level they think their work is worth. This can at times be illuminating, both of student misconceptions and frustrations. I found myself answering these comments in my marking feedback and students liked the personalised touch, looking at these comments first, which encouraged me further to develop this assessment 'dialogue'. When Sam observes that he should 'use PEEL more', I can answer 'yes, agreed – compare how much better your paragraph 3 was to 2 because of its clearer structure'. When Hannah gives herself a level 2 'because it just isn't good enough', I can encourage her with 'but you have the makings of a good essay here – be more confident in your claims (I liked your focus on the weaknesses of the Royalists rather than the strengths of the New Model Army) and think how further to support them with own knowledge'. This approach seems more 'user-friendly' than more formal feedback. I am now attempting further to develop this dialogue, with the students responding to my feedback on their previous essay in their next essay, on the lines of 'I think I have improved my paragraph structure this time', so that the students can gain a clearer idea of their progression.

Summary

This extract refers to practical examples of assessment strategies to promote tangible and immediate progress in essay writing. Peer assessment and self-assessment are at the forefront here in helping pupils find out how they can improve their essay-writing skills, although it is not clear how far these methods are used to challenge pupils' understanding of the past and the way it is presented. The idea of assessment as dialogue is raised towards the end of the extract. This approach could be extended beyond the confines of essay structure to include the content and argument of the essay.

Questions to consider

1. What evidence is there that Facey's students now understand how to get better at writing essays?
2. Is there an affective side to assessment? How important are confidence and motivation in terms of nurturing students' progress in your classroom? How might these be sustained and strengthened through the assessment process?
3. Is it possible to get better at writing essays without developing more powerful understandings of history? How can we ensure that students get better at both?

Investigations

Devising markschemes: Burnham and Brown both devised individual markschemes for particular assignments in their departments. What do your markschemes look like? Are they informed only by the level descriptions or also by your knowledge and understanding of the small steps your pupils need to make to develop in their understanding and communication of the subject? Work with your department to devise a markscheme you could all use for a particular assessment.

Revising marking: Audit a selection of comments that you have written when marking the work of pupils you teach. Chart whether comments encourage progress in simple skills, retention of detailed information or whether they promote the development of an understanding of the discipline of history in terms of second-order concepts and processes.

Pupil perspectives: Talk to a sample group of pupils across the age range you teach. Do they feel motivated and informed by your current methods of assessment? Are they aware of what they need to do to develop their understanding of history? Do they feel that there is a possibility for dialogue in the assessment process? Do they have any suggestions about making assessment more helpful for them?

Think deeper

Taking part in any form of assessment depends on a deep understanding of progression and a shared view of what it means to get better at history. Any further reading or reflection on assessment in history should be underpinned by consideration of the issues raised in Chapter 18, particularly Lee and Shemilt's (2003) discussion of the nature of progression in history in Extract 1.

Aside from the formative, frequent assessment that takes place in all history lessons, the term 'assessment' can often refer to a more summative piece of work that brings together the thinking from a number of lessons. In recent years practitioners have developed some alternative approaches to this form of assessment in the history classroom. One example of such an alternative is Fullard and Dacey's (2008) use of oral forms of assessment, particularly a structured debate on the English Civil War, which is discussed in detail in Chapter 16 (Extract 3). Matt Stanford (2008) also wanted to move away from a constant focus on the written word in his history assessments. His department was already creative in its approach to assessment with students designing statues of Cromwell, posters for the Richard III museum in York and DVD sleeves for a Hollywood version of Stalin's life. With these, however, Stanford found himself assessing understanding through the written explanation that accompanied the artwork rather than the artwork itself. An enquiry focused on the Renaissance seemed to offer the perfect opportunity to take a more radical approach, and Stanford decided to assess pupils' understanding of the historical period from the actual artwork they produced. The enquiry, 'What was so remarkable about the Renaissance?', was assessed through the task of designing a cartoon for the city hall in sixteenth-century Florence. Even the markscheme moves away from a traditional to a visual format; a series of sliding scales ask the assessor to consider 'Things from the Renaissance', 'Ideas from the Renaissance' and 'Artistic techniques from the Renaissance'.

Think wider

Paul Black and Dylan Wiliam (1998) wanted to draw attention to what was going on inside the classroom, which they refer to as the 'black box' and see if they could find ways to help teachers raise levels of achievement. The focus of this seminal pamphlet is on formative assessment, defined as 'when the evidence' from assessment 'is actually used to adapt the teaching work to meet the needs' (1998: 2). The authors carried out an extensive literature review to explore whether there was evidence that improving formative assessment raises standards, and came to a positive conclusion. However, they warn that formative assessment is not a magic bullet for education. They suggest formative assessment can be used to raise the self-esteem of pupils if it concentrates on specific problems with work, what is wrong and how to put it right. The pamphlet also promotes self-assessment by pupils but suggests that for this to work pupils need a sufficiently clear picture of the targets that their learning is meant to attain.

A follow-up pamphlet by Black et al. (2002) sets out some core findings from initial work with teachers. It is organised under four main headings: questioning, feedback through marking, peer- and self-assessment, and the formative use of summative tests. The authors point out though, that while teachers were able to develop the generic skills of 'assessment for learning' quite quickly, it became clear that the generic strategies could only go so far. For example, choosing a good question depends not only on a detailed knowledge of the subject, but also 'a thorough understanding of the fundamental principles of the subject, an understanding of the kinds of difficulties that pupils might have, and the creativity to think up questions that can stimulate productive thinking'. Furthermore, pedagogical content knowledge is crucial to interpreting the responses and deciding what comes next. A further publication by Black et al. (2003) expands this research further and includes stories of teacher change, ideas for management and support in introducing assessment for learning. Here assessment for learning is defined as 'any assessment for which the first priority is to serve the purpose of promoting students' learning' (2003: 2).

A more recent publication by Wiliam (2009) provides some hindsight to the promotion of assessment for learning. He does raise a concern about whether the ideas of assessment for learning, at this point firmly established as part of the government's National Strategy for schools, might become diluted and therefore ineffective. He is keen that the term 'formative assessment' be used accurately and feels there can be a disjuncture between formative intention and formative action. While he admits that long-term and medium-term formative assessment may be possible, he highlights the importance of 'minute-to-minute and day-by-day' formative assessment as this has the greatest impact on student achievement. He suggests (2009: 10) that

> if students leave the classroom before teachers have used the information about their student's achievements to adjust their teaching, the teachers are already playing catch-up. If the teachers have not made adjustments by the time the students arrive the next day, it is probably too late.

His focus is on improving the classroom practice of teachers by making it more responsive to students' needs.

Jo Philpott (2011) has been quite explicit in her use of assessment for learning techniques in the history classroom. She makes the distinction between day-to-day assessment, periodic assessment and transitional assessment. Where day-to-day assessment involves 'immediate feedback and next steps for [the] pupil' (2011: 264) and transitional assessment might be reported to parents/carers and the next teacher, periodic assessment provides a broader view of progress for teacher and learner. The main focus of the periodic assessment is to ensure pupils know what is expected of them from the beginning of a unit of work, they are able to connect together lessons along the way and make use of feedback in a formative manner.

References

Barzun, J. and Graff, H.F. (1970) *The Modern Researcher*. New York: Harcourt Brace.

Black, P. and Wiliam, D. (1998) *Inside the Black Box*. London: King's College London.

Black, P., Harrison, C., Lee, C., Marshall, B. and Wiliam, D. (2002) *Working Inside the Black Box: Assessment for learning in the classroom*. London: King's College London.

Black, P., Harrison, C., Lee, C., Marshall, B. and Wiliam, D. (2003) *Assessment for Learning: Putting it into practice*. Buckingham: Open University Press.

Fullard, G. and Dacey, K. (2008) Holistic assessment through speaking and listening: An experiment with causal reasoning and evidential thinking in Year 8. *Teaching History*, 131, 25–9.

Lee, P. and Shemilt, D. (2003) A scaffold, not a cage: Progression and progression models in history. *Teaching History*, 113, 13–23.

Philpott, J. (2011) Assessment. In I. Davies (ed.) *Debates in History Teaching*. London: Routledge, 261–72.

Stanford, M. (2008) Redrawing the Renaissance: Non-verbal assessment in Year 7. *Teaching History*, 130, 4–11.

Wiliam, D. (2009) *Assessment for Learning: Why, what and how? An inaugural professorial lecture by Dylan Wiliam*. London: Institute of Education..

Inclusion

History is generally regarded as an important subject that all young people should study. As Section 1 on the nature and purpose of studying history illustrates, there are debates about the precise reasons why young people should learn about the past, but these debates, and the often heated nature of them, reveal that history is regarded as central to a young person's education. However, history is often regarded as a difficult subject for children. There is a vast body of knowledge to become familiar with, while the concepts and processes that underpin the subject are complex. Time itself can be a very abstract concept. The fragmentary nature of our understanding of the past can be frustrating to some students who wish to 'know what happened' or believe there is an objective 'knowable' past. Pupils are often required to engage with mindsets very different to ours; this requires an ability to see the world from the perspectives of others (often from an adult perspective as well), which requires a level of sophisticated contextual knowledge. History is also regarded as a literary subject in many societies, requiring students to be very competent in reading and writing, and to be orally proficient. There is a danger that history is seen as too 'difficult' for some students, who therefore receive a different level of historical education. This is potentially divisive, disenfranchising and denies some young people access to important social capital. The teaching of history therefore presents teachers with many challenges, one of which is the question, how do teachers help *all* young people to learn history successfully?

Extract 1

Source

Harris, R., Downey, C. and Burn, K. (2012) History education in comprehensive schools: Using school level data to interpret national patterns. *Oxford Review of Education*, 38 (4), 413–36.

Introduction

This article draws upon a series of online surveys carried out on behalf of the Historical Association, which persistently highlighted major differences in the nature and extent of history education being offered to pupils of secondary school age in England, and the impact this has on the numbers of students going on to study the subject at examination level (GCSE). Independent schools and grammar schools (where they still exist) tend to give pupils on average more discrete history, both in terms of how it appears within the timetable and the time allocated to its study. The provision for history education in comprehensive schools, which most pupils attend, is far more varied. Within this article the authors examined the variance within comprehensive schools and identified those factors that often characterised schools where less time and energy was devoted to history; two factors, the level of socio-economic deprivation and the numbers of pupils identified as having special educational needs, were generally associated with lower levels of history provision in school.

Key words & phrases

Inclusion; history for all; accessibility; socio-economic status; comprehensive schools; curriculum access; special educational needs

---

Extract

Analysis of the data reveals that schools with good pass rates are more likely to see higher numbers of students studying history at GCSE. Given the links between academic success and socio-economic background it is likely that most of the schools in the survey with high GCSE pass rates are located in more affluent areas, as indicated by their IDACI [Income Deprivation Affecting Children Index] scores. The implication of this is that students in more socio-economically deprived areas are also less likely to study history. This suggestion is borne out by the strong association found in the data between less wealthy socio-economic areas and lower numbers of students studying history at GCSE. The similarly strong association between a high percentage of students with SEN [special educational needs] and low GCSE uptake also suggests that schools with significant proportions of students with SEN are also less likely to enter students for subjects such as history that are often seen as more 'academic'. Schools with high numbers of students with SEN and poor IDACI scores are also more likely to reduce curriculum time for history at K[ey] S[tage] 3 and therefore have fewer students opting to continue with the subject at GCSE ….

Does it matter if some students, especially those from areas of poor SES [socio-economic status] and students with SEN, receive less history teaching than others?

Clearly all students within state maintained comprehensive schools are supposed to be taught history in some form during the compulsory stage of the National

Curriculum. However, as this research and previous studies have shown, the extent of their history provision varies considerably from school to school (Burn and Harris, 2009 and 2010, Harris and Burn, 2011). Although there are general differences determined by type of school attended, and, as the analysis in this paper shows, by the specific nature of the different comprehensives surveyed, students from poorer socio-economic backgrounds and/or with special educational needs are likely to receive less history teaching at Key Stage 3 and are less likely to study history beyond K[ey] S[tage] 3. This restricted access to an historical education should be a matter of concern.

Summary

This extract highlights the difference in provision within comprehensive schools. Although such schools serve a broad pupil population and follow the National Curriculum, in reality there is a major difference in provision. Clearly this raises the question why there is such disparity, which the paper explores. The research reveals a complex picture, but the socio-economic status of the local area and the number of pupils identified with special educational needs is more likely to be associated with lower levels of history being taught. Restricting access to an historical education for such pupils raises further questions about why this should be the case, but also the potential damage this can have on future informed civic participation.

Questions to consider

1. What access (e.g. length of lesson, number of lessons, how many years history is studied for, access to examination courses) do *all* pupils have to an historical education in your context?
2. What do pupils gain from studying the past, or miss out on by not studying the past?
3. How appropriate is it to restrict the study of history to a proportion of the school population?

Extract 2

Source

Hart, S., Dixon, A., Drummond, M.J. and McIntyre, D. (2004) *Learning without Limits*. Maidenhead: Open University Press; see pp. 138–46.

Introduction

This book is based on a project that explored the practice of a number of teachers and the values that underpinned that practice. The book starts by rejecting what is referred to as 'the fallacy of fixed ability' and argues that a preoccupation with putting pupils into ability groups, either in class, or as a class, has held back the educational achievement of many young people. The teachers in the project were observed and interviewed precisely because they had rejected the notion of pupils having a 'fixed' ability and attempted to find ways to ensure all pupils were able to learn successfully. The extract is drawn from interviews with Julie, a history teacher, which explore the key principles that inform her classroom practice, and how she uses these to construct activities that allow pupils to be successful. Such activities can be very challenging, e.g. she outlines how she uses extracts from Chaucer's *Canterbury Tales* to learn about medieval medicine, but the principles that shape her classroom practice mean pupils are willing and able to engage with a range of activities and materials, which pupils in other contexts may find too daunting.

Key words & phrases

Inclusion; history for all; accessibility; emotional well-being; achievement

---

Extract

Accessibility of learning opportunities

The first principle is to make sure that the learning activities and experiences provided for the group genuinely do offer everyone something that they can do. This may seem self-evident, but Julie is concerned that much challenging behaviour is attributable to students being given work that they cannot do ....

What comes across as Julie describes what she does to ensure that learning experiences are accessible to all is a conviction that accessibility is a quality that is produced through teachers' judicious choices and actions – and the choices and actions that they enable and encourage on the part of young people – rather than an objective quality inherent in the relationship between particular learning objectives and the characteristics of particular students. The teacher's task is not a technical one of matching tasks and learning activities, but a creative one, involving careful design and sequencing of learning activities ... in order to make it possible for whatever knowledge, understanding and skills are intended to be the focus of the lesson to be made accessible to everyone.

Emotional well-being

Just as much attention to students' emotional well-being plays an essential part in achieving accessibility for all, so accessibility plays an essential part in securing students' emotional well-being. 'I think if a student can't do something then, well they're going to react in one of two ways, they're either going to get quite aggressive as a defence mechanism ... or they are just going to withdraw into themselves and just not contribute at all because they feel scared or stupid.'

These two principles of 'accessibility' and 'emotional well-being' work together in a mutually complementary way to help lift limits to learning. In making work accessible, Julie is noticing and removing possible barriers to learning that might otherwise cause learners to fail, and do further damage their self-esteem. Attending to the emotional dimensions of learning helps learners to overcome psychological barriers that might otherwise limit their ability and willingness to engage with learning opportunities provided.

Gaining a sense of worthwhile achievement

... Tasks and activities have to be designed in such a way that not just participation but success, something that both they and their teacher recognise as worthwhile, is a genuine possibility for every student. What Julie does is to establish a 'baseline', the minimum worthwhile achievement to be expected of all students ... if they can see for themselves that they have done the work, and feel good about what they have achieved, this helps to build confidence that they can be successful on further occasions.

By defining achievement more broadly, and making such opportunities for achievement routinely available for students in her classes, she helps to make it possible for all students to demonstrate their abilities and understandings more fully – and so gain a greater sense of achievement and satisfaction than would be available to them if formal recognition is given only to traditional forms of achievement.

Summary

In this extract, Julie outlines her beliefs about how pupils should be taught so that they can all be successful when studying history. Noticeably there is a strong emphasis on the psychological barriers to learning – barriers that Julie seeks to overcome by demonstrating to the students that they can succeed: success breeds success and therefore boosts self-confidence. These psychological barriers are not inherent within the children, but result from the conditions in which learning takes place, as a response, for example, to particular school grouping policies. The research evidence about setting pupils in schools by ability sometimes produces contradictory results, however one consistent message that comes through very clearly is the harm done, both in terms of self-esteem and academic outcomes, to those pupils placed in lower groups. The book raises serious questions about a child's overall educational experience from pre-school through to formal schooling at primary and secondary levels, and the way in which children's emotional needs are met in order that they can be academically successful. The book challenges many assumptions in education, both philosophically and in terms of classroom policy and practice.

Questions to consider

1. What factors do you think influence a child's attainment?
2. To what extent are these factors influenced by (a) the educational system; (b) individual schools; (c) individual teachers?
3. To what extent do you agree with the key principles that underpin Julie's approach to creating an inclusive learning environment?

Extract 3

Source

Harris, R. (2005) Does differentiation have to mean different? *Teaching History*, 118, 5–12.

Introduction

This article explores classroom practice and challenges some assumptions about how best to support a range of needs within the history classroom. Traditionally differentiation often means that teachers prepare different materials, resources and tasks for students, and therefore means 'different' things are presented to pupils. Not only does this label students, which can have unintended consequences on self-esteem and motivation, it can also mean more work for teachers and present issues around where to 'pitch' a lesson. This extract examines three key principles that underpin a possible approach to creating an inclusive classroom environment where differentiation is not seen as doing different things for different pupils.

Key words & phrases

Inclusion; history for all; engagement; accessibility; challenge; emotional well-being

---

Extract

In my experience the following principles are far more successful in allowing pupils of all abilities to succeed:

1. Make the work engaging.
2. Make the work accessible but challenging.
3. Decide where you want to place the obstacles.

Make the work engaging

Engaged pupils are ready to deal with the complexity of the past. Given a suitable stimulus, pupils will care about what happened to people in the past, see the relevance of events to real people at the time or simply be intrigued and puzzled. Personalising the past or making links to the locality can all help to grip pupils' imaginations.

Consider how you might deliberately arouse curiosity. The story of the death of Abbot Richard Whiting in 1539 is a gripping tale. Dimming the lights and telling the pupils they are about to hear a dreadful tale sets the scene and gets pupils listening expectantly. Small details help to conjure up images in the pupils' minds that culminate in the graphic details of Whiting's last moments. Suitably captivated, the pupils readily settle to a sorting activity to explain his death. The result is an introduction to the dissolution of the monasteries and the English Reformation – and whatever you do, do not set out the learning objectives on the board at the start of the lesson, as it will spoil the surprise! Do the pupils need differentiated materials to tackle this? In most cases, no, the process of engagement has got the class wanting to find out more. That is a far more powerful means of getting pupils to learn than giving them different resources or worksheets to complete ….

Make the work accessible but challenging

The following example shows how access and challenge can be provided for a mixed ability group. The task is deceptively simple. The pupils have to produce a written account of Charles I's execution. It is essentially a descriptive piece of writing, but it must be based on the evidence, much of which is contradictory. This provides an open-ended challenge. The pupils have to complete a grid drawing information from the sources.

The table is simple to complete but because of this, the task can now be tackled at a number of different levels. Discussion is vital here if pupils are to work through their thinking. 'Think, pair, share' is a useful technique in promoting talk. It involves pupils thinking on their own initially, and then talking as a pair before sharing ideas with the rest of the class. It has the benefit of not putting pupils on the spot, with the possibility of lengthy embarrassed silences as the teacher waits for an answer. It also means any pupil can be expected to provide an answer as they have all had time to think and discuss ideas. It can be done very quickly and is flexible enough to use in a variety of questioning and discussion situations.

In order to write their accounts pupils either need to reconcile the differences between the sources and/or use the language of uncertainty … The task is challenging, but the way it is set up allows all pupils to gain access at the 'ground floor', so they can all achieve something.

Decide where you want to place the obstacles

We teachers set the parameters of any task. We therefore decide where we put the degree of challenge. We have to consider our learning objectives carefully and use these to identify which obstacles we remove for pupils and which ones we deliberately leave in.

For example, how much writing do we want our pupils to do? I mean how much serious writing are we really going to cherish? How much writing do we need in order to gain understanding of pupils' progress and to consolidate their learning? If we expect pupils to write copious amounts each lesson, then we may be needlessly creating barriers to learning if that writing is not really necessary.

Summary

The extract highlights the positives of engaging pupils with topics and tasks, providing a 'way in' for pupils, but also not shying away from difficulties. To simplify things actually can make them more incomprehensible to pupils, so they need to work with the complexity of the past, but to be supported in doing so. It does challenge what might be considered more traditional ways to approach differentiating lessons, but offers a potentially more inclusive approach to teaching about the past.

Questions to consider

1. How do the approaches outlined here differ to other approaches to differentiation with which you are familiar?
2. What do you see as the strengths and weaknesses of the approaches outlined in the article?
3. The extract is based upon professional practice and reflection, rather than research. Does that strengthen or undermine the ideas presented?

Investigations

Pupil perspectives on the challenge of studying history: Gather the views of pupils, either through a survey or focus group. How 'hard' do pupils think history is? Do they perceive history as difficult and, if so, is this due to the nature of the content, the tasks they are required to do or the way they are taught?

Pupil perspectives on the classroom environment: Get pupils to complete a 'thought cloud', which presents the statement 'I feel secure and happy to work in the classroom when …'. Identify common themes from the pupils' responses and reflect on the extent to which your history classroom is somewhere pupils feel 'safe' and willing to work. If any issues are raised, use pupil focus groups to explore how the history classroom could be made more welcoming.

Teacher perspectives: Get teachers to discuss their understanding of inclusion and how they set out to create an inclusive classroom. Identify areas of difference between teachers and/or key principles that underpin their inclusive practice. Carry out a series of peer observations to see how well these principles are being enacted and whether further work could be done to embed them.

Think deeper

Inclusion is a complex concept, covering as it does issues to do with classroom climate, barriers to learning, means of making the subject accessible and so forth. It also raises philosophical questions about approaches to inclusion (e.g. should all types of pupils be educated together in the same class or should there be some separate special provision for particular types of pupil) and practical questions about means to cope with the range of needs within a class.

In 2003, Christine Counsell raised some fundamental questions about the nature of history education, by examining how we can create meaningful learning experiences for all pupils regardless of ability. Her argument is that history is a subject that is of value to all young people and therefore the role of the teacher is to make sure all pupils can access a subject that allows them to make sense of the world in which they live, and so offer them the opportunity to appreciate and participate effectively in society. Counsell explores four challenges, namely what is acceptable simplification in teaching history, how to promote an intrinsic motivation to study the past, what it means for lower achieving students to get better at history, and how history could combine intelligently with other subjects. In her discussion, Counsell presents a series of propositions, which are fundamentally to do with inclusion since the driving force behind each of them is to ensure that all pupils are able to access a meaningful historical education.

Richard Harris and Ian Luff (2004) offer a more practical approach to dealing specifically with the area of special education needs. The opening chapters of the book explore issues that relate to policy and special educational needs, and outline some general approaches to dealing with a range of special needs. The remainder of the book deals with specific issues within history teaching, ranging from assessment and progression to working with teaching assistants effectively and the use of role play and practical demonstrations to make history accessible. The basic premise of the book is that teachers should find ways to make the past accessible rather than making it simple, and as such is in tune with Counsell's (2003) desire to keep the past complicated.

The Historical Association's professional journal, *Teaching History*, also contains a number of articles that examine different elements of inclusive practice. Maria Osowiecki (2004, 2005) outlines an approach that uses a variety of aural, oral, visual and kinaesthetic activities as a means to create variety in a sequence of lessons, to secure an inclusive learning environment, and as a way of addressing concerns about boys' underachievement. She based a sequence of lessons around the concept of significance and an enquiry question 'What was so remarkable about the Renaissance?' The result was:

> the completed essays not only demonstrate that pupils had retained, processed and applied a great deal of the factual and conceptual content of the enquiry, they also suggest that most pupils had engaged in a relatively sophisticated consideration of historical significance. The standard of work elicited from a number of boys in the class was particularly remarkable, since they had previously struggled with extended writing tasks. Perhaps then the range of VAK activities had, if not appealed to particular learning styles, provided a suitably wide and stimulating variety of activities to ensure access and challenge for all pupils. Moreover, whatever their learning styles, we had used the wide range of VAK [visual, auditory and kinaesthetic] activities to lead them into high-quality, conceptually framed writing, not to avoid writing.

(Osowiecki 2005: 24)

In another article, Stanford (2008) experimented with alternative approaches to assessing pupils, which avoided the traditional emphasis on written work, while Foster (2008) also looked at capturing pupils' sophisticated understanding of change and continuity through drawing a 'road map'. Both of these articles are discussed at greater length elsewhere: Stanford in the 'Think wider' and 'Think deeper' sections in Chapters 11 and 19 respectively; and Foster in Chapter 12.

Think wider

Enabling pupils to be successful is a complex business, which encompasses issues beyond simply teaching the subject, and there is much to be gained by looking at research that examines barriers to learning both from a sociological and psychological perspective.

David Gillborn and Heidi Mirza (2000) carried out an interesting mapping exercise of pupils' attainment, exploring the differences between those from different gender, socio-economic and ethnic backgrounds. Although attainment is connected to these different variables, ethnicity and socio-economic background account for the biggest levels of disparity, for example pupils from lower socio-economic backgrounds and students from a number of minority ethnic backgrounds perform far worse in state examinations. They do identify local authorities that 'buck the trend' and so emphasise that it is possible to adopt approaches that foster achievement of all students. The reasons for the lower attainment of groups of pupils are not easy to disentangle. Gillborn (2008) draws upon Critical Race Theory (which originated in the US to explore the prejudice within the legal system and was then applied more widely to aspects of society) to analyse the UK education system to highlight ways in which racism is, often unwittingly, embedded in the educational system. Louise Archer (2008) presents a fascinating article that explores the ways in which teachers talk about pupils and what this reveals about their expectations of them; it seems that teachers often hold inappropriate expectations of many pupils from minority ethnic groups and these expectations become self-fulfilling prophesies.

Exploring psychological barriers to success reveals a wealth of interesting insights. The work of Albert Bandura (1997) has been hugely influential. His idea of self-efficacy can be used to explain why students perform so differently; efficacy is essentially an individual's belief in their ability to do something, and the higher the sense of self-efficacy the more able someone is able to do something. Obviously this sense of self-belief is shaped by a number of factors, but it emphasises the need to develop an individual's sense of confidence. This clearly overlaps with issues such as self-esteem and motivation, which all feed into someone's willingness to engage with work and their belief in their ability to be successful. Martyn Long (2000) provides a very accessible and comprehensive guide to a range of psychological theories that are pertinent to a deeper understanding of education.

Inclusion also embraces wider issues about the curriculum and the extent to which pupils feel they are represented within the curriculum. Terrie Epstein's (2009) study shows the ways in which pupils can feel excluded from school because they do not see 'themselves' or feel unable to connect with the portrayal of 'themselves' in the curriculum. This can be related to ethnicity, as in the case of Epstein's work, or it can be related to other factors such as social class. It is worth looking at other chapters such as Chapter 5 on history and identity and Chapter 15 on diversity, where this type of issue is explored further.

References

Archer, L. (2008) The impossibility of minority ethnic educational 'success'? An examination of the discourses of teachers and pupils in British secondary school. *European Educational Research Journal*, 7 (1), 89–107.

Bandura, A. (1997) *Self-efficacy*. New York: W.H. Freeman.

Burn, K. and Harris, R. (2009) *Findings from the Historical Association Survey of Secondary History Teachers*. Available at: http://www.history.org.uk/news/news_415.html (accessed 21 February 2011).

Burn, K. and Harris, R. (2010) *Historical Association Survey of History in Schools in England 2010*. Available at: http://www.history.org.uk/resources/secondary_resource_3754_8.html (accessed 21 February 2011).

Counsell, C. (2003) History for all. In M. Riley and R. Harris (eds) *Past Forward: A vision for school history 2002–2012*. London: Historical Association, 25–32.

Epstein, T. (2009) *Interpreting National History*. New York: Routledge.

Foster, R. (2008) Speed cameras, dead ends, drivers and diversions: Year 9 use a 'road map' to problematise change and continuity. *Teaching History*, 131, 4–8.

Gillborn, D. (2008) *Racism and Education: Coincidence or conspiracy?* London: Routledge.

Gillborn, D. and Mirza, H. (2000) *Educational Inequality: Mapping race, class and gender*. London: Ofsted.

Harris, R. and Burn, K. (2011) Curriculum theory, curriculum policy and the problem of ill-disciplined thinking. *Journal of Education Policy*, 26 (2), 245–62.

Harris, R. and Luff, I. (2004) *Meeting SEN in the Curriculum: History*. London: David Fulton.

Long, M. (2000) *The Psychology of Education*. London: Routledge.

Osowiecki, M. (2004) Seeing, hearing and doing the Renaissance (Part 1): Let's have a Renaissance party! *Teaching History*, 117, 34–9.

Osowiecki, M. (2005) Seeing, hearing and doing the Renaissance (Part 2). *Teaching History*, 118, 17–25.

Stanford, M. (2008) Re-drawing the Renaissance: Non-verbal assessment in Year 7. *Teaching History*, 130, 4–12.

Issues of acceptable simplification

History is complicated – the sheer extent of the past and the complexity of human life in its various forms can make history appear overwhelming. At the same time, the way in which we create an understanding of the past is a sophisticated, intellectual exercise, and often results in competing views of what happened. Given this degree of difficulty it is not surprising that history presents challenges for many adults, and so it is natural that history in schools will offer a simplified version of history for young people. Yet the question of how far history should be simplified, without it degenerating into a 'mythologised' past is central to many debates about how to teach history. The extracts presented here explore different aspects of this issue and consider how to maintain a balance between complexity and simplification. The first sets out some of the dilemmas and the need to develop period sensitivity, the second explores the issue of stereotyping and the third examines the use of analogies in history teaching.

Extract 1

Source

Counsell, C. (2003) History for all. In M. Riley and R. Harris (eds) *Past Forward*. London: Historical Association, 25–32.

Introduction

This extract comes from a position paper in which Christine Counsell explores the issue of 'history for all' and the different challenges this presents for history educators. In this extract, Counsell argues that too often the temptation when teaching history to those seen as academically 'less able' is to simplify what is taught and present a less sophisticated picture of the past. Yet this in itself may make history less intelligible.

Key words & phrases

History for all; acceptable simplification; lower attainers; pedagogy; sense of period

Extract

In a review of a CD Rom in *Teaching History* 93, Ben Walsh [1998] wrote:

> There is a belief in some quarters that history is too complicated. The problem with this argument is that if history is to stop becoming complicated then it must become simple. Then we are in real trouble, as in the minds of our students all Catholics hate all Protestants … for all time. All Jews live in Germany and are persecuted. All Indians work on tea plantations or emigrate to Britain. Similarly, all black people in the eighteenth and nineteenth centuries sit around bemoaning their lot as slaves until that Wilberforce bloke comes along and sets them free.

Walsh neatly summarises a central challenge of teaching history to the less able child. A key aspect of history is the diversity and complexity of past society ….

How on earth does the beleaguered teacher of the 'bottom set' or of the mixed ability class of 32 children cope with this when clearly there is a need to simplify complicated historical stories and situations? Pupils aged 11 to 14 with concentration or literacy difficulties are not going to grasp complex narratives or concepts at the same level that more able pupils of 16 to 19 will understand them. Naturally the teacher will try to make an account or activity as faithful to the complex reality as they possibly can but a degree of simplification is inevitable. Simplification means some skating over complexity. So we have our central pedagogic problem: what is the acceptable simplification?

My concern is that we do not dumb down. How do we secure some intellectually honest, historically rigorous way of teaching the causes of the Second World War or the development of the franchise in the nineteenth century without offering excessively simplistic and therefore damaging accounts? There will never be an easy answer to this but it is possible to debate principles.

The reason why I feel it is important to air this as a problem is that many experiments with teaching less able pupils not only do not come up to a basic standard of historical rigour but actually make it harder to improve pupils' overall historical understanding. Such experiments include, for example, certain kinds of 'empathy' activities that encourage anachronism and militate against pupils' sense of period. For example, the 'write a medieval rap about …' or 'imagine you are a reporter working for a medieval radio or television station commenting on the peasants' revolt'. Pupils who already struggle to realise that values, institutions, language and technology were utterly different in the fourteenth century from today are not helped by activities that confuse past and present values and media. This is not an argument against good empathetic work, far from it, but against activities that invite trivial or ahistorical responses, so feeding pupils' weaknesses rather than helping them to overcome them.

Summary

Counsell acknowledges that learning about the past is complicated, but instead of simplifying the past, history educators need to ensure that pupils are allowed to appreciate its complexity. Clearly there is a fine dividing line between over-simplifying and over-complicating the past, but Counsell argues that the type of activities pupils are often engaged with are ahistorical and weaken pupils' sense of period, making it more difficult for them to understand the past. This raises another issue, namely the tension between motivating pupils through the choice of engaging activities and developing a sensitivity to the lived realities of the period they are studying.

Questions to consider

1. Think of a particular class and/or a particular period/topic. What challenges do pupils face in understanding the past? What are the particular challenges for the lower attainers in the group?
2. To what extent are the challenges for these to do with the content, concepts and processes associated with history, as opposed to the literacy demands of the subject?
3. If, as Counsell argues, we should avoid ahistorical activities, what type of activities would allow these pupils to develop a richer sense of period?

Extract 2

Source

Kitson, A. (2001) Challenging stereotypes and avoiding the superficial: A suggested approach to teaching the Holocaust. *Teaching History*, 104, 41–8.

Introduction

In this article, Alison Kitson discusses the problems associated with teaching and learning about the Holocaust. In particular she identifies many common misconceptions that pupils have about this topic. These misconceptions represent a simple view of the events, in which Jews are condemned to be victims, anti-Semitism is seen as a peculiarly German phenomenon, all Germans are Nazis and so forth. In one sense such misconceptions are 'comforting' as they make the events of the Holocaust intelligible, and remove any strong need to question deeply human actions. In another sense such misconceptions are pernicious as they allow the 'blame' for the events to be placed on someone else, again avoiding the need to consider the complexity of the events and the situation.

Key words & phrases

Stereotypes; Holocaust; complexity; human experience; generalisation

---

Extract

What was 'the real opinion of the German people'?

The diarist Viktor Klemperer [1998], a German Jew who survived the war and who kept a diary throughout the Nazi period, wrote at one point 'What is the real opinion of the German people?' His diaries provide a brilliant insight into the complexities of German responses to Nazi persecution of the Jews. On some days, Klemperer would benefit from acts of kindness from complete strangers; on others he would suffer rejection by non-Jewish friends. A great deal has been written about the German people's attitudes towards the Jews and towards the anti-Semitic policies of the Third Reich. This has largely been the consequence of two things: first, being able to raise awkward questions about complicity and consent during the Nazi period due to the passing of time and the relative stability of modern Germany and, second, having such a wealth of scholarship available which seeks to illuminate everyday life between 1933–1945.

Daniel Goldhagen's bestseller, *Hitler's Willing Executioners: Ordinary Germans and the Holocaust* [1996], raised some troubling questions on this issue. His insistence that 'the model of Nazi anti-Semitism had taken shape well before the Nazis came to power … for it was deeply embedded in German cultural and political life and conversation' and his argument that, as a consequence, the Germans were in some way uniquely anti-Semitic and the 'willing executioners' of Nazi persecution and murder has been rejected as too extreme by almost all historians. The reality was much more complex. Certainly, it appears that the German people did consent to many of the regime's policies, and this included anti-Semitism. This might have been because of their overall support for a regime which was restoring Germany's economic stability, it might have been out of personal self-interest or it might, in part, have been because of existing anti-Semitic feeling. But the key point is that it was complicated. As the historian Robert Gellately [2001] recently put it, 'It is of course difficult to generalise about the German population whose reactions were often mixed and whose real opinions, at least if they were negative, could not be freely expressed'.

So why tackle this complicated and difficult issue in the classroom? I would argue that such an enquiry is essential for two reasons. First, because it challenges the stereotype that 'all Germans were Nazis' and 'all Germans were anti-Semitic', even if the reality is still far from comfortable. Second, it provides a further context for the Holocaust. Part of understanding why the Holocaust happened is thinking about where it came from. If studying the Holocaust is – at least in part – about gaining an insight into human behaviour, then this context becomes very important.

The three activities outlined below are intended to extend pupils' thinking about:

- the reasons behind Nazi anti-Semitic policies (causes and causal reasoning);
- the complexity of German responses to these policies (diversity of experience, views and attitudes);
- the outcomes of these policies on German Jews (consequences or effects).

These activities are also intended to develop an affective response that must balance and support this cognitive work. By stressing the human perspective, pupils can be helped to see Jewish and non-Jewish Germans as individuals rather than as mere categories. Rigorous historical thinking necessarily involves classification and the exploration of categories, so the history teacher's challenge is considerable: he or she has constantly to balance and even offset this with opportunities for human connection and human response.

Summary

The activities that Kitson outlines are worth reading in full, as the sequence of work directly challenges pupils' preconceptions. Using a combination of enquiry questions, such as 'What was it like to be Jewish before 1933?', she attempts to humanise the past by looking at specific stories of individuals and their experiences. This serves to disturb many of the stereotypes pupils may well hold. The activities also present the past as complex, with individuals facing or finding themselves in extraordinary circumstances and required to make decisions about how to act. This in turn raises important questions about humanity and how people treat each other. There are no ready answers provided through these activities; this is in part due to an unwillingness to present simple answers to an event as complex as the Holocaust.

Questions to consider

1. What makes events such as the Holocaust complicated to understand and teach?
2. What would you consider to be an overly simplistic portrayal of the Holocaust? Why would it be inappropriate to teach such events in an oversimplified form?
3. How, and to what extent, do you think you can/should make an event, such as the Holocaust, intelligible to young people?

Extract 3

Source

Rollett, S. (2010) 'Hi George. Let me ask my leading historians ...': Deconstructing lazy analogies in Year 9. *Teaching History*, 139, 24–9.

Introduction

This article explores the work of a teacher, Steve Rollett, working with his department to address a number of issues. In part they were looking for a way to help pupils appreciate the value of history, but they also wanted pupils to understand the complexity of the past, without recourse to simple, 'lazy' analogies. They found a useful way to bring these two issues together by evaluating the use of analogies within current discourse and subjecting these to critical evaluation. This approach allowed pupils to see how history could be valuable in better understanding the present, while also deepening their insights into contemporary issues.

Key words & phrases

Relevance; meaningful; purpose; analogy; Iraq; appeasement; simplification

---

Extract

A regular conversation with some pupils in my own school convinced me that there is still an over-simplification of the purpose of history to deal with. The view of Pupil X sums up this over-simplification: history was apparently 'useful' because it 'stopped us from repeating the mistakes of the past'. Whilst this has more depth of understanding than the vocational 'it helps you to work in a museum' response, something here still jarred with me. This is not to say that Pupil X's remark is not true – an orientation that takes in knowledge of the past most certainly can help us to 'avoid mistakes' in some instances – but to make this a general rule or history's main purpose is to over-simplify the relationship between the past and present – a relationship that is always fraught with difficulties ....

I have noticed from my own practice and from observing others that when we history teachers struggle to make a connection between the pupil and the past it is more often than not an analogy that we deploy in order to fill the gap in understanding. Sometimes these are carefully planned vehicles for creating understanding and on occasion they are quick fixes, parachuted in at the last minute during explanations that seem to be flagging. As such, they can be useful and powerful. At their worst, however, lazy analogies undermine the very complexities of historical understanding that make history relevant and meaningful. Recent developments in my own school show that if we get students to unpick analogies and to develop a critical awareness of their limitations, this can have considerable benefits, both for students' historical thinking and for their appreciation of history's role and value.

…

It is important to remember that analogies are always constructs, used by historians and teachers alike as a way of building meaning for a particular purpose. Having reflected upon this I became interested in how we might help pupils to deconstruct meaning or, at least, get them to challenge particular analogies. In my experience, such an evaluative, reflective approach always characterises the deepest historical learning ….

It is the potential of evaluating analogies that I would like to explore. This goes beyond the ways in which many history teachers have written about the issue, where analogy is called upon as a way of motivating or interesting students by showing some sort of human continuity across time. Of course, there is a strong case for using analogy to foster interest in the past …. But if we are to nurture reflective, questioning minds then surely we have to be more intellectually ambitious than simply building 'interest'.

…

All that I needed was an analogy with enough substance for us to grapple with, something that cried out for deconstruction. Images of Alistair Campbell squirming in front of the Chilcot Inquiry under questioning about the decision to go to war in Iraq proved to be fruitful. I was reminded of the speeches given in 2003 by both George Bush and Tony Blair. These summoned up a populist condemnation of Chamberlain's appeasement of Hitler in order to justify declaring war on a modern tyrant. We were warned to 'learn the lessons of the past'. Here was something for us to get our teeth into – an analogy with a highly contentious aspect of the past being used to justify an equally contentious issue in the present.

In order to deconstruct this analogy it was important to do so from both ends – to contextualise both the situation with Iraq and the role of appeasement in the 1930s. To this end, the learning sequence was planned to follow on from our usual investigation into appeasement as part of our 'Modern World' GCSE course. Pupils therefore already had a reasonably developed perspective of appeasement. In order for there to be sufficient depth to deconstruct the analogy I realised that the process had to cover several areas:

1. Clarity concerning the analogy in question – what were its users' intentions?
2. Knowledge of the justifications provided for going to war with Iraq.
3. Analysis and evaluation of these justifications.
4. Comparison between 2003 and 1930s contexts.

Summary

Rollett uses a standard tool in teaching about the past, i.e. the use of analogy, and carefully explores how it can be used to deepen pupils' insights into the past. Too often analogies are used to generate interest and/or provide a foothold for pupils to grasp an insight into the past. Although not denigrating these uses of analogy, Rollett and his department appreciate that these can create or perpetuate misunderstandings about the past, as analogies, by definition, provide simplified ways of understanding. By making pupils evaluate the validity of an analogy, through careful building up of contextual knowledge, pupils are able to develop more sophisticated insights into both the present and the past (and the way the past is used).

Questions to consider

1. What do you think Rollett means by 'lazy analogies'? What analogies do you use in the classroom and for what purpose?
2. To what extent do you feel analogies are an acceptable form of simplification?
3. How might you adapt any analogies you use in the way Rollett suggests, so that they are used to evaluate the past?

Investigations

Evaluating your own practice: Take a unit of work you teach. To what extent do you present a simplified version of the past? To what extent is this an acceptable simplification? How might you adapt your work in the light of these extracts? What challenges might this present for you? To what extent are these to do with subject knowledge, insights into pupils' understanding of the past, pedagogical issues or other factors?

Exploring pupils' perceptions of the past: Before staring a unit of work, get pupils to create a mind map of their understanding of the topic. What pre/misconceptions do they appear to hold? How might you address these in the light of this knowledge?

Analysing textbooks and other classroom resources: Take a sample of classroom resources. Look at both the images/visuals used and the text/audio. To what extent do these present a simplified view of the past, and to what extent is this an acceptable level of simplification?

Think deeper

The issue of acceptable simplification permeates many areas of teaching history. This can be a level of substantive knowledge, i.e. how much should young people know about the past or how much do they need to know about something to make sense of it. It can be at the level of sophistication in their conceptual or procedural thinking. Or it can be at the level of providing some form of vicarious experience to help pupils understand a situation in the past that is beyond their lived experience.

Husbands and Pendry (2000) explore the challenges pupils face in understanding the past. As they explain, the past is distant and it requires young people to appreciate a different mindset, but all too often young people are asked to examine this past through an adult's perspective and frequently that of someone who holds a position of supreme authority. In this chapter, Husbands and Pendry look at the ways in which pupils respond to Elizabeth I's dilemma about her cousin, Mary, Queen of Scots and whether she should be executed. Few children have had such an experience in their own lives and so the frame of reference on which they can draw to make sense of this dilemma is extremely limited. In this context it is not surprising that teachers will try to simplify the issues or that children will draw upon their own understanding of the world to make sense of them.

Kitson et al. (2011) also explore the challenges of history for young people. They talk about different mental 'blockers' to pupils' understanding of the past. For example many pupils believe that we know everything there is to know about the past and therefore accept what they are told, and they believe that people in the past were stupid because they lack the technology that we have access to today. They also highlight the problem of language and the level of abstraction that pupils need in order to understand concepts such as 'revolution'. However, they argue that

> it is possible to make history accessible to all pupils, while remaining faithful to its fundamental principles and aims ... successful inclusive practices depend on sensitivity to the nature of history as a discipline *in the light of* the challenges pupils face.
> (Kitson et al. 2011: 121)

Kitson et al. (2011) go on to discuss key principles for teaching history in ways that make it accessible to all. One of these principles is to make history satisfyingly difficult. As Counsell (in Extract 1) stresses, making history easier or 'dumbing it down' can make it harder to understand. For example when working with sources, it is tempting to provide a simplistic attribution to explain its provenance, yet this makes it more difficult to evaluate the value of such evidence, and means that students are often forced to resort to generalisations about bias.

Think wider

As part of exploring the area of acceptable simplification, it is important to understand better how young people view the past and the challenges it presents them. There is a wide range of material that provides insights into such issues. A particular contribution has come from the CHATA project (which is mentioned elsewhere in this book, but Chapter 18 provides references to several of the main publications). The work from this project has focused on identifying the misconceptions that can block a student's understanding of the past, and teachers need to be aware of these when seeking to simplify complex ideas. Without an awareness of likely misconceptions, teachers' intended simplifications can often compound and reinforce the student's mistaken ideas. Much of this research has necessarily examined pupils' conceptual understanding as opposed to their understanding of substantive content. This raises another series of questions, for example, what is an acceptable level of causal understanding? When studying the origins of the First World War, what would be an acceptable explanation for a 13-, 16- or 18-year-old? Clearly this is tied into the area of progression (see also Chapter 18), but forces us to think about what pupils should be able to understand and explain at different points in their education.

Wineburg (2001) examines the ways in which school pupils and university history lecturers differ in their reading of historical texts. Although it is to be expected that university lecturers would have a more sophisticated understanding of historical texts, what his work does reveal is the way in which students read and understand texts: 'For students, reading history was not a process of puzzling about authors' intentions or situating texts in a social world but of gathering information, with texts serving as bearers of information' (2001: 76). Such insights help history educators to step back and reconsider how they approach teaching young people about the past.

Levstik (2000) explores the differences in the ways that teachers and adolescents conceptualise historical significance. Again, it is unsurprising that there are differences, but the study reveals the ways in which young people think about the past and the misconceptions that they hold. Levstik and Barton's (2008) book presents a range of studies, covering both the primary and secondary age ranges, which examines the ways in which pupils try to make sense of the past, and the often simplistic (but understandable) reasons why they hold such views.

References

Gellately, R. (2001) *Backing Hitler.* New York: Oxford University Press.

Goldhagen, D. (1996) *Hitler's Willing Executioners: Ordinary Germans and the Holocaust.* London: Little, Brown & Co.

Husbands, C. and Pendry, A. (2000) Thinking and feeling: Pupils' preconceptions about the past and historical understanding. In J. Arthur and R. Phillips (eds) *Issues in History Teaching.* London: Routledge, 125–36.

Kitson, A. and Husbands C. with Steward, C. (2011) *Teaching and Learning History 11–18: Understanding the past.* Maidenhead: Open University Press.

Klemperer, V. (1998) *I Shall Bear Witness: The diaries of Viktor Klemperer 1933–1941.* London: Phoenix.

Levstik, L. (2000) Articulating the silences: Teachers' and adolescents' conceptions of historical significance. In P. Stearns, P. Seixas and S. Wineburg (eds) *Knowing, Teaching and Learning History.* New York: New York University Press, 284–305.

Levstik, L. and Barton, K. (2008) *Researching History Education.* New York: Routledge.

Walsh, B. (1998) Review of 'Homebeats: Struggles for Racial Justice CD-ROM'. *Teaching History,* 93, 47.

Wineburg, S. (2001) *Historical Thinking and other Unnatural Acts.* Philadelphia: Temple University Press.

Technology in the history classroom

Educational policy in England and Wales, through successive versions of the National Curriculum, has encouraged the use of different kinds of technologies across all subject areas. This chapter focuses on how the use of different information technologies should be integrated into the process of learning history in order to further enrich the experience. The first extract in this chapter deals explicitly with how to plan for the integration of technology use and progression in history; the second focuses more precisely on the use of databases; and the third explores the use of online web-debates to further students' understanding of historiography.

Extract 1

Source

Counsell, C. (2003) The forgotten games kit: Putting historical thinking first in long-, medium- and short-term planning. In T. Haydn and C. Counsell (eds) *History, ICT and Learning in the Secondary School*. London: RoutledgeFalmer, 52–108.

Introduction

In this chapter from a book that she co-edited, Christine Counsell argues that high-quality use of information and communication technology (ICT) is dependent upon teachers' clarity about the kind of historical thinking and historical knowledge they want to develop in pupils. The chapter includes sections on long-, medium- and short-term planning with the first of these being developed in most depth. In this extract Counsell justifies the need to integrate planning ICT use into broader thinking about historical progression. Asking whether a certain activity 'works' is simply not enough when teacher thinking and planning play such a large part in the success of any activity.

Key words & phrases

Planning; progression; purpose; historical thinking; historical knowledge

Extract

If we are to address some of the problems inherent in unsatisfactory use of ICT in history we will not get far if we look only at ICT. We need to look at rationales for history teaching and how these manifest themselves at the level of teachers' planning. This ought really to be obvious. If we were analysing the reasons for poor history practice and inadequate historical learning generally we would not examine in detail the pens and books, tables and televisions that teachers use. We would look at the hidden connections in the lesson, at teachers' links and emphases between ideas, at the reasons for fluctuation in pupil motivation across different historical activities. We would look at the quality of pupils' historical thinking and how it connected – or otherwise – with teacher conceptions ….

The fundamental questions about securing quality historical learning for pupils can only really be tackled through an emphasis on:

- Establishing what progression means, or what we want it to mean (long-term planning);
- Identifying and structuring the best enquiries for sustaining historical rigour and securing pupil motivation (medium-term planning);
- Examining closely how the best history teachers turn that rationale into reality in individual lessons (short-term planning) ….

A measure of the problem that confronts us is that it is still relatively common to come across history teachers who ask whether or not an ICT activity 'works'. While this might be an appropriate question if one were examining whether or not the focus of the activity is historically sound or rigorous (i.e. does it 'work' histori-cally) any attempt to relate it to generic effectiveness with all learners is bound to be rather meaningless. Surely this is the wrong question to ask. Too much is depend-ent on how the teacher implements it and in what planning context it is deployed. It is hard for an ICT activity to be 'good' or 'bad' in its own right ….

This chapter argues that high-quality ICT use is dependent on our own clarity about the kind of historical thinking and historical knowledge we want to develop in pupils. Our willingness to keep up debate and exploration concerning its cat-egories and distinctions is therefore key. The chapter further argues that blanket references to something called 'ICT' are unhelpful and sometimes even damaging. The activities that take place under the umbrella of ICT are now so diverse as to defy generalisations about it.

Summary

Later in this chapter, Counsell distinguishes between 'ICT-dependent and non-ICT-dependent' planning for progression within history. In the first of these categories she describes four types of ICT use in which regular and progressive revisiting is desirable: the use of websites as interpretations; testing hypotheses through the use of large data files; experimenting with the wording of an historical argument using the functions of a word-processor; and the art of finding historical material on the Internet. Counsell goes on to look at what progression might look like in various types of ICT use, for example progression in using computer databases and spreadsheets. This is essential reading for anyone involved in long-term planning for the use of ICT in history education.

Questions to consider

1. How is ICT used in your history department? How far does student use of ICT support the department rationale for history teaching and learning? What might be the advantages and challenges of carefully integrating ICT use into long-term history planning?
2. What should progression look like in students' use of websites as interpretations? How might long-term planning ensure that such progression in ICT–dependent historical thinking takes place?
3. How do you evaluate the use of ICT in your history department? To what extent does the introduction of new software and hardware affect what you are able to do in history lessons?

Extract 2

Source

Martin, D. (2003) Relating the general to the particular: Data handling and historical learning. In T. Haydn and C. Counsell (eds) *History, ICT and Learning in the Secondary School*. London: RoutledgeFalmer, 134–51.

Introduction

Dave Martin wants to promote the use of databases in school history. He argues that databases in various forms can be an engaging and useful way of helping students navigate the vast amounts of information that might exist in an overview of, for example, the fall of the Roman Empire. Equally, however, more local, personal databases can be used to raise questions during depth studies and give pupils a sense of ownership over their particular strand of enquiry.

Extract

The use of databases in the history classroom has been slowly growing and many of the documented examples are about the interplay between the big narratives or analyses and the smaller details. Because of the volume of data that a database can store, and the sophistication of its manipulation tools, pupils can be taught to look for worthwhile patterns, to frame hypotheses about 'big stories', to question accepted pictures of the long-term view and to place interesting little details and stories into broader historical contexts that they have set up and tested for themselves.

For example, one of the key questions a history teacher might want to pose of the Roman Empire is: why did it fall? In order to answer that question in a meaningful way, pupils must consider aspects of the reigns of many emperors to find the patterns and trends that, over three centuries, led to the fall. The best way to do that is by using a data file of emperors. Of course, it is interesting for pupils to study an individual Roman emperor in depth, but such a depth study acquires wider historical meaning only if it contributes to the overview, to the resolution of some searching analytical question (NCET/HA, 1998; HABET, 1992).

But the overview–depth relation works both ways. Too much concentration on the bald facts and endless figures of a succession of emperors would tend to excessive abstraction. Children and teenagers need to be motivated by the *human* connection. Data files can take us into the small stories, too, raising fascinating questions for further enquiry at the detailed, or local level, and helping students to think about the value and function of those questions within a wider picture ....

The Great War 1914–19 is certainly a 'big' event, potentially yielding myriad lines of enquiry. The data file to be found on the Commonwealth War Graves Commission website (www.cwgc.org) provides an ideal opportunity for pupils aged 13–16 both to investigate the lives of individuals and to do so for a clear historical purpose.

This searchable online data file contains information on the 1.7 million members of the Commonwealth's forces who died in the First and Second World Wars. Pupils need a focus to help them to come to grips with this mass of information. This is true of any data file, large or small. In the first place, pupils need guidance on searching. Their directed enquiries will help them to understand what information there is in the data file, which in turn will enable them to devise suitable enquiry questions of their own ....

It is not just large data files that can help the classroom teacher. Small data files also can move pupils between the general and the particular. Take, for example, the typical treatment of the Middle Ages current in history departments in England

and Wales. Teachers usually begin with an examination of the Norman Conquest and then stop off at various points over the next 450 years to examine the relations of the monarchy with the Church, with the barons, and with the peasants and their neighbouring monarchs …. One of the key difficulties for teachers is how to help their pupils to put these disparate pieces together within the big picture ….

Year 7 pupils can set up their own data files on medieval kings. This 'set-up' process is both surprisingly straightforward and surprisingly rich in the learning that it affords, especially in relation to historical analysis and the nature of historical significance …. A good question, one that the data file will be reasonably helpful with, would be: 'How big a problem was rebellion for medieval kings?'

Summary

This extract includes several practical examples of how data files of varying content and size can be used to enrich the experience of exploring history. Data files can be used to promote curiosity as they are a particularly useful way of encouraging students to ask questions and take ownership of their own enquiry. Data files have also become a simple but effective way of bringing relevant, rigorous local history into the classroom.

Questions to consider

1. How do you currently use data files in your department? Would it be appropriate to introduce one such activity for each year group? What could progression look like in students' use of data files to encourage historical thinking? How might long-term planning ensure such progression takes place?
2. Martin focuses on the importance of teaching both overview and depth. How do you currently approach the teaching of large-scale overviews? What data files might be useful to cover periods that currently receive scant attention?
3. Martin describes students setting up their own data files and devising their own enquiry questions. What are the advantages and challenges of this approach to student learning in the history classroom? Why does ICT particularly lend itself to this type of independent learning?

Extract 3

Source

Thompson, D. and Cole, N. (2003) Keeping the kids on message … One school's attempt at helping sixth form students to engage in historical debating using ICT. *Teaching History*, 113, 38–43.

Introduction

Denise Thompson and Nathan Cole teach A-level history to 16–18-year-old students. They were keen to create a sense of real engagement and to encourage their students to read widely and engage in historiographical debate. They found the answer in an online message board that was set up at the beginning of an academic year. Students were given key times to contribute and teachers set up key questions for debate, moderating throughout. The results included a more engaged class, with all students contributing to debate both online and in the classroom. The online forum also helped teachers come to a better understanding of their students' misconceptions.

Key words & phrases

Online message board; professional historian; argument; historiographical debate

Extract

We wanted to explore ways of persuading all our students to think and argue as budding historians. In other words, we were committed to teaching history, and looking beyond levels of skills and responses both to creating real engagement, and to fostering genuine pleasure in learning ....

We decided that the medium of the on-line message board might have something to offer our students. A basic conference type board that was user friendly and cheap to operate – the one we use is free – could provide a forum for discussion, debate and argument outside of the confines of the classroom and allow us to develop reflection and extended thinking in our students. The message board offered a way to encourage discussion which linked directly to the reading required and recommended as part of the course of study. Once students began informally to discuss on the message board what they were reading they could be encouraged to develop their arguments. As they made their argument and responded to challenges on-line they began to realise that argument, to be effective, needs shape and purpose. Our students realised that to win the argument on-line, they needed to select evidence carefully to support their contentions. They had to be specific and analytical. It was not good enough just to express an opinion ....

We focused ... on two key strands – discussion and reading. In seeking in the first instance to stimulate discussion we had a number of concerns in mind. We wanted to foster an atmosphere of enquiry that could be shared by all our students. All too often in the classroom some students can be intimidated by others (or even by the teacher) and so clam up. They remain silent, apparently hard-working and interested and yet never really included in the cut and thrust of debate. Others can be too lazy to join in, whilst some dominate the discussion and rarely give the rest a chance ....

Many of our most quiet and reserved students found their voice on the message board. They welcomed the time for reflection that the board allowed. In the classroom responses are expected instantly – this was one of the key reasons given by students for not joining in discussion.

We, like many, want to see our students read for a purpose but to go beyond the basic texts and not simply use historians to illustrate points. Many of our students have stated that they believe they are reading 'for information' rather than for argument and this is perhaps a reason for their lack of motivation. The love of history is fostered through argument and debate – not (hopefully) through even diligent learning of facts! In this sense we wanted to foster some real historiographical debate – to see our students engage with historians' interpretations, not just accept them, or even worse accept them as facts in themselves. This, of course, is all part of our encouraging students to see history as the construct of the historian and not some monolithic received truth. In this, the message board has proved invaluable. No matter how much we required or recommended reading we still found many reluctant readers among our student body. Once we managed to persuade professional historians of the eminence and standing of Philip Morgan and Aristotle Kallis to contribute to our message board our students found a whole new motivation. One element of this was the 'wow' factor – yes, this really is the man who wrote the book that we have been encouraging you to read and think about! Yes, you really can argue with him and disagree … but only if you can support what you are going to say! All of a sudden there was a desire to challenge – a reason to read ….

Summary

Thompson and Cole decide to use an online discussion board in order to foster real engagement among their A-level pupils. They focus on encouraging skills of argument and set particular reading tasks that are then discussed online. The use of professional historians on the discussion board clearly enlivens the debate and gives students a reason to read, but other teachers might want to consider a different audience for their students.

Questions to consider

1. What are the advantages and challenges inherent in using online forums in the history classroom? These authors use the message board with older students. How might the technique be best adapted for use with younger students?
2. Thompson and Cole describe great success when they introduce professional historians to their message boards. Would it be possible for you to replicate this method in your department? Who might you approach?
3. Students seem to respond well to an audience on a message board. Could you set up different classes to argue against one another or even approach another school? Which topics might be best suited to this approach? What resources would you need?

Investigations

Information technology (IT) audit: Create an audit of how students use different technologies across the full age range in your department. Is there a full scope of activities including databases, message boards and evaluation of websites? Do you explicitly teach your students how to research using the Internet? To what extent do the activities support learners in focusing on authentic, higher-order historical thinking? What would you need to change to move towards this goal?

Working with the IT department: Liaise with the head of the IT department to find out what particular technologies students are learning to use at different stages. Compare schemes of work for a particular year group. Are there some complementary areas that your departments both focus on, such as critical use of the Internet? Plan a joint scheme of work for one topic that enables students to make progress in both history and IT use.

Pupil voice: Select a focus group of students. How do they use different technologies in their own lives? Do they use computer games based on aspects of the past? Do they research aspects of the past on the Internet? Do they create films and share them with others? How might you harness your students' knowledge of technology to develop your history lessons?

Think deeper

Each of the articles referred to in this chapter makes it clear that ICT should not be used for its own sake in history lessons, but rather integrated into deeper planning in order to develop historical understanding. Terry Haydn (2003) sets out a background to the use of ICT in the history classroom, and highlights some of the inherent dangers of ICT use. One is the danger of 'leaving the learning until later'. For pupils he suggests this can manifest itself as ' "*Encarta* syndrome" where pupils print off large chunks of digital resources without reading and assimilating the content'. However, he suggests that teachers can suffer in the same way, accumulating large collections of resources without necessarily 'digesting them and translating them into worthwhile learning experiences for pupils'. Another danger Haydn highlights is that ICT might help learners to do many 'low-order' tasks more quickly, but this does not necessarily follow into spending more time focusing on 'authentic, higher order, historical thinking' (2003: 20).

Ben Walsh (2008) also highlights potential dangers for students in ICT use, this time in the use of the Internet. He suggests that people tend to believe what they see on a website rather than question its nature, origin and purpose and argues that it is the role of the history teacher to encourage good habits in students when accessing websites. Walsh argues for historical thinking in an information age, as 'proper historical thinking can encourage students to think critically about how social, racial or ethnic groups have been manufactured or reinforced over time' (2008: 9).

Using technology to communicate beyond the history classroom can offer opportunities for new perspectives on the past. When Richard Kerridge and Sacha Cinnamond

(2012) were given video-conferencing facilities in a history classroom they took the opportunity to extend their practice and enrich the experience of the students studying history. This article describes, in depth, a particular collaboration with a German history department, through video-conferencing on the teaching of the First World War. The aim was to move students beyond an 'us' and 'them' sense of the war to understanding the suffering that all soldiers would have faced. There was also a second project around the similarities and differences in the two countries' development after the Second World War. Students produced materials that were 'beamed' into the German school and vice versa through the video-conferencing facilities. New perspectives were therefore brought to students that would have been difficult to access in the past.

Think wider

A plethora of different software and hardware has entered classrooms over the last two decades and provided opportunities for deepening understanding of history in a number of different ways. Diana Laffin (2008) was at first wary of the fashion for using voting pods in the classroom, seeing most activities as reductivist factual recall. However, she decided to see how she could use the devices to further the understanding of her own students, specifically the understanding of different perspectives within past scenarios. Each student had to research a character in a particular historical scenario, for example Tudor Britain. Various decisions were then made using the voting pods, but the students had to vote in character and be prepared to justify their choices. The voting pod technology put pressure on each individual student to come to a confident understanding of a particular perspective in order to be able to contribute confidently to informed debate.

Sally Burnham (2008) describes a similar scepticism when she first came across Movie Maker. However, she found that in order to be successful in using Movie Maker pupils must research their clips carefully and plan them to the last detail. As Burnham says, it is this, 'rather than the making of the clip' that really secures the historical learning. Movie Maker therefore played a very specific role in getting students to understand what historical explanation really involved. One example that Burnham illustrates in the article is the use of Movie Maker to teach about the Public Health Act of 1875. Students had to email her relevant images for homework, then in class make a very short documentary about why the Act was passed. Groups of students had to select appropriate images and write a voice-over to go with them. Here the use of technology emphasises the role of careful selection in creating effective explanation.

When a set of laptops arrived in Maria Osowiecki's department, she decided that changes needed to be made to integrate them effectively into schemes of work. Her article (2006) describes three key activities that focus on using ICT to develop an understanding of overview. The first of these involved pupils role-playing and then photographing key images from Renaissance medicine. The photos were imported to Microsoft PowerPoint and the students then created voice-overs to explain the changes in medicine through the Renaissance. Further examples include 'The rise and fall of Mister Germ' and 'Surgery Top Trumps'. In these examples it is the ease with which the software allows manipulation of several different factors that justifies the use of ICT in the activity.

Sometimes, the most familiar software can have a positive effect on the struggling history student. Ben Walsh (1998) describes a number of activities that use simple word-processing skills to help students build a line of argument in extended prose. Walsh suggests that using the word-processor can not only teach students how to select ideas and shape an answer, but it can also provide the confidence to attempt the abstract thought 'essential to historical analysis'.

References

Burnham, S. (2008) Making pupils want to explain: Using Movie Maker to foster thoroughness and self-monitoring. *Teaching History*, 133, 39–44.

HABET (1992) *Teaching History Using IT*. London: Historical Association.

Haydn, T. (2003) Computers and history: Rhetoric, reality and the lessons of the past. In T. Haydn and C. Counsell (eds) *History, ICT and Learning in the Secondary School*. London: RoutledgeFalmer, 11–37.

Kerridge, R. and Cinnamond, S. (2012) Talking with the 'enemy': Firing enthusiasm for history through international conversation and collaboration. *Teaching History*, 148, 8–15.

Laffin, D. (2008) 'If everyone's got to vote then, obviously … everyone's got to think': Using remote voting to involve everyone in classroom thinking at AS and A2. *Teaching History*, 133, 18–21.

NCET/HA (1998) *History using ICT: Searching for patterns in the past using databases and spreadsheets*. Coventry: NCET/HA.

Osowiecki, M. (2006) Miss, now I can see why that was so important: Using ICT to enrich overview at GCSE. *Teaching History*, 125, 38–42.

Walsh, B. (1998) Why Gerry likes history now: The power of the word processor. *Teaching History*, 93, 6–15.

Walsh, B. (2008) Stories and their sources: The need for historical thinking in an information age. *Teaching History*, 133, 4–9.

History textbooks

Textbooks are used in history classrooms around the world, but the way they are put together, the pedagogical assumptions that underlie them and the selection of material can differ greatly. This may depend on the intentions of the government and education system in a particular country, how a particular country was involved in key events in the past, the dominant pedagogy in that country and how far textbooks are intended to instil a sense of national pride and common identity. The first extract, from an Israeli perspective, discusses what the aims of history textbooks are now and what they should perhaps in the future. The second, from a comparative study of textbooks in different countries, focuses on the English experience and why it might differ from others; the third suggests a pedagogical approach to using textbooks as interpretations. In many countries there is no choice over textbooks as they contain the officially sanctioned views of the past. However, whether books are officially approved or not, it raises questions for teachers as to how to handle the material contained within.

Extract 1

Source

Porat, D. (2001) A contemporary past: History textbooks as sites of National Memory. In A. Dickinson, P. Gordon and P. Lee (eds) *Raising Standards in History Education: International review of history education, volume 3.* London: Woburn Press, 36–45.

Introduction

In this chapter Dan Porat explores Israeli history textbooks over five decades and, in particular, their changing depiction of the Bar Kokhba Revolt (the last of the

Jewish–Roman wars in 132–6 CE). He shows how the depiction changes according to wider social and political considerations. He concludes the chapter with this extract, arguing that although textbooks can achieve a goal of passing down memory, if the purpose is for students to think historically either textbooks need to change or teachers need to focus on the conceptual tools of thinking historically.

Key words & phrases

History textbooks; narratives; alternative narratives; authoritative accounts; knowing historically; historical scholarship; community of enquiry

---

Extract

History textbooks narrate history for students and, in so doing, suppress alternative narratives. Textbooks present students with a supposed factual account. In some instances authors conceal, in others they select, but in all they interpret. In an essay written more than 30 years ago, Peter Schrag [1967] explained:

> History textbooks are bad, not because they are too biased, but because their biases are concealed by the tone. History texts are written as if their authors did not exist at all, as if they were simply the instruments of a heavenly intelligence transcribing official truths. The tone of the textbook is the tone of a disembodied voice speaking in passive sentences, it fosters the widespread confusion that the text is history, not simply a human construct composed of selected data, interpretations and opinions.

Furthermore, authoritative accounts of history textbooks, points out Peter Seixas [1993], do not convey the essence of knowing historically. When historical scholarship is transferred into textbooks and is presented as 'reality', it loses what signified it in the historical community of inquiry. Historical arguments among historians are 'tentative and invented, to be challenged and revised, contributions to an ongoing discussion within a community of inquiry. When taken out of that context, they dry up', as happens in textbooks ….

Some scholars have argued for a change in the authoritative tone of textbooks. 'If we want students to read historical texts differently from their driver's education manuals, if we want them to comprehend both text *and* subtext', points out Wineburg [1991], 'we will have to change our lesson plans – not to mention our textbooks.' …

The social role of textbooks dictates their tone. The authoritative tone and the narration of the past serve to pass down a memory from one generation to another. The goal is for students to have pride in their tradition, for them to cherish their origins, for them to join, identify and benefit their social group. Textbooks represent the socially valid and truthful knowledge. Competing viewpoints do not serve to communicate a heritage to the young generation; they do not enhance the group's cohesion. We should not expect the complexity of historical knowing to come from textbooks which are social tools ....

The narrative of textbooks is an important means for communicating society's account of events to students. As we have seen, with all the changes textbooks have gone through in the past decades, they still remain primarily tools for the enhancement of national identification among students. History education must, however, go further and educate students to know in a critical sense, as well as to understand the limits of their ability to know. For students to know in historical terms, we need to focus our efforts on the instruction of history, on transferring the conceptual tools for thinking historically.

Summary

This extract points to some of the advantages of textbooks, representing the knowledge that society finds valid in the contemporary moment. However, it also points to the dangers of such a narrative approach, if we want students to understand the 'limits of their ability to know'. It is important to note that this research is based on Israeli textbooks, which might include more of a narrative framework than textbooks in some other countries, notably England, as Extract 2 will show.

Questions to consider

1. How are textbooks used in your classroom, as a narrative resource or as a construct in their own right? What are the advantages and limitations of each of these strategies?
2. The author writes of students understanding 'the limits of their ability to know'. Is this an important objective in teaching history? What are the risks involved in deliberately seeking to develop young people's understanding of the tentative and provisional nature of historical accounts?
3. To what extent are the textbooks you use tools for the enhancement of national identification among your students? How far do you agree with this purpose?

Extract 2

Source

Nicholls, J. (2006) Beyond the national and the transnational: Perspectives of WWII in U.S.A., Italian, Swedish, Japanese, and English School History Textbooks. In S. Foster and K. Crawford (eds) *What Shall We Tell the Children? International perspectives on school history textbooks.* Charlotte, NC: Information Age Publishing, 89–112.

Introduction

In this chapter Jason Nicholls reports on a rigorous comparison of textbooks across five countries, each focusing on the Second World War. He finds many differences dependent on the role and final outcome of the different countries in the war and the current approach to history education within those countries. This selected extract focuses on English history textbooks.

Key words & phrases

English history textbooks; Second World War textbooks; interpretation; pluralism; relativism

---

Extract

A wide variety of perspectives are adopted in English textbook portrayals of World War II. Thus, while the transnational ideological struggle between liberal, fascist and communist visions of the world are acknowledged, so too is the intensely political power struggle between the nation states themselves. What is more, local and individual perspectives are included, often in the form of numerous sources, purposely offering contradictory points of view on particular events. As for regional perspectives, major battle arenas on the Eastern Front, in the Pacific and in Western Europe are covered in roughly equal measure across the sample with, somewhat surprisingly, less attention devoted to events in North Africa ….

English textbooks give a strong sense that the war is open to interpretation. On one level, this should be welcomed since it offers a platform for high levels of critical engagement and analysis. On another level, it is not difficult to see how this pluralism may slide into a kind of relativism, particularly where students are not positioned to critically engage (for whatever reason) with perspectives. In addition, the incorporation of such a wide range of perspectives may in fact serve to elevate Britain's role as a member of the Allies in the conflict, from third of the big three to a relative equal ….

School history education in England is located within parameters set by the National Curriculum and the external examination syllabi. In contrast to the sweeping survey courses found in the U.S. and Japan, historical studies are typically based around themes and topics. Qualifications are based on results through continual assessment as well as examinations. In particular, course objectives routinely emphasize the importance of interpretation as well as knowledge retention. Since curriculum and syllabi are relatively prescribed, textbooks are commonly conceived as a resource only, used less frequently than in many other countries. The textbook market is liberal and competitive …. Textbooks tend to include a multiplicity of perspectives and numerous sources with a relatively minimal narrative component. Assignments and questions are usually oriented around the comparison and interpretation of evidence as opposed to the retention of knowledge ....

Critical engagement with multiple perspectives in history education should be clearly defined, not only in terms of an intrinsic suspicion of singular 'catch all' perspectives, national or transnational, but also in contrast to the relativist notion that all perspectives are valid. Above all, critical engagement requires the student to evaluate and assess, and to make judgments, in addition to simply describing differences. Grounded in a particular definition of the subject and with it, the extent and limits of agency, the essential question becomes not what is the 'correct' perspective to adopt, to learn or to teach, but rather: How is it possible to engage with plurality meaningfully and critically?

Summary

This extract focuses on some of the distinctive features of English textbooks and why they might exist. It highlights potential dangers of presenting multiple perspectives in the history classroom, not arguing against this, but questioning how pupils can be helped to avoid a relativist approach and engage meaningfully with plurality. The full chapter should be referred to in order to compare perspectives in English textbooks on the Second World War with those from the USA, Italy, Sweden and Japan.

Questions to consider

1. How far are local, regional and national approaches to the Second World War evident in your schemes of work? What is the balance between the national experience and a more trans-national approach? To what extent do the textbooks you use guide the approach to content that you take in the department?
2. To what extent do you support a multiple-perspective approach to teaching the past? If teaching with this approach, what strategies need to be put in place to avoid pluralism sliding into relativism?
3. To what extent might your approach clash with that of the textbook or textbooks you use? Is this down to differences in pedagogy or differences in the substantive content that you deem significant to the debate? What might be the benefits, if any, in sharing that clash with your students?

Extract 3

Source

Edwards, C. (2008) The how of history: Using old and new textbooks in the classroom to develop disciplinary knowledge. *Teaching History*, 130, 39–45.

Introduction

Chris Edwards is determined that students in history classrooms should not become passive consumers of textbooks. He believes that there is an alternative way of using history textbooks to develop students as critical readers. In this article he suggests approaching older textbooks as historical interpretations and gives a variety of examples of how this might be achieved in the classroom.

Key words & phrases

Textbooks; historical interpretations; discipline of history; class; gender

Extract

Treating textbooks as historical interpretations in the classroom requires us to author the text. In the same way, and for the same reasons, that we would talk about 'Simon Schama's account' when examining *A History of Britain*, we should equally recognise the authors of our textbooks. For students this has the effect of personalising the text and immediately points to its constructed nature. Working with textbooks currently in use plays out on three levels. Firstly, students can examine the text's surface qualities – how the text has been organised and what choices the author has made regarding style, content, questions, the use of illustrations, and types of history? Secondly, the text can be analysed – to what extent is the account reliable, substantiated, adequate or balanced? Thirdly, the text can be mined more deeply for what Sam Wineburg (2001) calls the polemic of the text, piercing beneath the surface of the text to gauge something of the author's personal values.

To compare a pre-1945 textbook account with a recently published one is to set up a problem of historical interpretation. The study of historical interpretations is one of the main ways students can develop their understanding of the nature of the discipline ....

The treatment of the working class in textbook accounts has also undergone revision. In earlier accounts, they are hidden or subsumed under the more general term 'the people'. When given an occasional mention it is largely in negative terms such as the 'poor', the 'mob' or the 'common people'. Typically, they are portrayed as being without culture and judged in terms of their loyalty to the Crown ... Thompson's (1973) 'working class' is divided between a hot-headed unreasonable group of Chartists and a sensible majority who want to support the Government. Comparing Thompson with a recent and more sympathetic account of working class movements in class would allow our students to discuss the fundamental question: who decides what is included in textbooks and why some topics are favoured and others not?

During the past thirty years textbook authors have sought ways to include the distinctive contribution of women within their accounts. Prior to this development textbook authors' coverage of women was confined to the lives of a few individuals and, generally, women were hidden from view. The amount of textual coverage and the choice of illustrations are a measure to some extent of an author's gender bias. For example, Macmillan's *New History* published in 1912 contains forty portraits of men and four of women – Queens Elizabeth, Anne, Victoria and Mary – and, in a detailed account of Victorian and Edwardian English history, it chose to remain silent on the topic of the Women's Suffrage Movement.

Whereas *Recent Times* by Mowat and Kelly, published in 1962, includes fifty portraits of men and ten of women. In their text Mowat and Kelly include a brief account of the Women's Suffrage Movement but do not feel it necessary to include the contribution of women in the two World Wars of the twentieth century. It would be interesting to apply this simple analysis to a recently published textbook. Would you expect the ratio of female to male illustrations to be smaller and the textual coverage to be wider? In addition, textbook illustrations open up for analysis the diverse ways women have been represented at different points in time. For example, Macmillan's 1912 account includes only one illustration of a woman apart from the four portraits of queens. This Elizabethan family scene is the female viewed from a 'separate spheres' perspective. Why was this single illustration chosen by the author? Textbooks can be used as markers for the debate on the place of women in history. As such they provide us with a rich point of entry to a major contemporary historical issue.

Summary

Edwards suggests that teachers should make their students aware of the constructed nature of textbooks. He suggests various questions that should be asked of textbooks, from examining surface qualities such as organisation and selection to less obvious issues such as reliability. The examples Edwards provides in the article range from across the twentieth century, but if such texts are not readily available then students could still benefit from a comparison of the approaches in a variety of contemporary textbooks.

Questions to consider

1. To what extent do your students take the information in textbooks at face value? How might you help your students to see textbooks as interpretations?
2. Who decides what is included in textbooks and why some topics are favoured and not others? What answer would your students give to this question? At what stage in their education would it be most appropriate to raise such a question?
3. Edwards focuses his examples on gender and class, portrayals of which have changed a great deal over the last five or six decades. What other changes in interpretation might you expect your students to be able to identify in a selection of textbooks since the Second World War?

Investigations

Pupil review of history textbooks: When starting a new topic, give pupils the task of auditing the textbook they are going to use. What is the gender or class balance in the written and pictorial sources used? What is the balance between narrative material and source material? How far does the textbook tell a national story and to what extent does it incorporate regional or local perspectives? Who are the authors and to what extent do they substantiate the claims they make in the book?

Department review of history textbook use: Use a department meeting to share experiences of using current textbooks. How do members of the department use the textbooks? Are there topics they always avoid using the textbook for? Do teachers feel there is a match or a clash between their personal teaching approach and that supported by the textbook? How do other members of the department help students to understand the notion of textbook as a construct?

Pupil comparison of textbooks: Give students chapters from different textbooks that cover the same topic. Ask them in what ways and how far the textbooks differ. Can they account for the differences? Use any student misconceptions that emerge from the exercise to help plan the next stages of your teaching.

Think deeper

Textbooks can be very influential in creating a convincing picture of a past society; selection of detail and visual images is obviously key to the accuracy of such a portrayal. Audrey Osler (1994) reviewed the way women were represented in 36 English history textbooks published soon after the inception of the National Curriculum. She found that while sexist language had been avoided, there was still a long way to go to achieve a more balanced historical record and to move closer towards a real understanding of the lives of women in the past. She suggested that textbook illustrations in particular were a cause for concern. With the 2008 version of the National Curriculum emphasising an ethnically diverse portrayal of the past, it would be interesting to repeat such research on more recent textbooks and see how women and other groups in society are now portrayed. Osler provides a useful methodology for textbook analysis, carefully explaining her consideration of illustrations, text and language used, activities and exercises suggested and the authors themselves. This could prove very useful to anyone wishing to undertake further research into the portrayal of different groups within history textbooks.

The selection of textbooks for use in class is an important decision facing all history departments. Robert Stradling (2001), writing on the teaching of twentieth-century European history, provides an extensive guide for teachers evaluating a textbook before deciding whether or not to purchase and use it. This involves 40 questions under the subtitles 'Content', 'Pedagogical approaches', 'Intrinsic qualities of history textbooks' and 'Extrinsic factors in evaluative history textbooks'. Useful questions include 'How is the past portrayed? Is the present perceived as the inevitable outcome of past events? Is history portrayed as "the triumphal march of progress"? Will it challenge the student to think about history as a discipline?' and 'Does the material in the textbook reflect recent research or current thinking among historians?' (2001: 257–63).

Sometimes there is a clash between the pedagogy used by a class teacher and the pedagogy implicit in a textbook. Jacques Haenen and Hanneke Tuithof (2008) re-designed a Dutch history textbook with the explicit aim of promoting cooperative learning and pupil involvement, reflecting the chosen pedagogy of many teachers. In this article they describe their aims and offer some examples from the textbook. The style of cooperative learning builds on the work of Spencer Kagan (1992), so explicit instructions are given for activities such as brainstorming, pairwork, placemat, jigsaw and think-pair-share.

Think wider

Different countries have their own specific, and often very passionate, debates about their national past that are often played out in discussions around history textbooks and suitable content. Section 3 in a collection edited by Irene Nakou and Isabel Barca (2010) includes chapters examining several such debates, from Greece, Israel and Turkey. The chapter by Yonghee Suh and Makito Yurita (2010) shows that the precise content of textbooks can cause international debate; in this case specifically in Japanese and South Korean textbooks on the Second World War. The chapter concludes that history textbooks in both countries avoid discussing controversial issues by representing the war either as a chronological account or as a one-sided narrative.

There is a similar theme in Stuart Foster and Keith Crawford's (2006) edited selection of chapters on international perspectives in school history textbooks. This book includes pieces on the construction of European identity since the Second World War, the portrayal of immigrant groups in US history textbooks since 1800, the Islamisation of Pakistani social studies textbooks and the dynamics of history textbook production during South Africa's educational transformation. The introduction, on the critical importance of history textbook research, points to the power of history textbooks as the keepers of ideas, value and knowledge in any given culture.

The particular controversies surrounding the teaching of the Second World War and the textbooks involved in this are followed up in another book, this time authored by Crawford and Foster (2007). The ideas in the initial chapter on 'War, nation and memory' could provide a useful backdrop for older students interested in evaluating how the Second World War has been portrayed in a variety of interpretations. Later chapters focus on different textbook portrayals of specific events or groups within the war such as the Holocaust, the destruction of Dresden, French resistance and collaboration and the role of the British Empire and Commonwealth.

References

Crawford, K. and Foster, S. (2007) *War, Nation, Memory: International perspectives on World War II in school history textbooks*. Charlotte, NC: Information Age Publishing.

Foster, S. and Crawford, K. (2006) *What Shall We Tell the Children? International perspectives on school history textbooks*. Charlotte, NC: Information Age Publishing.

Haenen, J. and Tuithof, H. (2008) Cooperative learning: The place of pupil involvement in a history textbook. *Teaching History*, 131, 30–4.

Kagan, S. (1992) *Co-operative Learning*. San Juan Capistrano, CA: Kagan Cooperative Learning.

Nakou, I. and Barca, I. (2010) *Contemporary Public Debates over History Education: A volume in international review of history education*. Charlotte, NC: Information Age Publishing.

Osler, A. (1994) Still hidden from history? The representation of women in recently published history textbooks. *Oxford Review of Education*, 20 (2), 219–35.

Schrag, P. (1967) The emasculated voice of the textbook. *Saturday Review* (21 January), p. 74.

Seixas, P. (1993) Parallel crises: History and social studies curriculum in the USA. *Journal of Curriculum Studies*, 25 (3), 313.

Stradling, R. (2001) *Teaching Twentieth-century European History*. Strasbourg: Council of Europe.

Suh, Y. and Yurita, M. (2010) International debates on history textbooks: A comparative study of Japanese and South Korean history textbook accounts of the Second World War. In I. Nakou and I. Barca (eds) *Contemporary Public Debates over History Education: A Volume in international review of history education*. Charlotte, NC: Information Age Publishing, 153–68.

Thompson, E. (1973) *The Historical Course for Schools History of England*. London: Macmillan.

Wineburg, S. (1991) On the reading of historical texts: Notes on the breach between school and academy. *American Education Research Journal*, 28 (3), 495–519.

Wineburg, S. (2001) *Historical Thinking and other Unnatural Acts*. Philadelphia: Temple University Press.

History teachers' professional learning

Professional development for history teachers

The nature of professional development as a teacher within any subject discipline is a complex and contested process. The importance of *subject-specific* professional knowledge was first highlighted in 1986 by Lee Shulman, who referred to the relationship between subject knowledge and pedagogic knowledge as the 'missing paradigm' within research into teacher effectiveness. Shulman's specific contribution in addressing that neglect was the concept of pedagogical content knowledge, which he suggested represented a blend of content and pedagogy: an understanding of how particular topics, problems or issues could best be organised, represented and adapted in response to the needs of diverse learners and presented for instruction. Although Shulman's rather simplistic assumptions about the processes by which subject matter is transformed from the knowledge of the teacher into the content of instruction have since been challenged, the questions to which he drew attention by asking about the knowledge bases on which teachers draw, and how they can be developed, remain extremely important. However, conceptions of professional learning as the development of specific knowledge or skills have also been called into question, both for their neglect of teachers' attitudes and beliefs and for failing to pay attention to the wider contexts and cultures within which teachers work. While career-long continuing professional development is recognised as a responsibility of each individual teacher and a vital component of school improvement, questions also arise about how history teachers can draw on the wider resources of the professional subject community, and work together with subject colleagues in school to create expansive learning environments within their departments.

Extract 1

Source

Husbands, C. (2011) What do history teachers (need to) know? In I. Davies (ed.) *Debates in History Teaching*. London: Routledge, 84–95.

Introduction

In this chapter Chris Husbands both summarises and builds on a research study originally undertaken with two other history teacher educators, Alison Kitson and Anna Pendry (Husbands et al. 2003), in which they examined the practice of eight heads of history departments, using classroom observation and interviews (both about the observed lessons and the history curriculum within the school), supplemented by analysis of their departmental handbooks and further contextual data. Here Husbands seeks to construct a framework for thinking about the relationships between the different sorts of knowledge deployed by teachers and to consider some of its implications for teachers' professional learning.

Key words & phrases

History teachers' knowledge bases; pedagogic content knowledge; substantive content knowledge; procedural knowledge; conception of history as a discipline; knowledge about pupils; knowledge about classroom practices

---

Extract

Unpacking teachers' knowledge about history

Detailed content knowledge is characteristic of successful teaching, but it is not sufficient. Teachers' knowledge about history is not defined by their knowledge of the historical past alone …. On Shulman's model, what should happen is that teachers would 'acquire' knowledge from engagement with the subject and then derive from that pedagogic content knowledge. In practice, something different seems to happen in the relationship between substantive and procedural knowledge ….

Teachers in our study made reference to the substance, or content, that they wanted their pupils to understand but this was almost invariably seen in terms of procedural concepts such as evidence, changes, continuity or causation. A lesson on nineteenth-century public health, for example, might be about specific developments, but it was also about pupils' understanding of change over time …. Not surprisingly, a distinction between novice and experienced teachers lies precisely in their different approach to procedural concepts …. One important way of thinking about learning to teach a subject is, therefore, that it involves the acquisition of increasingly sophisticated understandings of the procedural concepts.

A third feature of subject knowledge relates to the notion of history as a discipline. For many history teachers this has a particular prescience given the pressure on their subject in the curriculum ….

What teachers know about pupils

… Our own work suggested that teachers have strong images of pupils' understanding in history, and that, in some cases there is an awareness of the results of recent research which suggest that pupil learning is not stage-related, that structures of learning depend on engagement and revisiting. It may be that for experienced history teachers this is so interlinked with their knowledge of school history and their knowledge of how pupils learn that it does not make sense to try to disentangle it. Nonetheless, there is evidence to suggest that *in addition to* general ideas about how pupils learn, successful history teachers have a developed understanding of progression in learning history.

Knowledge in action: knowledge about resources and approaches

... [W]e found a deliberate matching of resources and activities to goals, as teachers drew on a wide repertoire to make decision about what would be most appropriate .... It is not surprising that this broad repertoire was most evident in the talk of the most experienced teachers: they have had the time both to develop and use a wide range of strategies, and also to see their effects with a range of different classes and individuals ....

Although teachers' descriptions of their practice are often couched in terms of activities, what is often clear is that there is a profound understanding of pedagogy underlying these.

A framework for thinking about knowledge: history, pupils and resources

Three dimensions to teacher knowledge have been explored, and they are summarized in Figure 24.1. As the discussion above has suggested, these three are not separate: they inter-relate and draw off each other. However, as a schematic representation of the argument, Figure 24.1 has some merits: it draws attention of

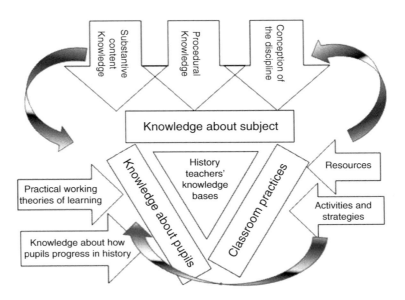

Figure 24.1 A framework for teachers' knowledge.

the multi-dimensionality of history teachers' knowledge; it suggests that each element in the model then draws on other components, and at the centre it suggests that they sit in a dynamic relationship to each other. Approaches which place subject-matter knowledge itself at the core fail to capture the inter-relationship and dynamism of the different sorts of knowledge we found teachers routinely deploying.

There are some potentially profound implications of this model for teacher learning and teacher development. Teacher education programmes – whether initial or in-service – frequently construct artificial barriers between different sites of learning – between library, seminar room and the classroom. This chapter suggests that these boundaries are artificial: understanding flows between the different sources and forms of knowledge, as each becomes a lens through which the others are perceived. For novices, the model here has implications too. The model reminds us that learning to teach involves the acquisition of diverse knowledge. It points to the school, and the classroom as the critical site in which learning is acquired, and provides foci for knowledge development. Equally, it reminds us that while the school is a critical site for knowledge development, focused support is needed to maximize the potential of schools to support teacher development.

Summary

Although Husbands sets out the study's findings in terms of three different types of teacher knowledge – knowledge about *history,* knowledge about *pupils* and knowledge of *classroom practices, resources and activities* – he is anxious to stress the dynamic interplay between the different elements. And indeed each of the three main types of knowledge represents a combination of different elements working together. Knowledge of history, for example, involves far more than the factual knowledge necessary to teach about specific events or developments in the past, since this is shaped by – and serves to shape – teachers' understanding of the procedural concepts that provide – and reflect – their understanding of the nature of history as a discipline. In a similar way, teachers' practical working theories of learning and their deep knowledge of individual pupils interact with their knowledge of how pupils make progress in history. Their knowledge of resources or learning 'activities' is not something separate from, but in fact richly imbued with, their knowledge of pedagogy. The development of history teachers' expertise therefore certainly does not proceed *simply* from their knowledge of the subject matter; and while it needs to draw on sources beyond the classroom, it can only be realised in the context of teaching. This has important implications for educational researchers and teacher educators who have a critical role to play, both in presenting their ideas as suggestions *for* practice with which teachers can experiment and in strengthening and sharpening their critical reflection *on* practice.

Questions to consider

1. Husbands claims that it was easier to track the influence of teachers' 'practical working theories' about learning (in general) than it was to see the influence of more specific knowledge about pupil understanding *in history*. What *general* theories of learning influence your own practice and why do you subscribe to them? To what extent are you aware of *specific* theories or research claims about students' learning in history, and how do they inform your teaching?

2. Husbands' choice of a triangle to represent the three main types of knowledge base suggests that they are all equally important, with each informing the other, rather than subject knowledge forming the central core. How far does this match your own experience of learning as a teacher?

3. If the classroom is the 'critical site' for teachers' learning, how can you ensure that it also draws effectively on wider frames of reference (including educational research)?

Extract 2

Source

Counsell, C. (2011) Disciplinary knowledge for all, the secondary history curriculum and history teachers' achievement. *Curriculum Journal*, 22 (2), 201–25.

Introduction

This article was written in 2010 as a response to the announcement of a new National Curriculum Review in England. In responding both to recent curriculum trends that had tended to reduce history to 'generic skills' and to new calls for a history curriculum that would foster 'narrowly celebratory versions of Britain's past', Christine Counsell argued for the fundamental importance of teaching the 'disciplinary knowledge and concepts' necessary to reach or challenge claims about the past. The relevance of this article to teachers' professional development is that her argument is built from history teachers' own published discourse. She sets out to show how teachers themselves have set out to solve the problems associated with 'uniting content and concept': engaging in practical theorising and more formal kinds of action research, to find ways of motivating and engaging all students in developing genuinely *historical* knowledge and understanding.

Key words & phrases

Disciplinary knowledge; teachers' published theorising; research orientation; second-order concepts

---

Extract

Developing pupils' understanding of the distinctive properties of disciplinary knowledge and its difference from the 'everyday' is what history teachers have been attempting to do for about 25 years. Moreover, history teachers' published theorising has rendered the principles of that practice increasingly explicit. Where practice published as articles or shared through websites and workshops is openly cognizant of others' efforts, it adds up to a coherent discourse of some power. Such discourse shows teachers renewing their pedagogy through disciplinary reference. There is therefore a case for using that discourse to examine the scope of teacher-led problem-solving, its curricular referents and curricular potential.

This is not to say that all history teachers are engaged in such efforts or have a research orientation. It is fair to say, however, that most are trying to solve problems or to find creative resolutions to sets of tensions (Husbands, Kitson and Pendry 2003). Undoubtedly an 'accessibility agenda' dilutes some teachers' disciplinary goals (Hawkey 2006). Nonetheless, even though some practice is more limited, much addresses directly the complex difficulties of integrating disciplinary product and process, content and concept. This article explores the nature and significance of such teacher efforts and reflects on their implications for curricular review.

Although by no means universal, what is noteworthy is the capacity of teachers to discern problems, to generate solutions ... and to give these currency through public discussion ....

Teacher-led practical exploration of second-order concepts

Teachers have also built activities designed to shift pupils' ideas within particular conceptual domains. The most powerful of these eschew reductive 'quick fix' tasks and show pupils the nature of the generalisations that they are forming or testing. Examples of history teachers doing this are extensive, often spinning from a single, starting example that teachers pick up, reshape and then throw back into the community for continued debate. Chapman's (2003) approach to teaching counterfactual reasoning was one such catalyst. His 'Alphonse the Camel' has influenced many other activities, such as those designed and researched by Buxton (2010), whose pupils compared eighteenth-century France and Britain as a way of furnishing counterfactual possibility. Woodcock (2005) was inspired by the camel metaphor to seek greater precision in pupils' classification and linking of causes. Choosing from words such as 'underlying', 'latent', 'emergent', 'inexorable', 'inevitable', 'exacerbate', 'shape', 'determine', 'mitigate' and 'temper', his pupils' writing gained new explanatory power.

Perhaps the most illuminating concept when exploring disciplinary structure and boundaries is 'historical significance'. 'Significance' is revelatory because of its special ontology: it cannot be a property of the phenomenon under study. Always ascribed by others, it shifts according to questions asked, as well as cultural or political context. Present in every National Curriculum since 1995, it only found its way into the Attainment Target of the National Curriculum in 2008, largely in response to burgeoning teacher discussion, by then spanning over 20 articles, many web discussions and new textbook activities. Discussion was enriched by international work (e.g. Seixas 1997; Cercadillo 2001). The taxonomies of Lomas (1990) and the practical ideas of Phillips (2002) became referents for work on nurturing progression (Bradshaw 2005), on pupils' preconceptions (Conway 2005), on stretching post-14 pupils (Hall 2008) and on using significance to engage pupils with local history (Brown and Woodcock 2009).

Summary

The development of teachers' practice has been driven, Counsell argues, by their attempts to resolve the tensions that they encounter in seeking to offer young people meaningful forms of engagement with the discipline of history. The fact that they have shared their own endeavours in online or journal publications or at conference workshops means that their solutions are not only passed on, but debated, tested, refined and extended by others. A single teaching idea intended to help students to appreciate the different roles or functions that causes could serve, and so to evaluate their importance, equipped other teachers to explore the potential of counterfactual reasoning and the importance of linguistic development in supporting students' conceptual reasoning. The work of professional researchers and educational theorists certainly informs and enriches teachers' conceptions of progression – as in the case of historical significance – but that work is transformed as teachers apply and test it in relation to their particular classroom concerns.

Questions to consider

1. Counsell's argument in this article is addressed to policy-makers, urging them to consider the ways in which history teachers are transforming our understanding of how to teach history effectively. How appropriate do you think it is to base curriculum development on the ideas of teachers?

2. In what ways do you seek to access ideas developed through the practical theorising of other history teachers? How have these ideas been modified through your own application of them and experimentation with them? What steps do you or could you take to share the outcomes of your own practical problem-solving with others?

3. In your experience, how do the findings of educational researchers come to influence the work of practising teachers?

Extract 3

Source

Burn, K. (2012) 'If I wasn't learning anything new about teaching I would have left it by now!' How history teachers can support their own and others' continued professional learning. *Teaching History*, 146, 40–9.

Introduction

Katharine Burn's research into history teachers' professional learning has been pursued both as an 'insider' – as a head of department and PGCE mentor in schools – and an 'outsider' – as a university tutor and educational researcher. This article draws on three different research projects to examine the interaction between individual teachers (with their own particular dispositions towards professional learning) and the specific departmental contexts within which they work. In this extract, based on comparative case studies of teachers' informal learning in one history and one geography department (which shared a team room) and two science departments in different schools, she outlines some of the factors that influence the learning cultures of subject departments and the way in which individuals operate within them and contribute to their creation.

Key words & phrases

Learning departments; habitus; subject cultures; departmental leadership; interplay between individual dispositions and departmental context

Extract

Learning departments

Physical space and the way in which heads of departments chose to use it was of crucial importance. Access to tea and coffee, and routines that encouraged staff to gather together (often over cakes and biscuits too!) were very significant in bringing people together, but the ways in which they interacted and the kinds of conversation that they had were also influenced by the shared, if unspoken, assumptions that Bourdieu [1977] has described as 'habitus'. These can perhaps be regarded as a system of dispositions – schemes of perception, thought and action – that an individual develops in response to the social conditions that they encounter. While they are rarely articulated, essentially functioning at an unconsciousness level, they frame the way in which 'we do things here' – the kinds of things it is possible both to say and even to think.

The influence of particular subject cultures

Ways of working within different subject areas also obviously have a history that graduates bring with them: traditions of team-working in science and individual scholarship in history. While this is perhaps beginning to change in universities, as on-line archives reduce the need for silent research in rare-book rooms and history departments become more engaged in international and multi-disciplinary collaborations, history teachers may still tend to see research in terms of personal reading. While the head of history whom I observed was profoundly committed to continued professional learning and was an avid reader, he tended to regard engagement with the wider scholarly community as much more of an individual responsibility than one that was conducted collaboratively. His high expectations were reflected in the very careful and thoughtful advice that he gave to the student–teacher in history, but he always tended to do so privately and quietly, tending to arrange separate meetings to talk in detail about her ideas and the next steps forward.

The influence of departmental leadership

The head of history's approach was in marked contrast to that of the head of geography, who regarded almost everything that was happening as an opportunity for learning, welcoming questions or requests for advice and frequently asking others for their ideas, always at a volume that could be heard across the (admittedly small) room. She often provided a commentary on her own and others' on-going work, as well as outlining the particular issues that she happened to be wrestling with, or giving feedback to others …. While she regularly offered advice, she also sought it out, canvassing views from junior as well as more senior colleagues and urging them all to seek feedback on what they were doing from students too. The distinctive feature of her commitment to continued learning was its highly visible and public nature.

The impact of individuals' choices

Differences in the two approaches adopted undoubtedly reflected differences in personality, as well as age and career stage; … but they also reflected conscious policies, rooted in their understanding of the nature of professionalism and processes of professional learning, and they undoubtedly made an important difference to the ways in which their respective teams tended to operate. While the other history teachers regularly joined in discussions initiated by the geography teachers about ways of teaching a particular concept, or offered their own reflections on how an idea being discussed by the geographers might be adapted for use in history; they rarely asked their own questions except about specific aspects of factual information and they too always worked essentially privately with the student teacher, as they evaluated lessons or liaised with her about future planning. While they undoubtedly drew on their own experiences in offering her advice, she rarely gained any insight into their own processes of planning *as* they happened, or saw exactly how they drew on different kinds of resources.

Although leadership was undoubtedly extremely important, as indeed were some of the enduring ways of working shaped by previous incumbents, we also saw powerful examples of the ways in which individuals, even at a very early career stage, could take responsibility for their own learning not merely finding ways to work within existing structures, but beginning to re-shape the learning contexts that they found, making them more conducive to their own learning …. A teacher in his second year stood out in terms of his willingness to ask questions and to seek advice – part of a very deliberate strategy that he had chosen to adopt [following a long period of illness in which he had reflected on] his professional ambition to become the best teacher he could be …. The impact of his approach was profound in terms of the opportunities that he created for other teachers to share, explain and evaluate the specific teaching ideas that were planning or had recently deployed.

Summary

While the physical environment of departmental team rooms has a vital part to play in creating informal opportunities for teachers' learning, the way in which those opportunities are exploited depends on often unspoken assumptions about what it means to be a professional, and the extent to which all teachers are encouraged to see themselves as learners. Conventional academic practices that shape how history is learned at undergraduate level may continue to shape expectations of professional learning for history teachers. While the attitudes and routine practices of heads of department have an important influence, individual teachers at all stages of their career can also choose how they respond to the cultures they encounter and so influence their development.

Questions to consider

1. How appropriate or important do you think it is to regard teachers' informal interactions in the team room as opportunities for professional learning? How effectively does the physical layout of your department team room, and the way in which people use it, encourage such interactions?
2. What prior experiences of learning – including those as an undergraduate learning history and previous professional experiences (in other schools or other contexts altogether) – have influenced the way in which you think about learning as a teacher?
3. How can heads of history model an approach to teaching that is rooted in respect for continued professional learning?

Investigations

Conduct a case study of teachers' professional learning within your own department: Interview the different members of your department to explore their views of the nature of history and their main purposes in teaching history. Then ask about their experiences of learning – as a history student *and* as a history teacher. What has exerted most influence on the ways in which they teach and on the ways in which they now learn to develop their practice?

Undertake the introduction of a new scheme of work with a deliberate emphasis on teachers' professional learning: In planning for the development of a new scheme of work (or any other departmental initiative) consider the range of sources (including historical research and scholarship) on which you could draw to inform your practice, and how you could work together with colleagues not merely to reduce the demands of the planning task, but to learn as productively as you can from external sources and from each other. Evaluate the process of planning in terms of teachers' learning as well as the effectiveness of the new scheme for students' learning.

Review the ways in which your departmental team room is used: Review the way in which your team room is laid out and how it is used by different teachers at different times. Think about display space as well as the way in which resources are shared. Are there ways in which you can promote more informal interactions focused on teaching and learning, and encourage *all* teachers, at whatever career stage, to ask questions and learn from one another?

Think deeper

An article by Paula Worth (2011), a history teacher wrestling with the challenges of adapting lessons for a low-attaining class of 12–13-year-olds, is one among many in the professional journal *Teaching History* that exemplifies the kind of practical theorising that Counsell describes. The approach that Worth adopts provides a rich illustration of a history teacher drawing on academic research, professional literature and other teachers' suggestions for practice, first to analyse the nature of the difficulties she is experiencing and carefully define the specific objectives that she is seeking to achieve, and then to hypothesise a potential solution and undertake a systematic action research enquiry to investigate its effectiveness. The specific 'demons' that Worth sought to tackle included two aspects of conceptual development in history: an empathetic understanding of attitudes and beliefs held in the past, which initially seemed alien or absurd to the students, and the use of that understanding to construct a causal explanation. The strategy that Worth chose to adopt, extended reading of a fictional historical play that she devised, obviously presented a third challenge for a group struggling with literacy but it reflected the insights that Worth had gained from her own reading – that her usual practice of simplifying texts for this particular group effectively robbed the history of its drama and interest. The article explains how Worth approached the issue as an action research enquiry with specific research questions focused on the nature of students' engagement in the reading and the ways in which they responded to the challenge of explaining why some women were persecuted for witchcraft. It also illustrates the process of analysis by which themes were generated inductively from various data including the students' work and interviews both with the students and various teaching assistants who supported them.

The tradition of teacher research that is illustrated by Worth's article and praised by Counsell (2011) (Extract 2) for illuminating our understanding of what it means to take a disciplinary approach to the teaching of history is rooted (as the original Schools Council History Project itself was) in the tradition of action research advocated by Lawrence Stenhouse, who famously argued that curriculum research and development ought to belong to the teacher. A clear introduction to his ideas and fundamental conviction that 'it is not enough that teachers' work should be studied: they need to study it themselves' (Stenhouse 1975: 142) can be found in Chapter 10 of his seminal work *An Introduction to Curriculum Research and Development*.

The process by which departmental teams construct new professional knowledge together, and induct newcomers into that process, is explored in a fascinating article written jointly by three successive members of one history department, Whitburn, Hussein and Mohamud (2012), the last of whom was a student teacher. The fact that the substantive history that they were seeking to teach, and that each of them had to learn specifically in order to so, was the history of pre-colonial Africa, makes this account of professional learning particularly fascinating. Since this history is fundamentally based on oral traditions that the teachers sought to respect, understand and explore with their students, it called for considerable risk-tasking in terms of pedagogy and assessment. It also demanded a profound commitment to dialogue between teachers as the source of their learning as they sought to do justice to the history. The discussion of departmental ethos, in relation to the South African concept of *ubuntu* (in which personal creativity flourishes within a community of similarly creative individuals committed to mutual support) serves as an interesting parallel to Burn's (2012) (see Extract 3) socio-cultural analysis of the complex interplay between individual teachers' learning dispositions and the context in which they are working.

Pendry et al. (1998), in the final chapters of their book examining history teachers' learning from initial teacher education through induction and on into continuing professional development, focus both on the role of subject departments in supporting such learning, and on the role of the individual teachers themselves, seeking to set their professional development as history teachers in the context of their professional life cycles. The hypothetical case studies that they use to illustrate the complexity of professional learning owe much to Burn's (1995) year-long study of the members of her own history department, and serve to illustrate the interplay between teachers' professional and personal lives as it impacts on their commitment and sense of identity as subject teachers. The implications of this relationship on teachers' sense of agency, well-being and resilience, and so on their continued learning, have since been explored in a substantial mixed-modes study of 300 primary and secondary teachers across different professional life phases (Day et al. 2007), examining how they, in turn, impact on students' attitudes and attainment.

Think wider

Barton and Levstik (2004), who survey a number of studies in the US exploring the relationship between history teachers' disciplinary knowledge and their pedagogical practice, conclude that the most important determinant of teachers' practice, and thus the most important element to focus on in promoting professional development, is a teacher's conception of the *purposes* of teaching and learning history. In the final chapter of their book, reflecting on their own quest to help teachers to understand history as 'an interpretive and enquiry-oriented endeavour' (2004: 246), they hold up examples that demonstrate that developing a better knowledge of historical process has no *necessary* impact on classroom practice. Even secure convictions about the enquiry-based nature of the discipline are simply not enough, they argue, to help overcome the combined pressures towards conformity that teachers face. These pressures derive from the fundamental assumption that a teacher's role is essentially to secure control in the classroom so that he or she can cover the curriculum efficiently, limiting the opportunities for potentially disruptive student discussion. The pressures are so strong, Barton and Levstik suggest (in a claim that directly contradicts Counsell's arguments about the concerns that have driven history teachers' practical theorising) that securing teachers' loyalty to the principle of teaching disciplinary history is not sufficient to generate the 'intellectual and emotional commitment necessary to reform practice' (2004: 259). The only force they believe will provide sufficient motivation for history teachers to resist narrow, 'transmission' modes of pedagogy is a commitment on their part not to producing mini-historians but to equipping young people to play their part within a pluralist, participatory democracy.

Flora Wilson (2012) makes a passionate plea for teachers' active engagement in research as part of the commitment expected of them as professionals. The research, for which she calls, however, is focused less on pedagogy and more directly on the development of substantive historical knowledge. Her argument for teachers to go on extending their knowledge of history derives not only from the scope that it provides to enrich the curriculum with fascinating stories and engrossing details, but also from the important model of 'intellectual curiosity' that it presents to students. She shares two examples of her own engagement in reading beyond the current curriculum, both focused on the lives of individual women, one involving local archive research and the other drawing on a published collection of four short biographies. The account that she gives, both of the process of developing her own knowledge and of supporting her colleagues in developing new schemes of work, illustrates the importance of engagement with the wider academic community – in Wilson's case through the Women's History Network – and with the teachers in her own department, planning lessons collaboratively to build on their distinctive strengths.

While teachers' accounts of their own action research studies tend to include quite a lot of data about the impact of their new ideas on their students' learning, there are relatively few evaluations of more formal professional development programmes that examine the impact of teachers' learning on their *students'* achievement. In an attempt to address this deficit, Susan de la Paz and her colleagues (2011) set out to investigate the impact on students' learning of one professional development course within the Teaching American History programme (a programme that they claim has, since 2002, invested nearly a billion dollars in professional development for history teachers). The researchers focused on students of three different ages, examining their construction of written responses to document-based questions as their main data set, alongside qualitative analyses of the teachers' activities to try to tease out the connections between classroom lessons and student outcomes. The study is particularly interesting not only because it seeks to distinguish between those teachers who merely attended an intensive professional development programme and those who built on that initial input with at least 30 hours of further networking activities, but also because of its approach to measuring impact both in terms of the students' substantive historical knowledge (their mastery of the content) and on their abilities to use sources effectively as evidence in the construction of a written argument. The findings confirm the critical importance of involvement in ongoing networks of support as the teachers seek to apply new ideas, and also provide a rich illustration of the ways in which their practice changed.

References

Barton, K. and Levstik, L. (2004) *Teaching History for the Common Good*. Mahwah, NJ: Lawrence Erlbaum Associates; see Chapter 13: 'Teacher education and the purposes of history'.

Bourdieu, P. (1977) *Outline of a Theory of Practice* (translated into English by R. Nice). Cambridge: Cambridge University Press.

Bradshaw, M. (2005) Creating controversy in the classroom: Making progress with historical significance. *Teaching History*, 125, 18–25.

Brown, G. and Woodcock, J. (2009) Relevant, rigorous and revisited: Using local history to make meaning out of historical significance. *Teaching History*, 134, 4–11.

Burn, K. (1995) Teachers' perceptions and experiences of professional development: A case-study of a school department during an academic year. Unpublished MSc dissertation, University of Oxford.

Buxton, E. (2010) Fog over channel; continent accessible? Year 8 use counterfactual reasoning to explore place and social upheaval in eighteenth-century France and Britain. *Teaching History*, 140, 4–15.

Cercadillo, L. (2001) Significance in history: Students' ideas in England and Spain. In P. Lee, P. Gordon and A. Dickinson (eds) *International Review of History Education, Vol. 3*. London: Woburn, 116–45.

Chapman, A. (2003) Camels, diamonds and counterfactuals: A model for causal reasoning. *Teaching History*, 112, 46–53.

Conway, R. (2005) What they think they know: The impact of pupils' preconceptions on their understanding of historical significance. *Teaching History*, 125, 10–15.

Day, C., Sammons, P., Stobart, G., Kington, A. and Gu, Q. (2007) *Teachers Matter: Connecting work, lives and effectiveness (professional learning)*. Maidenhead: Open University Press.

de la Paz, S., Malkus, N., Monte-Sano, C. and Montanaro, E. (2011) Evaluating American history teachers' professional development: Effects on student learning. *Theory and Research in Social Education*, 39 (4), 494–540.

Hall, K. (2008) The Holy Grail? GCSE history that actually advances historical understanding! *Teaching History*, 131, 9–18.

Hawkey, K. (2006) Mediating narrative in classroom history. *International Journal of History Learning, Teaching and Research*, 6 (1), 1–10.

Husbands, C., Kitson, A. and Pendry, A. (2003) *Understanding History Teaching: Teaching and learning about the past in secondary schools*. Maidenhead: Open University Press.

Lomas. T. (1990) *Teaching and Assessing Historical Understanding*. London: Historical Association.

Pendry, A. and Husbands, C. with Arthur, J. and Davison, J. (1998) *History Teachers in the Making: Professional learning*. Buckingham: Open University Press.

Phillips, R. (2002) *Reflective Teaching of History 11–18*. London: Continuum.

Seixas, P. (1997) Mapping the terrain of historical significance. *Social Education*, 61 (1), 22–7.

Shulman, L. (1986) Those who understand: Knowledge growth in teaching. *Educational Researcher*, 15, 4–14.

Stenhouse, L. (1975) *An Introduction to Curriculum Research and Development*. London: Heinemann.

Whitburn, R., Hussein, M. and Mohamud, A. (2012) Doing justice to history: The learning of African history in a North London secondary school and teacher development in the spirit of *ubuntu*. *Teaching History*, 146, 18–27.

Wilson, F. (2012) Warrior queens, regal trade unionist and warring nurses: How my interest in what I don't teacher has informed by teaching and enriched my students' learning. *Teaching History*, 146, 52–6.

Woodcock, J. (2005) Does the linguistic release the conceptual? Helping Year 10 to improve their causal reasoning. *Teaching History*, 119, 5–14.

Worth, P. (2011) Which women were executed for witchcraft and which women cared? Low attaining Year 8 use fiction to tackle three demons: Extended reading, diversity and causation. *Teaching History*, 144, 4–15.

Author index

Subject index